Praise for

Women's Experi

"Reflect[s] a shift in consciousness regarding the Divine, one that is shaped by a deep and personal relationship with the Sacred within us and all around us, a knowing that is beyond images and names, a unifying energy that weaves into one all life on our planet. Shows how this Spirit-driven force within feminist spirituality continues to add to the universe story a multifaith, multicultural dimension steeped in wisdom and compassion and oriented toward planetary justice and peace. May these sacred stories give rise to many more."

—**Miriam Therese Winter**, professor, Hartford Seminary; author,
Paradoxology: Spirituality in a Quantum Universe

"Amazing ... restores balance to our human understanding of the Divine [and] brings readers face to face with a Divinity who empowers and accompanies women of many religious traditions and blended faiths. A must read!"

—**Joan Borysenko, PhD**, author, *A Woman's Journey to God*

"Heartful, multifaceted ... generous and inspiring. As a Buddhist practitioner, I generally don't use theistic language to describe deepest connections of love or clarity, so I found many of the perspectives in *Birthing God* to be especially interesting and thought provoking."

—**Sharon Salzberg**, author, *Real Happiness: The Power of Meditation: A 28-Day Program*; co-founder, The Insight Meditation Society

"[A] valuable resource [and] a real eye-opener.... Many insights into how this translates into traditional worship services. It is also a journey of self-discovery with the help of questions for reflection and a marvelous collection of meditations and visualizations."

—**Kay Lindahl**, co-founder, Women of Spirit and Faith; co-editor,
Women, Spirituality and Transformative Leadership: Where Grace Meets Power

"Offers a kaleidoscope of opportunities to invite in the Divine Feminine in myriad forms ... it can't help but expand our ways of thinking how we can experience the Divine. Helps all women realize we belong to God/dess."

—**Carolyn Bohler, PhD**, author, *God the* What? *What Our Metaphors for God Reveal About Our Beliefs in God* and *God Is Like a Mother Hen and Much Much More ...*

"As women's stories are told, the depths of women's souls begin to be known. Speaking of the presence of Goddess and God in their lives, women transform religions."

—**Carol P. Christ,** author, *Rebirth of the Goddess* and *She Who Changes*

"Challenge[s] us to understand divinity and spirituality beyond traditional ideas of gender and dogma. Offers reflection, inspiration and even practical guidance for anyone seeking to experience her faith more deeply."

—**Lisa Catherine Harper**, author, *A Double Life: Discovering Motherhood*

"How diverse is your Spirit, Holy One, as these women testify. How many and varied are your Paths. Readers, explore these stories to clarify your own Way."

—**Mary E. Hunt**, co-director, Women's Alliance for Theology, Ethics and Ritual (WATER); co-editor, *New Feminist Christianity: Many Voices, Many Views*

"Crosses boundaries to unite human and Divine.... Both draws on and departs from religious traditions ranging from Islam to Lutheranism, Catholicism to Zen Buddhism, simultaneously diving deeper into and transcending the limitations of that which we think we already know about the Divine."

—**Caryn D. Riswold, PhD**, associate professor of religion and chair of gender and women's studies, Illinois College

BIRTHING GOD

Women's Experiences of the Divine

LANA DALBERG

FOREWORD BY KATHE SCHAAF

Walking Together, Finding the Way®

SKYLIGHT PATHS®
PUBLISHING
Woodstock, Vermont

Birthing God:
Women's Experiences of the Divine

2013 Quality Paperback Edition, First Printing
© 2013 Lana Dalberg
Foreword © 2013 by Kathe Schaaf

For information regarding permission to reprint material from this book, please mail or fax your request in writing to SkyLight Paths Publishing, Permissions Department, at the address / fax number listed below, or e-mail your request to permissions@skylightpaths.com.

Library of Congress Cataloging-in-Publication Data

Available upon request.

10   9   8   7   6   5   4   3   2   1

Manufactured in the United States of America
Cover Design: Jenny Buono
Cover Art: ©iStockphoto.com/Liliia Rudchenko
Interior Design: Heather Pelham

SkyLight Paths Publishing is creating a place where people of different spiritual traditions come together for challenge and inspiration, a place where we can help each other understand the mystery that lies at the heart of our existence.

SkyLight Paths sees both believers and seekers as a community that increasingly transcends traditional boundaries of religion and denomination—people wanting to learn from each other, *walking together, finding the way.*

SkyLight Paths, "Walking Together, Finding the Way" and colophon are trademarks of LongHill Partners, Inc., registered in the U.S. Patent and Trademark Office.

Walking Together, Finding the Way®
Published by SkyLight Paths Publishing
A Division of LongHill Partners, Inc.
Sunset Farm Offices, Route 4, P.O. Box 237
Woodstock, VT 05091
Tel: (802) 457-4000   Fax: (802) 457-4004
www.skylightpaths.com

CONTENTS

Foreword ix

Part I
DIVINE LOVE AND LOVE OF SELF 1

Esperanza: Great Courage within Me 9

Lindsey: Where We Find God 16

Lori: Rocking in the Mother's Arms 21

Hyun Kyung: From the Palms of God into
  the Vortex of Becoming 26

Susan: Worthy to Stand Here with God 34

Sridevi: Rooted in the Divine Feminine 40

Arisika: The Body as Gateway to the Divine 44

Rachel: The Sacred within Me 53

Anna: Circling into the Womb of the Mother 58

Alice: Resonating like Home 64

Sarah: Hanging Out the Wash like Prayer Flags 70

Ann: Seeing Ourselves with Love 75

Rhina: The Church of the Open Door 81

Part II

DIVINE CONNECTION   87

Jeanette: Dropping into the Hands of God   93

Irma: A Mother's Embrace   99

Kimberly: Welcoming Occasions to
  Know God   106

Elena: Celebrating the Mother's Diversity   112

Belvie: Who Can We Become Together?   119

Malisa: Seeing the Divine in Each Other
  (*Namaste*)   128

Sadaya: The Womb of God through Which
  We All Come   134

Carolina: Light and Love in All Beings   140

Debbie: Experiencing the Divine
  in the Multitude   147

Teresa: God among Us   152

Susan: Appreciating the Sacredness of Life   157

Marci: Like Family   162

Emily: Seeing the Glory   165

Alison: Restoring Our Sense of
  Interconnectedness   172

Judith: Swirling in the Mandala That
  Connects Us All   177

Part III

DIVINE CHANGE

181

SaraLeya: Under the Wings of Shekhinah   187

Lucy: Embracing Our Imagination   192

Ayesha: Madly in Love with God   198

Allison: Not Fearing Death   204

Viviana: All of Us Spirit   210

Zoharah: Who Am I and Why Am I Here?   219

Kristin: Listen to Mother Earth—
She Has a Lot to Tell You   228

Dionne: Drumming to Heal the Mother   235

Stacy: Climbing into Her Branches   242

Virginia: Stirring the Ashes   250

Jann: Let Justice Roll Down Like Water   256

Katie: Would You Hug Me, Jesus?   261

Epilogue   266

Acknowledgments   268

Meditations and Visualizations   269

The Interview Questions: Eliciting Spiritual Stories   278

Notes   280

Suggested Resources   287

FOREWORD

by Kathe Schaaf

I was approaching my fiftieth birthday when the powerful events of 9/11 reached into my heart and activated a new gyroscope there. That morning I was across the country from New York, watching flaming towers on the television in my home in southern California with my husband and my two sons, ages eight and twelve. Weeping as the second tower collapsed on the screen in front of me, I heard a voice inside say loudly and distinctly, "This would not happen in a world where the voices of women are heard."

I could feel the truth of those words in every cell of my body and in my spiritual DNA. And so I began following that voice out into the world and deep into myself, spiraling around on a journey with no maps and no plan. I was guided, pulled along by a subtle yet strong knowing. For the first time in my life, I allowed myself to know that I knew much more than I was ready to admit I knew. I was called to acknowledge my own inner wisdom before I could be ready to witness the wisdom of other women. I was asked to face my own unspoken fears, the ones that were written in my bones, so that I could inspire other women to be faith-filled. I was required to recover my own authentic voice before I could really listen deeply to the voices of other women. I was invited to step into my own true leadership so I could testify passionately to the tide of women's leadership that is rising now. Through it all, I was lovingly held in the embrace of the Divine Feminine where I began to remember my own natural spiritual authority just in time to celebrate the transformative spiritual leadership carried by so many other women.

When I hear the voices of women, spoken in a safe and sacred space and spoken from a deep place of knowing within, I hear Her voice. When I listen deeply to Her, I am awakened anew at some place within me to sing my own precious holy song in answer.

Such a lovely maternal circle of giving and receiving, of speaking and listening, of knowing and seeking is walked round and round in *Birthing God*. The voices of these women are strong and clear, called forth by the safe and sacred space Lana Dalberg offers them with her deep curiosity and the purity of her witnessing. Each voice is unique, and yet there is a lyrical melody that runs through these stories about major traumas and everyday life, about moments of boldness and experiences of keen vulnerability.

Several years ago, my friend Julie Raymond shared a vision that came to her in a meditation. She is drawn into an opening in the earth at the base of an ancient tree and finds the Sacred Mother entangled in the roots, weak and depleted. Julie frees her and carries her gently up to the open air. As they emerge from the underground cave, they see women streaming toward them from all directions, thousands and thousands of women. Each woman is carrying a piece of the Mother; every piece is different and every piece is essential in order to re-member the Sacred in its original wholeness.

DIVINE LOVE
AND LOVE OF SELF

Part I

"Birthing God. Kenosis." These three words come to me in the middle of the night. The first two words provoke an apt title for this book. But the third stumps me. Not remembering "kenosis" from my seminary days, I fling back my covers to look it up and discover that it signifies self-emptying in ancient Greek.[1] Back in bed, I try to sleep, but the notion of self-emptying echoes inside me, reminding me of the Buddhist concept of no-self: not a cipher or empty sack, but a receptivity to Spirit that makes incarnation possible.[2]

Women, I realize, empty themselves all the time, making room for the spouse, or the child and his or her attendant needs. I think of Mary—an unwed woman, a girl. What is her response to a divine being who tells her that she is pregnant when circumstances dictated that she could be stoned for that condition?

"Let it be with me according to your word,"[3] Mary is said to have responded, opening her life to the risk and the potential of divine inspiration. Receptivity, desire for connection, making room for another: these attributes express women's most fundamental ways of being in the world. Conception, when women's bodies take in foreign DNA in order to gestate new life, is but one example. Arisika Razak, one of the women I interviewed, is a nurse-midwife as well as a spiritual teacher. She shares a conception story and later characterizes birthing as "a totally sacred moment ... the moving of essence, from that side of the veil to this, from there to here." She goes on to describe the incredible risk and resistance a woman meets in childbirth and how a birthing mother must marshal all her resources in order to bring new life into the world.

But this power to bring forth life has long vexed those who aspire to dominate. In centuries past, men condemned childbirth as divine punishment, blamed women for the advent of sin, and even claimed that their semen was the seed of life, relegating women to the role of incubators. In much of the Western world, women's connection with the earth and their sacred knowledge of plants and healing herbs were destroyed or driven underground. Our mothers' mothers' mothers' bodies were raped, flogged, and burned. Even today, debate rages over the power of government to regulate and control women's reproductive abilities. The femicides of the Inquisition and, for non-Western women, slavery and genocide, burn deep within our collective unconscious, manifesting as self-doubt, dread, and fear.

Plenty of fears—of pain, rejection, unworthiness, inadequacy, un-lovability, and abandonment—came out in the interviews I conducted for this book. These fears and self-condemnations were not news to me. They'd been part of the soundtrack of my life for years, particularly the dirge beating out the heavy refrain, "Not good enough, not good enough, not good enough."

But in my early forties, an amazing thing happened. I began meditating daily, at first in my bedroom closet so as not to awaken my husband, and later in a small room he built for me in the garage. In those precious moments of meditation, I emptied myself, letting go of fears and other distractions, and resting gently in the breath and in timeless silence. Visions appeared, fragrant from another realm: oceans and forest streams with eddying pools where four-legged animals gathered to drink.

During that period, as my body shifted toward change, toward menopause, my inner spirit opened itself to the larger Spirit, and I came face-to-face with God as Mother. Scenes unfurled on my inner eye in undulating landscapes, and she stepped into them. A tall African woman, the Mother was someone my heart recognized instantly, even though I had been raised with male images of God. I recorded each vision as soon as I opened my eyes.

> July 1, 2002: The Mother takes my hand, and we walk along a seashore. She hands me a shell necklace and reminds me of my gifts that have been hidden in the dark. She places a cape upon my shoulders and says, "Remember I am the mantel you wear, and I am in your heart. I am always with you. I love you."

In the visions, the Mother cared for me, providing nourishment, clothing, walking sticks, and gemstone necklaces that spoke to me of my inestimable worth in her eyes. She midwifed my children, helping me to birth them into the world. And there were later visions of death and rebirth. I typed each one into my laptop.

> August 3, 2002: Today I saw myself emerging from the water, clothed in buckskin and with long black braids. But as I emerged, I saw pieces of myself break off like shards—shards of me falling away, splashing into the water. I was afraid, and I reached toward the sun, my Mother. The sun voice said, "Behold, here is my daughter, with whom I am well pleased." And I was a woman's body again: curvy, voluptuous, pregnant, and, although pregnant, old. I walked with a cane. I carried age in my bones. The time came for me to bring forth the child in my womb. I gripped a pole, and my Mother Midwife soothed me, stroking my hair, patting my brow dry, feeding me water to drink, and whispering words of encouragement in my pain. My pain was the labor of birth, but the pain of not knowing, too. I heaved and groaned through the pains, and I birthed an adult—an androgynous human being that was as big as me, that merged with me, swirling like the symbol of the yin and the yang. This was *my* birth, I realized.

I searched for my Mother God, and I heard her say, "I am here: in the rain, in the sun, and in the earth. I will always be there for you."

The waking visions were reinforced by dreams and gave rise to my desire to know other women's stories and to hear their experiences of the Divine, however they named it. I made room in my professional and domestic life for a new project, asking women to share their stories with me. I started closest to home, in my church community,[4] and broadened the circle to draw in others who were interested. Many of the women had been involved in courageous, compassionate work for years, and they were just now recognizing the injustices thrust upon the collective female soul. Some were creating women's circles, others were collaborating in ecofeminist ventures to safeguard the earth, and others were involved in healing and creative work to lift up the Divine Feminine. Instead of disparaging themselves, these women were embracing themselves as cherished and one with the Divine.

I learned many things as I interviewed these women, but everything they shared reinforced one simple treasure: however we name Spirit, we receive it with deep-hearted openness. Our receptivity is active, recognizing the value we bring to relationship by trusting and honoring the God within; by experiencing Spirit as soul mate; by glimpsing the Divine all around us; and by allowing God to cradle and nourish us. At the same time, our spirituality is a process, unfolding and growing with each passing day. Our spiritual stories are full of missteps and unabashed celebration. They are narratives of suffering and of hope; lessons in shedding fear and learning to love ourselves. Ours are embodied stories that begin with emptying so that we can glimpse the Holy Other, this Light who appears in ways unplanned, unexpected, and unsettling. Our lives are the surprise that begins with the response, "Let it be."

Treatment of Important Terms

I have used title case for all nouns that the interviewees use with the intention of denoting God. Just as God, Allah, and Yahweh are capitalized, so are the following equivalents: Creator, Spirit, Holy One, Holy Other, Divine Feminine, Shekhinah, Wisdom, Divine Mother, Mother God, Goddess, Universe, Source, Higher Power, Inner Divine, and Divine Presence, Light, or Energy.

Phrases in other languages are italicized, and translations are offered parenthetically. Lastly, the alternate name of Ebenezer Lutheran is herchurch, which is spelled in lowercase (and run together), except when it begins a sentence.

Esperanza

Great Courage within Me

Suddenly, I felt this tremendous courage in my body.... This knowledge born from within gave me energy, and I felt a great confidence in my own person, that I could do what was needed.

ESPERANZA ORTEGA, GRANDMOTHER AND
COMMUNITY ORGANIZER

E speranza Ortega is one of El Salvador's historic women, having survived the country's twelve-year civil war and its many atrocities. Her petite frame is compacted from years of working the fields, and her face is eagle-like. Her black eyes watch me as she awaits my first question. When asked how she has experienced the Divine's presence, Esperanza answers, "Really, every day, each step we take, is through God."

Because I know her community history, Esperanza's response surprises me. Like many people in this mountain village I am visiting, Esperanza suffered terribly during El Salvador's civil war. She was one of thousands of subsistence farmers who'd worked the rocky hills of northern El Salvador for generations when the Salvadoran military dictatorship, in an effort to isolate and destroy an expanding guerrilla movement, began a "scorched

earth" campaign in the rural areas. The Salvadoran Armed Forces
burned peasants' crops, fruit trees, and homes. They killed union-
ized farmworkers as well as priests and catechists—anyone they perceived as a threat to their continuing rule. Esperanza was one of an
estimated two million Salvadorans—a third of the nation's total
population—who fled their homes in terror.

She recounts the *Guinda del Mayo* (the Flight of May,
1980),[1] when she and her neighbors ran for days, finally hiding in thorny underbrush and capping their children's mouths
to avoid detection. "We were surrounded by the troops. They
were combing the whole zone, helicopters machine-gunning
from above, and we were under the *chupamiel* (flowering vine),
praying for our lives." She says they had been running away from
the massacre that had taken place at the Sumpul River and they
had been without food for two days. "The soldiers were so close
that we could see them eating the mangos from the trees. How I
longed to eat one of those mangos! We were hungry and so were
our children. Instead, we covered the mouths of our babies to
keep them from crying. But thanks be to God, even though in
our group there were three of us who had recently given birth,
our babies didn't cry. The soldiers were close by, but they didn't
detect us."

Esperanza explains that in that moment, God accompanied
her and gave her strength. "I thought to myself, 'This is the Spirit
of God that gives strength and trust.'" She says that this moment
is an example of what she calls *la fe vivida*—a faith that is lived.
"It is confidence in your own self that God is within you. We
had to trust in ourselves with that confidence. For example, there
were moments when we felt we could uncover the babies' mouths
because we sensed that they wouldn't cry. And they didn't cry.
We were not discovered." Esperanza survived many such encounters, learning to trust the Spirit of God that was within her to
guide her.

In another incident, Esperanza, her husband, and several others were fleeing an army incursion when her husband was hit by gunfire. "It was another experience with this lived faith, this really deep trust in myself. My husband was shot through the back, through his shoulders." Using her hands, she shows me how the two G3 bullets exited his body. Her left hand, starkly brown against the canary yellow of her T-shirt, bursts open beneath her left breast, and her right hand splays above her right breast. "Two giant holes, here and here, and the flesh hanging out, and the blood running. And I thought to myself, 'He's going to die,' because just looking at him you could see that. But a health promoter—one of our own, trained in first aid—cleaned the wounds and then covered them so that they wouldn't get infected. It was a miracle of God! Not a single organ was touched! No infection! And we were there hiding in the mountains, in the brush, for a month! I say this because we need to have faith in our own capacities. Sometimes you think that only the doctor can heal, but no, it's faith that heals." The health promoter, she emphasizes, was a *campesino*—a subsistence farmer like herself—who had faith in his abilities to save her husband's life.

Esperanza gives a firm nod with her head. "You have to have trust in your own self. *Esta es la fe vivida* [this is a lived faith]. The importance of having faith is to see it concretized in your own self."

Raised Roman Catholic, Esperanza grew up in a blend of Catholicism and the beliefs stemming from rural Salvadorans' indigenous roots. Before the war, Esperanza received training as Celebrator of the Word, since priests were rarely able to come to their isolated area. "When I was learning to become a Celebrator of the Word, I realized that there was an unjust system in place here in El Salvador and that all of us have responsibilities, but we also have rights to be treated equally. Struggle is necessary to gain these rights. So from the very beginning, faith and social justice went hand in hand for me."

When asked about the Divine Feminine, Esperanza alludes to a God who is continually birthing from within and likens it to her own motherhood. "As women, we always pray for our children, 'Holy God, bless my children with health. Protect them.' That's because within us, there is that God who accompanies us, and that God is good, compassionate, and works miracles within us."

Esperanza tells me that her mother was the village midwife, and she helped Esperanza to give birth to eight children, of which two died, one in the *Guinda del Mayo* mentioned earlier. Despite (or perhaps in keeping with) these many ordeals, Esperanza freed herself of the notion of innate female inferiority and birthed a new understanding of the Spirit within her, manifested as confidence and trust in her own intuition and that inner voice she identifies as the God within.

She shares another example of this God within. "During the war, the Jesuits invited me to tell my story in Italy. I was a country woman; I didn't know cities, not even the township of my province, Chalatenango. When my companions took me to the airport, they could only accompany me so far. Then they said, 'From here on, you're on your own. You alone will have to defend yourself.' It was my first experience of traveling outside the country. I was afraid. I was worried. I didn't know what to do."

Alone in the airport, Esperanza was seized by fear, and rightly so, for she was vulnerable to capture and torture simply because she was a peasant from a war zone. But the thought came to her: "'When we come into this world, we come alone. We are born alone, and everything is learned on the way, as part of a process. I can learn this. But first, I have to break through this fear!' And then suddenly," she continues, gesturing to her chest, "I felt this tremendous courage in my body—*un coraje en mi cuerpo*—and then a voice, like someone inside me was saying, 'Esperanza, ask.' This tremendous courage, this knowledge that was born from within, gave me energy, and I felt a great confidence in my own person, that I could do what was needed.

"Just then, a man passed by, and I felt this urging to ask him for guidance." Despite the very real possibility that asking a question of the wrong person could result in detention or worse, Esperanza acted on her inner prompting and said, "Excuse me, sir, I need to take a plane, but I don't know which one or how."

"Show me your ticket," he said, and at first Esperanza thought she'd endangered herself. But to her great relief, he said, "You are going to Milano, and this is your number."

"And then," Esperanza says, "he took me by the hand. He said, 'I am on the same plane as you, but I am only going to Guatemala. After that, you go on alone. But you can do it!' And so for me, it was a miracle of God that I received because it illumined my mind of what I am capable of—*que puedo hacer yo*. And so you see, God is within us, helping us. *Dios pone los elementos a uno*—God gives us what we need."

In preparation for my next question, I motion to the hill-sides, lush with recent rains. Pointing to the corn sprouting in rows and the bean vines twisting up their stakes, I ask Esperanza about the earth.

She answers, "Everything on planet earth, God gave. All plants—plants for medicine, fruits for us to eat, leaves and roots that are medicine—all that we have. One day, walking to a neigh-boring village, I sat down next to a brook where the water was flowing. I was there for about an hour, alone, and it filled me with life—*me llenó de vida*! I was thinking about nature and about myself, listening to the rushing of the water. And I felt grateful that God gave us water, because we need it. And I saw the rocks there, and I thought, thank you for the rocks. God gave us rocks to build fences with, to build houses with, so many things that we do with rocks! And the trees! God gave us the trees also, so many things we can do with trees! God created everything in harmony, *bién ordenado*. We are the *destructores*, the ones who destroy. People are too quick to cut down the trees. Not all of us remember to take care of the earth, but it is something that God has given to all of us."

When I ask Esperanza for her advice for young women, she sighs, "Ay, so many things I would like to share with them: participate in the good things of the community, starting with church and community activities; learn good values. With good values, one knows how to treat others with affection and respect, from the aging to the children. Without values, we mistreat one another."

I would have liked to spend another hour with Esperanza, but her bus is approaching, and it is the last one of the day. I thank her several times, for I feel that she and so many of her compatriots have blessed me with their examples of faith, courage, and confidence. As her yellow-skirted, sturdy brown legs sprint for the bus, her words remain with me: "This is the Spirit of God that gives strength and trust.... It is confidence in your own self that God is within you." As with Esperanza, the insight gives me courage.

Going Deeper

1. In which moments did Esperanza experience God's presence most intensely?

2. How does Esperanza characterize God's presence within her? How do you sense this Spirit within you?

3. How does Esperanza draw on "the God within" when fear presents itself? How can you deal with fear differently?

Try This

Plan on sitting quietly for at least ten minutes, twenty minutes or longer being ideal. Close your eyes. Relax your body, allowing any tension or stress to dissipate. Inhale slowly and exhale thoroughly for at least ten cycles of in-and-out breaths. Focus your mind on the word "in" as you fill your lungs and "out" or "empty" as you empty your lungs of the last remnant of air. Breathe another ten or twenty cycles in this fashion, thinking "in" as you inhale and "empty" as you exhale, letting all thoughts drift away. Afterward, write what you felt inside, especially when you were "empty."

Or try this: If a moment of tension or fear arises for you, close your eyes and breathe through at least five cycles of slow, calm inhalations and exhalations, focusing your mind on the filling and emptying movements of your lungs. How does your awareness of breath and/or your awareness of the Inner Divine affect your fear?

Lindsey

Where We Find God

You have something beautiful within you. You have who you are. You have integrity. You have decency. You have goodness, and God loves that in you and that's always going to be there, no matter what happens.... Hold onto that message that you are loved for who you are.

LINDSEY CRITTENDEN, AUTHOR

Lindsey's face is serene—clear eyes behind brown-rimmed glasses—but her hands are in constant motion, reaching, gesticulating, folding inward in mock prayer. When I ask her to describe a moment when she felt the Divine palpably, she responds, "I was up at Bishop's Ranch[1] on a parish retreat. But I felt like being alone. I was having tons of anxiety, so I decided to go for a walk on the trail that goes up to the lake. I was totally in my head, you know, probably walking with a furrowed brow, when I got to this place in a clearing where you can go a couple of different ways. It was a hot afternoon, and the sun was shining. I stopped there, and I felt the sun and heard this voice. It wasn't a male voice or a female voice. It was like the wind or something, and it said, 'I love you.' Part of me was instantly critical of it. 'That's so hokey,' I thought. But then I felt this warmth in me, and for a split second, I felt my whole body relax." She motions from her heart outward and downward, her hands undulating at the wrists. "It was this physical sensation of inner warmth, like I had swallowed some warm liquid that was filling me up inside. My whole body went 'Ah.'"

When the feeling slipped away, Lindsey decided that she'd just imagined it. Almost immediately, she felt anxious again. "I was like, 'What was that? If that was God telling me God loves me, well then, why would I feel anxious again?' I got all up in my head again."

Later, after the retreat, she spoke to her priest. "I remember I said, 'If this experience was from God, why would it scare me?' And he said, 'How could it not?'"

His response gave Lindsey the permission she needed to stop analyzing the experience and allow other prayer experiences to fill her and calm her. That year, she had been going through a particularly bad bout of depression and intense anxiety. She'd come back to the Episcopal Church, the faith she'd been raised in, a few years beforehand when she'd been grieving the death of her younger brother, murdered at age twenty-six. As she describes in her memoir, *The Water Will Hold You: A Skeptic Learns to Pray*,[2] she'd experienced intense light and warmth at his deathbed in the hospital. Even then, a few years passed before she began an active prayer life. The words spoken to her on that solitary trail while she was on retreat were a mini-breakthrough for her.

"The experience on the trail was a step in coming closer to the idea that you can totally be yourself with God. You don't have to be on your best behavior. I don't think my parents ever told me this, but I had this notion growing up that God was the ultimate grown-up. You had to be on really good behavior around God. God was like the school principal or something," she quips, and we both laugh. "It wasn't that I didn't think God loved me, but

I really never thought that God *did* love me. People would say, 'God loves you,' and I'd think, 'Okay,' but I didn't really feel it.

"I still don't know what it means to say, 'God loves me.' I don't think of God as a person who loves the way people love. God's love is something we can experience, but it's ultimately incomprehensible. But that experience at Bishop's Ranch took me further along in the notion of the Divine as something other than this stern man with a beard. It was more like a maternal kind of love, something that was just very accepting."

Lindsey doesn't draw a direct parallel between how God is portrayed and how young women view themselves, but she explains that in adolescence, "I wasn't comfortable with who I was. Now I think the message I'd give to a young girl would be to point her to what Jesus said to his disciples: You have something beautiful within you. You have who you are. You have integrity. You have decency. You have goodness, and God loves that in you and that's always going to be there, no matter what happens. You're going to make mistakes and do things you don't feel good about, and people will make you feel bad. You're going to have days that test you. But you'll always have that integrity inside. Hold onto that message that you are loved for who you are."

Lindsey, who grieved the loss of both her parents not long after her only sibling's death, says in her memoir that prayer holds her just as water buoys a person who learns to trust, to float. Describing her current experience of prayer, Lindsey says, "Lately I've been praying the rosary again, because it's tactile and it gives me a focus. But the words I've been using are a meditation on the here and now. For one of the beads"—she thumbs an imaginary bead—"you say, 'The kingdom of heaven is within you and outside you,' which is something attributed to Jesus in the Gospel of Thomas.[3]

"I've been thinking a lot about that, and the notion that you have it inside you." Lindsey brings up a passage from the Gospel of John as an example. "Jesus is saying good-bye to the disciples and he gives that long, long, long talk about the fact that he's leaving, and he's basically saying, 'You already know everything you need to know.' And the disciples are like, 'What are we going to do?'" Mimicking their anxiety, Lindsey raises quivering hands and injects worry into her voice as she repeats, "'Just what are we going to do?'"

Lowering her hands, Lindsey quotes Jesus's response: "'Love one another.'"

I nod my head in agreement, and Lindsey continues. "In silence, in devotion, in personal prayer we can find that kernel of the Divine in all in us. It manifests itself in different ways in different people. But I also think it's outside of us, in relationships with other people and what we do for other people and what they do for us. We can create the kind of relationships based on love and based on integrity that can further that inner sense of communion with something bigger than ourselves."

She opens her arms in an inverted arch. "I've always thought of God as this idea that there is something bigger than ourselves. It's inside us, and yet it's bigger than we are. And it has a kind of consciousness. I don't know if God intervenes, but when there's suffering and pain, God feels that suffering and pain. I don't know how that happens, but I believe that it does, somehow. There's a kind of communion, connection."

I am reminded of the scene in Lindsey's memoir where she is standing next to her brother. In her book, she describes "his head swaddled in a turban of white gauze" and a ventilator working his lungs. There, at her brother's bed, she experiences inexplicable warmth when she puts her head to his chest and feels "[t]he strongest love I've ever known. A moment of pure, transcendent grace. My brother was not conscious—he would never be conscious again—and yet he felt it, too. I cannot explain that, but I know it.... In that small warm pocket of space, I did not hear my parents' sobs or the *whoosh* of the ventilator. I did not see the orange tint of my brother's skin or his brow beneath the turban of gauze. Everything outside of him and me fell away. Time expanded and stood still. I had never felt such sweetness before, such encompassing light.... Death reduces love to its essential, and there—in essence—is where we find God."[4]

Going Deeper

1. What spiritual moments did Lindsey describe, and how did she open herself to them?

2. How do you think Lindsey's experiences contribute to her ability to say, "You are loved for who you are"?

3. How do you experience divine love in your life, and how does it influence your view of yourself?

Try This

After a few moments of quiet, relaxed breathing, picture in your mind someone who is dear to you who has passed on. For as long as you like, hold onto that image. Treasure that person and what he or she shared with you. What would that person say to you about your worth or the ability to love yourself? Take a moment to write down your reflections.

Lori

Rocking in the Mother's Arms

God is revealed to us in so many ways. I asked; God answered; my life changed.... Each of us lives with the One inside our hearts who is everything we need and more than we can possibly imagine.

REVEREND LORI EICKMANN,
LUTHERAN PASTOR, SIERRA PACIFIC SYNOD

Lori Eickmann sits very straight. Her eyes are strikingly blue and her voice animated. She grew up in a churchgoing family, she says, but left home for college in the seventies during the height of the women's lib movement. Like many of her friends and colleagues, she began looking at the world through a new lens, one shaped by the women's movement. She jokes, "Sometimes I toyed with the idea of changing my last name to Eick*woman*." She got her degree in journalism and started working for the *San Jose Mercury News*, all without finding a church where she fit. But after getting married, and with children on the horizon, Lori and her husband began looking for a church community.

Within a few years, Lori and Steve started attending a Lutheran church in Dublin, California, that was pastored by a married couple. Lori felt that if one of the pastors was a woman, she would temper the male-dominant doctrine and language that Lori had endured as a child. But that was not the case, at least not at first.

Lori describes sitting in church and longing for something different, something more affirming of women. "I felt invisible, there in church. Maybe it was because I had children—one son and one daughter—and I was seeing the world through their eyes. I had to notice that the world offers a God who, as someone wrote, 'is somehow more like my father, husband and brother than like me.' I began to ache for all the daughters who couldn't see themselves reflected in the Divine. I ached for them and for myself, because I knew we were created in God's image, but mainstream Christian religion seemed unwilling to admit that."[1]

One day after church, Lori brought this up with the woman pastor. "Jan," she asked, "why does everything about God and religion seem to be about men and maleness?"

The pastor's response floored Lori. She said, "Oh, there are feminine images of God in the Bible." And Lori said, "Nobody's ever told me that!" The pastor gave her copies of *The Divine Feminine: The Biblical Imagery of God as Female* by Virginia Ramey Mollenkott[2] and *Biblical Affirmations of Women* by Leonard Swidler.[3]

In reading these books, Lori discovered several biblical passages where God makes self-references that use female imagery: as a woman in labor, as a she-bear defending her cubs, as a midwife, and as a nursing mother.[4] She read in Proverbs that Wisdom calls out in the streets, and in Matthew 11, "Wisdom is vindicated by her children," both references to a feminine characterization of God prevalent during Jesus's time.

These passages were a catalyst for Lori. Lori remembers kneeling to pray when she suddenly said, "Heavenly Mother," in addressing God. "It was a Spirit-led thing," she reflects. "Not an intellectual decision." She expresses that her feeling that something was amiss in church "was wiped away like a tear from a child's face."

With the words "Heavenly Mother," Lori says she named the God of her heart, expressing what she'd felt for years. God had long felt to her as much like a heavenly mother as like a heavenly father. But Lori clarifies that the God she names as Mother is one face of the Christian Trinity. To Lori, the three persons of the triune God, and the relationships they engender, are important; not just God the Parent, but also Jesus and the indwelling Spirit. The three persons of the Trinity are palpable to Lori. They rock her, literally.

The first time the rocking happened was the Monday after she had been on an intensive women's retreat. She had some symbols from the retreat spread out on a cedar chest in her bedroom and was kneeling in front of this makeshift altar when the rocking started. "It really terrified me. I was afraid I'd erupt into tongues or something like that. I'd never experienced anything like that, and the thought came to me: this is what it feels like to be filled with the Spirit."[5]

The rocking stopped, and Lori opened her eyes. She bent forward to get up for lunch, but then she decided to pray a little more. "I closed my eyes, and the rocking started up again. My first thought was, 'This is really inconvenient if it's going to happen every time I close my eyes!' But then I had this sensation of feeling Jesus. During the retreat, I'd had this intense feeling like Jesus was sitting right next to me and looking over me, and when I started feeling the rocking again in front of the cedar chest in my bedroom, I felt that same presence, this Jesus presence."

The lunch hour had come and gone, but still Lori felt like she should keep praying. When she closed her eyes the third time, she knew, as she later wrote for the *San Jose Mercury News*, "that [the rocking] would happen again because, the thought came to me, 'There are three of them.' When it started the third time, it was so different, so slow and gentle, so loving. And then I understood: this is my heavenly mother, because mothers rock their children gently."[6]

The rocking confirmed for Lori that she was on the right path. The gentle cradling she felt was so real, so tangible that she couldn't ignore it or explain it away. It happened at other times, even when she wasn't praying, and she viewed it as a confirmation of her "calling to show the feminine in the Divine." Lori started a women's group at the church and, through a series of synchronicities, entered the seminary the following fall, even though she'd initially believed she would enroll after her children were a little older.

After eight years of seminary (she went part-time) and two years of serving churches as an interim pastor, Lori was ordained as a pastor called specifically to serve churches that are in between pastors. In addition to helping churches discern their next pastor while serving as their interim pastor, Lori leads a three-week study on female imagery for God in the Bible. She discusses passages like Isaiah 42:14 (God giving birth), Isaiah 49:15 (God likened to a nursing mother), and Matthew 23:37 (Jesus likening himself to a mother hen).[7] "My passion is helping people see that there is a biblical basis for naming God Mother or she. It is not just something twentieth-century feminists made up!"

Lori affirms, "God is revealed to us in so many ways. I asked; God answered; my life changed. Even before I asked, God was the Heavenly One, my Sacred Mother, my Savior-Brother, the Passionate Spirit within. And I'm just one person. Each of us lives with the One inside our hearts who is everything we need and more than we can possibly imagine."[8]

Going Deeper

1. How did Lori make room for divine inspiration and divine love in her life?

2. What do you feel about Lori's experiences of being rocked? How did Lori's experiences contribute to her love of self and lead to a rebirth in her sense of vocation?

3. What are the ways in which you experience the Divine in your life? In which moments do you feel loved by God?

Try This

Get comfortable. Read "Meditation on Divine Love" in the section "Meditations and Visualizations" (page 270). If you can, record it for yourself or have a friend read it out loud to you as you breathe deeply and relax into its message. When prerecording, be sure to read slowly and pause for at least five seconds on the ellipsis (…) and at least ten seconds between paragraphs. These pauses allow you to go deeper into the meditation experience.

Hyun Kyung

From the Palms of God into the Vortex of Becoming

> Even if I had been killed in that torture chamber, I knew that I could not be separated from this great love of God ... whatever the outcome, whether I died or I lived. I felt myself to be in the palms of God.
>
> DR. CHUNG HYUN KYUNG,[1]
> ASSOCIATE PROFESSOR OF ECUMENICAL
> STUDIES, UNION THEOLOGICAL SEMINARY[2]

Dr. Chung Hyun Kyung's face is round and radiant like a full moon cresting a slender mountain. I strain to catch each accented word as she tells me of the time she was kidnapped, imprisoned, and tortured by the South Korean dictatorship. "My 'crime' was hiding another student activist, and they wanted this information from me. In the torture chamber I learned that whenever I made human contact with the torturers, they couldn't torture me anymore. But some torturers, their soul is not with them anymore, so no matter what you try, you cannot make contact. This one time, I got a lost-soul torturer. No matter how I tried to talk to him, smile at him, ask about his family or friends, I couldn't connect. He was really untouchable. Then the torture began."

Hyun Kyung's eyes transmit a glimpse of the beatings, hangings, and other tortures that made her lose consciousness. "So with this torturer, I was at a crossroads—either I had to tell him where my friend was, endangering my friend's life, or I could be killed myself. And in this life-and-death situation, I heard, coming from a distant place, this mantra: "God is my shepherd." I had recited the Twenty-Third Psalm as a child in church, and it came to me, over and over, like a mantra. Even though I was literally walking the valley of death, I knew God's staff would comfort me. And through the horrible pain, I felt very soft and warm hands holding me."

She touches the back of my hand gently and inclines her perfect, nearly shaved head toward me. "The hands were neither male nor female, just a round presence that was holding me, carrying me. Despite the pain, I felt sooooo peaceful. It was the most powerful experience of the Divine. I *knew* God existed. Even if I had been killed in that torture chamber, I knew that I could not be separated from this great love of God." She cups her hands together and brings them to her heart. "I had been very afraid, but after I felt those hands supporting me, I just felt so calm, and I felt that I could go through it, whatever the outcome, whether I died or I lived. I felt myself to be in the palms of God."

After she was released from prison, Hyun Kyung decided that she wanted to learn more about God and how God accompanied her people's struggle. "I wanted to become a theologian—a feminist liberation theologian. But in South Korea at that time, all liberation theology books were banned by the dictatorship. You could be imprisoned or executed for reading *Das Kapital* by Karl Marx. How could I continue to study in South Korea?"

Having obtained her bachelor's and master's degrees in Korea, Hyun Kyung came to the United States to pursue doctoral studies in theology. She wanted to explore feminist theology—the lived faith of Asian women—and not the "theology of dead European men." But when it came time to write her dissertation, the seminary did not approve her way of doing theology. The seminary's response paralyzed her, and she was unable to write a single word of her dissertation. Her marriage was also falling apart. She'd married a fellow student movement leader in Korea, but he had gotten involved in a fundamentalist Christian sect, opening a chasm in their marriage.

"I was at a crossroads again, but this time it was not between the life and death of my body; it was the life or death of my spirit—of my intellectual life, my love life, my spiritual life. So I created an altar with my Bible, some feathers, some candles, and I began to pray. I sobbed from morning until nighttime."

In this anguished, altered state, Hyun Kyung says she felt herself transported to the eastern seashore of Korea. "There I met a Buddhist monk who told me I must go deeper, and so I went deep into the forest, into the Seol-Ak Mountain." She came to a cliff below which frothed a river swirling with the failed-dragon snake-animal Ee-Moo-Ki. "I heard an urging: 'Touch the Ee-Moo-Ki.' As I stood there at the edge of the cliff, I thought, 'What have I got to lose? I'm dying anyway.' I took off my shoes and dove, and when I touched the slimy side of the Ee-Moo-Ki, it turned into a green dragon that carried me on its back as it flew." She describes landing at a gated farm. Inside was an old woman, "very much like my Korean grandmothers. I was hungry, and she fed me. She gave me the daily task of drawing water from the well so that she could water her fields." As the fields grew, rapidly bearing their fruit, Hyun Kyung felt joy arise within her, something she had not felt in a long, long time. But the old woman told her that she should prepare to leave. "I didn't want to leave. The impasse over my dissertation was not resolved. I still didn't know what to do about my marriage. But the old woman told me, 'You *do* know. All the answers you already know. You already have the power within you. Just trust yourself.'

"Before leaving, I asked her name. She said 'Quan Yin.'[3] Even though I didn't come from a Buddhist family—my family had been Christian for three generations—the collective unconscious of my ancestors' faith came to me, and Quan Yin, who I hadn't known about, came to me, encouraging me in my effort to do feminist theology from Asian women's struggle for liberation. My school was having a hard time accepting my style of feminist theology, but Quan Yin encouraged me, saying, 'Of course you can do this. Trust yourself.'"

After that experience, Hyun Kyung says the appropriate selections of more traditional theologians' works came to her in dreams, and she incorporated them into her dissertation on Asian women's theologies, a solution acceptable to the seminary. But there was no solution for her marriage, and she and her spouse separated and then divorced.

Later, when Hyun Kyung actually visited the eastern shore of Korea where she'd landed in her meditation, she discovered a temple dedicated to Quan Yin there. Piqued by the vision experience, Hyun Kyung began to study Zen Buddhism almost as soon as she'd passed her doctoral exams. "I wanted to know Buddhism experientially, so I went to the Korean Zen Center, and I became a student in the Kwan Um Zen School. I studied with Zen Master Seung Sahn. After twenty years of studying with Zen Master Seung Sahn, and at various moments with Thich Nhat Hanh, the Dalai Lama, and Maha Gosananda, I became a Buddhist dharma teacher in the Kwan Um Zen School of the Korean tradition of Buddhism."

Hyun Kyung laughs. "Zen Master Seung Sahn said that in Kwan Um Zen School, you have to practice hard, so experiences like the one I had with Quan Yin are 'dharma cookies' to entice us to do the hard practice!" He told me, 'You have to go deeper into the meaning of emptiness and don't-know.' He discouraged me from this kind of connection with Quan Yin."

Many years later, when Hyun Kyung was on silent retreat and had been meditating sixteen hours a day for one hundred days, she was once again taken by the dragon to Quan Yin's place beyond the gate, but Quan Yin was not there. Hyun Kyung describes how in the vision she cooked rice to feed a hungry boy, and when she looked in the kitchen mirror, the face looking back at her was that of Quan Yin. "In the earlier vision, I couldn't see my reflection when I looked in the well, but now I had the face of Quan Yin. My teacher told me, 'When you are a child, the mother is raising you in faith. But when you become an adult, you don't need mother's milk anymore. You *are* the Buddha. And you have to move beyond any image or word or shape into the vast emptiness, the don't-know. Everything comes from this vortex of becoming and energy and transformation.'

"Zen practice is shedding layer after layer, like an onion, shedding all your layers of being until you reach that emptiness. I have a very sweet memory of this personal encounter with the Divine Feminine, Quan Yin, but now, more and more I am entering the mystery of don't-know. Before the don't-know threatened me, made me anxious, but now, don't-know makes me so peaceful, enabling me to be with this very moment, the present, to be very wide open"—she extends her arms—"like *wow*! Let's see what's next!

"My teacher said that we all have power to make something life-giving. You have that power. So don't be swayed by any power. Whatever happens to you, you have the inner power to deal with it and make it better."

At Union Theological Seminary, Dr. Chung teaches Buddhist-Christian dialogue as well as ecofeminist theology and interfaith peacemaking. She also leads a daily early morning meditation class. "I can see that in the four months between the beginning of the class and the end of the class, the students' faces change! And their energy changes. It's just beautiful to watch," she adds in a tone of wonder and gratitude. "And I feel very privileged to nurture young people into this world of meditation.

"Zen taught me that meditation is mindfulness. Meditation is not something special. It's an everyday, every-moment activity. When you eat, you eat with a 100 percent of your attention focused on your food, 100 percent focused on the here and now. That's meditation. But I still need a sitting for one month or a sitting for one week. I call it housecleaning. You dust every day a little bit, but sometimes you do a spring cleaning of the whole house. I need that from time to time."

When I ask Dr. Chung about her communities and what she is doing to safeguard the health of the earth, she responds that she is joining with others in protesting the Korea-U.S. plans to build a navy base and harbor nuclear warships at the formerly protected and venerated Jeju island in South Korea. Remembering her recent trip to Jeju island to accompany the protesters, she says, "These young people have a bigger vision, to protect *life*, so I want to be with them. I feel most alive marching among the people: the women's movement, the ecological movement, the peace movement." Very softly she adds, "I feel the presence of God with every step."

When I ask if Hyun Kyung has anything to add, she says, "Another thing in my meditation practice, I had this big, big hole in my heart from when I was one year old because I had the Korean version of a surrogate mother. When I was one year old, I was taken from my biological mother to my father's wife, and I didn't discover this family secret until I was thirty-one years old! When I found out, I thought, 'Oh!'" Hyun Kyung gasps. "That's why I have this big hole in my heart! This was due to the loss of my mother when I was one year old! What a great trauma! And also, I was one of the first radical feminist liberation theologians in my country, and that's a lot of burden! I had so much trauma embodied in me, and I had a big hole here"—she places her hand over her heart. "And then, in meditation, this hole kept going down and down"—she lowers her hand to her abdomen—"to here, my *dan-jun*, my womb, and then it became crystal clear, and in that crystal I could see the whooole wooorld!"

I am amazed because Dr. Chung has indeed traveled the world in her work with grassroots eco-peace and women's rights movements, most recently touring seventeen Islamic countries and gathering women's stories for her forthcoming book, *Life Flowers in the Garden of Allah: An Islamic Pilgrimage.* But she is not yet finished with her "womb" story; her hand still hovers at her abdomen. "I learned in meditation that my biggest trauma was my biggest power when it was transformed. I almost felt like I was pregnant with the whole world because out of that deep [mother] pain that I had experienced, I realized that I no longer had any fear. People would say to me, 'How could you go to seventeen Muslim countries by yourself? Weren't some of them at war? Weren't you afraid?' And I said, 'No. In every country, I met a person who was my angel. They became my shepherd in every place!'"

Just like her recent experience with Hurricane Sandy barreling through New York. When the lights went out in Manhattan and the wind gusted against the windows of her high-rise, she felt tranquility, not fear. In the chaotic darkness, she rested and contemplated. She said, "When Mother Earth is angry, we have to listen to her anger. We have to hear her wake-up call for all of us. We have to trust her."

When I ask Hyun Kyung for her words of wisdom for young women, she tells me that was the topic of a book she wrote in Korea called *Letter from the Future: The Goddess-Spell according to Hyun Kyung.* "In that book, I write 'ten commandments' for a young woman to be fully who she is. The very first commandment is to love and trust yourself no matter what. That is the very beginning of everything. Whatever happens to you, never stop believing that you're lovable. Love yourself first—before everyone—and *trust* yourself. Sometimes I ask myself, 'Hyun Kyung, do you trust yourself?' And sometimes, like any woman, I lose confidence. But whenever that happens, I always come back to me"—she places her hand on her abdomen again—"to this womb place. I trust it more than anything." She smiles, and her eyes glimmer. "Womb power, womb intuition, womb wisdom!"

Going Deeper

1. How did Hyun Kyung's most difficult experiences affect her faith and the direction of her life? How were they transformative?

2. How did Hyun Kyung's deepest wound become transformed into her greatest strength?

3. Think of your deepest wounds. How might they become transformed into your greatest strengths?

Try This

Pick one household chore and do it mindfully, that is, in the presence of Spirit. Your chore could be folding clothes, chopping vegetables, or washing dishes. Whatever your task, focus all your attention on it. Complete it with devotion. Empty your thoughts to more fully experience God's presence—and your own—in the now.

Susan

Worthy to Stand Here with God

The experience of the Divine comes to us at any stage of our life, in big ways and small ways. It can come in nature, in other people, in amazing experiences of peace breaking out somewhere where there's been war, some good coming out of tragedy—all kinds of ways for it to happen if we keep our eyes and our minds and our hearts open.

SUSAN STROUSE, PASTOR, FIRST UNITED LUTHERAN CHURCH, AND INTERIM EXECUTIVE DIRECTOR, INTERFAITH CENTER AT THE PRESIDIO

Susan Strouse is an ordained Lutheran pastor with a doctorate in interfaith dialogue. Her brown eyes dance as she tells me a story about her seminary experience. "In seminary I got indoctrinated into 'correct' theology and 'correct' practice. I look back now, and I think they stuffed me into this box, and they did a good job of it. I got in the box, and I came out thinking, 'This is our theology, and we're right!'" Susan raises her fist in mock triumph. "Lutherans are right!

"Back then, interfaith work wasn't even on my radar at all. I was in Buffalo, New York, and in my second parish when I got involved in an interfaith group.

34

I only got involved because the bishop asked me to and because I was the dean of the conference. I sort of got dragged into it unwillingly, but once I was in, all of sudden I started having these experiences, and certain things in church no longer made sense to me."

I ask Susan about the experiences, and she responds, "Well, the first one came at a time of emotional turmoil for me. I was part of this prayer group, and we were all sitting on the carpet, and the spiritual director said we were to be in silent time and praying. Later I realized that I'd been hunched over." Susan curls inward. "And I had my hands folded and my head down. And suddenly I heard very clearly a voice within myself say, 'You don't have to hang your head in shame anymore.' And it was such an amazing experience of grace." Susan's voice brightens. "And every since then, I've never prayed with my head down, hunched over. Because I know that I didn't say those words to myself. They came from somewhere else. It was a very real powerful experience. It was life changing."

"How?"

"Well, some liturgies say, 'I'm not worthy to come here before you' or 'Have mercy on me, Lord, I'm a miserable sinner,' but I realized that I don't have to grovel before God. Instead I think I am worthy to stand here with God." Susan laughs. "Because God told me!

"The experience really changed how I thought about God. At the time, I was in the middle of a second marriage that was going bad, so there was that whole trauma. The fact that I was ordained by that time meant it was going to be a huge mess to have to deal with the church. Because [when you're a pastor] in that situation, you can't just resolve something between two people. No, you have to involve the bishop and the congregations and everybody else. It was a big deal. And I was feeling like a failure. Married and divorced twice." Susan rolls her eyes. "I felt crappy, telling myself things like, 'You did it again. What kind of person are you?'

"But the experience of the Divine felt very joyful, and it also opened me up to having more experiences in some very real ways.

It changed me. I realized that the Divine was accessible and affirming and created a sense of joy that I had not had before. So I was
able to go into that situation of difficulty with a different way of
thinking about how I was going to handle things. Not that everything was always joyful, but—" Susan's voice rings stronger—"it
helped to know that I'm okay and that no matter what happens,
I'm going to be okay. Really, I felt a sense of joyfulness and deep
gratitude for everything that I had received."

I prod Susan to tell another experience, since she'd alluded
to several. She responds, "The next one that comes to my mind is
when a spiritual director led me and two other women in a guided
visualization. In it, she had us going down a stairway, finding a
door at the bottom, opening the door, and going in. When I got to
the bottom of the stairway in my mind, there was this massive oak
door, like to a medieval castle, and I could not open it, it was so
heavy. But even in my mind I'm stubborn, and I kept pushing on
it and pushing on it. Finally, the door dissolved, and I was in this
space of bright light—intense orange, yellow, green light—but I
felt that I could not go further because I was not worthy. I couldn't
be in that light, so I was holding back. And then the light just
came and overwhelmed me, and I was within the light, and then I
was okay. The light was very intense, kind of swirling and glowing.
It was a wonderful, wonderful experience of grace.

"At the time, I was in this women's prayer group—all clergy—
and we started talking about spiritual experiences, and it was almost
like we were afraid to tell anybody these things because we knew that
as Lutherans we're not supposed to have these experiences. It was
like, 'Whoa, we're outside of the Lutheran box here a little bit!' But
we were also women discussing how women experience the Divine.
Because we'd all been in seminary, and seminary was like, 'Okay, we
let you women in, but we expect you to behave like us, think like us,
live like us, and dress like us.' They didn't want to hear about wom-
en's ways of theology or inclusive language. It was a joke to them.

I got to wondering, 'Gee, maybe all those women that our professors joked about, those early Christian women who were doing mystical kinds of things, maybe there was something there.'"

Susan's mystical experiences paralleled her deepening understanding of other religions. Her congregation wanted to study world religions. "They asked me to invite a Hindu woman I knew to our study group. After her presentation, an older member of our study group was distraught. She said to me, 'I don't know what to do about this. I love this group. I love learning about these other religions, and I loved meeting Pat and hearing about her religion. But I'm afraid that if I accept that her religion is valid, then I'm betraying Jesus.' That was a defining moment for me. My theology was changing so radically that I realized that I couldn't get up and say some of the things in the liturgy that I'd said before. I just couldn't do it, not with any integrity. And so I decided to leave, get my doctorate in interfaith dialogue. Mainly I wanted to help Christians understand what it means to be a Christian in an interfaith world. The next thing you know someone encouraged me to interview for First United Lutheran Church, and I discovered a Lutheran church that actually likes thinking in this way, likes living outside that Lutheran box."

Susan brings her hands together. "When you start talking to people of different faiths, they've had the same kind of mystical experiences. When you start talking on that level, all of a sudden the doctrinal differences go away. They just don't exist. You come from that place of pure devotion, where it's all about the Divine. And you don't have to worry about whose Divine. It's all the same One."

Susan likens her ongoing relationship with the Divine to that outlined in *Practicing the Presence of God*, a pamphlet attributed to a sixteenth-century monk named Brother Lawrence. "What Brother Lawrence says resonates for me, this sense of being present to God in every moment. It's the same with Buddhism and Taoism. There's no separation between you and me and the Divine. The Divine is within me, but the Divine is not impersonal. There is

Something that cares about me. It's around me and connected to everything else. It's like a web. I love the idea of the web.

"For example, prayer. Sometimes we agonize about prayer at First United because we're real obsessive about the details, like what is prayer exactly and who are we praying to? But in a way it doesn't even matter. It doesn't even matter what words we use, whether they're the 'correct' theological language. What matters is that we're in that state of prayer. We're vibrating the web. If we're praying for somebody's mother whom we don't even know, that's okay because we're connected. We're all the web, all of us together, and so whatever we're doing, with whatever words we're saying, to me that's prayer. And the web is vibrating."

Susan says she also believes there's a love that's overarching. "There's a sense of the whole, and it is always trying to draw out the best in us. We always have a choice, but the Divine is kind of luring us to the better choice. And if we make a bad choice, it's okay. God's going to work with that. What matters now is the next choice, and the next choice after that. God is always helping us to make the best choice. Even in bad stuff, there's always that lure into wholeness."

Our conversation turns to the Divine Feminine. Days before the interview, Susan had just attended a four-day conference called Women of Spirit and Faith.[1] "Philosophically I don't have any problem with the Divine Feminine, but in my own practice I am so far away from thinking about the Divine in any anthropomorphic way that neither Father nor Mother works for me. In fact, my own mother was not great, so reclaiming the Divine Mother for me is …" Susan grimaces, and we both laugh. "However, I do agree and appreciate and want to be talking about feminine energy, feminine leadership, and women's way of doing things."

"So, what would you say to a young woman about faith?"

For the first time, Susan looks flummoxed. "Wow, I was sailing until now!" she exclaims. "Now you hit me with the hard question!" She purses her lips in a thoughtful way. "Faith is a difficult word, but there's another word I can use. I can say I have experienced the Divine. I think the main thing is that we be as open as we can be to that Presence, whatever it is.

"The experience of the Divine comes to us at any stage of our life, in big ways and small ways. I think the main thing is keeping our eyes and ears open for flashes of it to come. It can come in nature, in other people, in amazing experiences of peace breaking out somewhere where there's been war, some good coming out of tragedy—all kinds of ways for it to happen if we keep our eyes and our minds and our hearts open. That is what I would say about the Divine. That, and knowing that the highest quality of it is love."

Going Deeper

1. What experiences of loss or of new understanding affected Susan? How did she conceive the Divine differently?

2. How has your spirituality changed, in relation to both your outer world and your inner experience?

3. How would you characterize your conception of God today vis-à-vis your previous conceptions? How is this birthing a new understanding of the Divine in your life?

Try This

Find a place and position where you can become very still. If helpful, read one of the selections in the section "Meditations and Visualizations." Get comfortable and breathe deeply for several minutes, until your breathing lengthens into a natural, calm rhythm. As you breathe, listen to your body. If you become aware of a particular area in your body, give thanks for it. Breathe in your awareness of your body's many gifts. Breathe out your gratitude, again and again and again.

Sridevi

Rooted in the Divine Feminine

When I look at these [goddess] portraits,
I think of the things that deeply touch me—my
mother, beauty, and love.

SRIDEVI RAMANATHAN,
EDUCATOR AND LIFELONG LEARNER

Sridevi Ramanathan's appreciation for beauty comes
out in her shimmery red tunic and glittery gold nails.
She slips easily into the school-desk chair adjacent to mine,
her black hair flowing over her shoulders in thick waves.

The classroom in the California Institute of Integral
Studies, where Sridevi is a doctoral student, echoes around
us. As a student of women's spirituality, Sridevi has come
to herchurch[1] conferences and Sunday worship several
times. She says, "I like to visit other places of worship like
herchurch. I enjoy that, and being Hindu, I can do that
because we believe that there are many faces to the Divine."

I ask Sridevi about her experiences of the Divine,
and her darkly outlined eyes light up as she recalls her
decision to switch career paths from law to teaching.
"In my bedroom, I had multiple pictures of Saraswati,
who is the Hindu goddess of wisdom and learning.
Sitting in my room looking at these images of Saraswati

40

on my walls, I made the connection. I was *supposed* to be teaching! I remember it being a very moving moment. I was like, 'Wow! *She* is speaking to me. I know I'm doing the right thing.' In all aspects of my being, it just felt right. With these pictures around me, it was like the Goddess was saying, 'Yes!'"

Earlier, when I had asked Sridevi for an interview, she had sent me a link to her article in an online journal. In "What the Goddesses Did for Me," she depicts her childhood home as "filled with beautiful and captivating portraits of Hindu goddesses who were lavishly dressed in colorful saris and adorned with glittering jewels." She adds, "When I look at these portraits, I think of the things that deeply touch me—my mother, beauty, and love."[2]

In the same article, she recounts her college classmates saying that they felt spiritually adrift, and she reflects on her own spiritual heritage. "I wondered if this was because they did not see women like themselves in their religions. My personal revelation was that my blossoming into a woman with deep spiritual roots had been profoundly nurtured by my exposure to the Goddess."[3]

Sridevi places her hands on the fold-down desk of her chair. Her rings glint in the light. "I didn't realize it when I was growing up, but in retrospect, I can see that I received a very strong spiritual foundation. Knowing the feminine aspect of that has empowered me to be in touch with my soul, rooted in ways that perhaps other women are not."

I ask Sridevi what prompted her to study women's spirituality. She responds, "I've always been interested in the women's perspective on things. Part of that has to do with my culture. Although there is this definite presence of the Divine Feminine, patriarchy has taken its toll on the religion and the culture. I was taught, in both overt and covert ways, that men are superior to women. That bugged me." She groans. "So as I continued my education in college, I was interested in the woman's perspective, the feminist perspective, on basically everything."

When I ask Sridevi to talk about her ongoing relationship with the Divine, she looks mildly baffled. "It's hard to put it into words because it is so natural. I'm always aware, mindful that there is a higher Presence. It's like water to a fish; it's just there."

Asked for an example, Sridevi responds, "I think being more in tune with my intuition. Knowing when I'm receiving a message from the Universe or the Divine versus something random. Knowing when I've put out a question and I'm receiving an answer."

"How do you distinguish between intuition and a fear or a worry?" I ask.

Sridevi fists her long fingers into a ball at her heart. "I think it's coming from a very rooted knowing. This kind of knowing in all aspects of my being—mind, body, spirit. There's something that's in alignment."

I ask about meditation and prayer, and Sridevi says, "My meditation practice hasn't been as strong as in the past. I think it's also shifting. I'm coming back to exercise as my meditation now. I lead group dance fitness classes, and I dance on my own, too. I do all different types of movement, so that's been more my form of meditation."[4]

Sridevi talks about the Hindu community and her women's spirituality community, adding, "I don't go to the temple regularly, but I will on occasion. Again, I see the Divine as being everywhere."

She tells me she contributes to community through her research and also through dance. "Through my master's thesis research, I looked at how the stories we read, specifically the fairy tales, and the mythology that we were exposed to in childhood, affect our self-esteem, our achievement, our body image, and various things about how we behave and who we are. For women especially, the messages tend to be negative and damaging. I'm continuing that work and empowering girls and women. Dance is another big one. I think dance is a means of connecting within ourselves and maybe cultivating that inner knowing that I mentioned earlier, that connection with the Divine. It's also a means of addressing that profound need for community." She grins. "I'm exploring these things still."

When asked how she contributes to the health of the earth, Sridevi responds that she is a vegetarian raised by vegetarian parents. "Environmental awareness has always been there, even in my school days. I wouldn't buy lunch because it had meat in it, so my mother would pack mine in a brown paper bag. I remember folding up the brown bag to bring home and use again and kids commenting, 'Why don't you just toss it? That's the convenience of a paper bag!' But recycling was something my family did. My parents immigrated from India. Recycling is a much bigger way of life there than it is here."

I ask Sridevi if she wants to add anything. With her gracious smile, she says, "Just the power of story, imagery, and dance. Spirituality is an ongoing process." When I thank her, she nods ebulliently and says, "You're welcome."

Going Deeper

1. How did Sridevi's upbringing inform her spiritual experiences as an adult?

2. Sridevi is aware of the Divine all around her. When do you feel this way in your life?

3. How do positive feminine images contribute to your self-esteem?

4. What beautiful images do you see within yourself?

Try This

Put on some music that you like. Relax however feels right for you, whether that is lying on the floor or sitting. After a few minutes of breathing deeply in that relaxed position, allow a hand or a foot or another body part to move to the music, however it wants to move. Allow it to expand its movement. Allow your whole body to respond to the music. After the music ends, take a few minutes to write down what you experienced.

Arisika

The Body as Gateway to the Divine

There's a point in every woman's labor … when all her attention to the outer world drops away, and she turns inward toward the world-making within her body. And in that moment, I see the face of Goddess birthing the world again.

ARISIKA RAZAK, CHAIR,
WOMEN'S SPIRITUALITY PROGRAM,
CALIFORNIA INSTITUTE FOR INTEGRAL STUDIES

Arisika Razak's face is open, unbroken by lines. Her dark hair grays at the crown where she has woven it into a wreath. Asked about her spiritual experiences, she responds, "I think that one of the first that comes to mind is the conception of my son. I was in East Africa, and my passport and birth control pills had been stolen. I'd had unprotected sex, but I thought that it was a safe time. I remember that I had planned to go to the independence celebration for Tanzania. It was on July 7, *Saba-Saba* (7-7 in Swahili). Instead I woke up, and I was really sick. A little voice—an inside voice, not an outer, audible one, but an inner one—said that I was pregnant and that I had a choice, yes or no." Arisika smiles and swoops her hands high. "And my whole being just said, 'Yes!'"

Arisika explains that she has always known the Divine through personal experience, not dogma. Nominally Christian as a child, she had a lax relationship with the black church but was taken with the Hail Mary prayer of her cousins' Catholic church. As a young adult in metropolitan New York City, she explored several religions, attending a Yoruba temple and later studying under a Native American shamanic woman. But Arisika is quick to clarify that her body has been her greatest teacher. "My experiences were not mediated by organized religion or traditional systems. They came through the body. I deeply believe in the body, the knowledge of the body, the gifts of the body. For me, the body has been absolutely a gateway to the Divine."

For example, a therapist once asked her to breathe into a place of pain. "I had some pain in the side, and he asked me to breathe into it, and I had this most incredible experience in which I was light. I was energy. Light is a moving, energetic process. I was that, shooting through the universe. I was not in the body, and there was no limit. I was limitless in an unlimited universe, moving through the universe, and what one perceives there cannot be perceived in the body in the same way. And then I had the experience of what it is like for energy to fall into matter, and how the perception in flesh is not the perception unbounded, that it is different. You know, in the Bible there's a phrase about seeing through a glass darkly?[1] It's like that. It was a profound experience."

Arisika's posture is calm, and her arms reach forward as if she were painting the moments she describes. Her hands dip and converge when she tells me about her twenty-plus years of midwifing children into the world. "Most of that time I was doing work in a county hospital, attending the births of women from over sixty countries, but I also did home births on the side, and my son had been born at home. I don't remember when I learned this, but there's a point in every woman's labor—she may have thought she wanted to have music, she may have thought she wanted to have people with her, she may have wanted all kinds of things in her birth plan—and then there's a moment when all her attention to the outer world drops away, and she turns inward toward the world-making within her body. And in that moment, I see the face of Goddess birthing the world again. It's an incredibly holy and sacred moment. It's not a moment of ease. I don't mean, when she turns to this inner work, that it's all peace and tranquility. It isn't. Birthing, the moving of essence, from that side of the veil to this, from there to here, takes all of her energy and more. It is something that every woman feels she cannot do. And in that moment, she meets that force." Arisika sweeps her knuckles together in a soft clash. "She meets whatever the resistance is. She meets her body being inhabited by what is greater than itself. It's a totally sacred moment. To be met by the body and the Spirit is the essence of what it is to be human. To be privileged to witness that moment again and again is to stand inside what it is to be matter infused with Spirit coming through. It's a very, very powerful sacred act."

Arisika describes sensing a Divine Presence when she was attending the birth of twins. "There was a holy moment when the first twin had been born, and we were waiting for the second twin to move down and to come out. Because we were still, I could feel that with the birth of that child, the energy of the universe shifted. For the universe, it's a tiny, infinitesimal shift. I mean, what is human life compared to the birth of stars and galaxies and their deaths? But it's still a shift in the energy of the universe when a soul moves from there to here, and I felt it, that shift in the universe."

Arisika's prenatal work was also a type of birthing—of the women themselves. Arisika describes how pregnant women waited for two hours for a fifteen-minute visit, and although she received pressure from her supervisor to hurry them up, she would not deny them their stories. She listened to them, even if it meant she left the clinic hours after closing time. "I couldn't change the lives of my homeless clients or my poor clients, but by listening to their stories, and by crying sometimes with them, I could say, 'Your life is worthy. Your story is worthy of being heard.'"

At the California Institute for Integral Studies, where Arisika is the director of the Women's Spirituality Program, people ask her if she misses being a midwife. She responds, "I am helping women to rebirth themselves. I listen to their stories. They tell the mother line, the stories of their mother's lineage. And often—I don't ask them to do this—they tell the stories of rape and incest, a legacy of women who were maltreated, who couldn't leave abusive husbands, time after time. And so we have room for them to tell their stories."

By encouraging women to tell their stories and honor their mother line, Arisika empowers them to reclaim their essence, their connection to Spirit. She midwifes their rebirth by helping them to value their existence. She also helps them express themselves through dance, which is her most sacred practice. "When I dance," she says, extending her arms into a graceful pose, "I am at one with the Divine. I go to a place, and sometimes that place is transmitted. Dance is how we speak Spirit, or if we're lucky, how Spirit speaks us, how Spirit speaks human. So I created a dance about the sacredness of our bodies, and I did that dance for about eight to ten years. And it moved women to go and claim something in their lives. There was something about having an ordinary body and doing these particular movements that touched something inside of women to say, '*Yes*!!'" Arisika claps a single bright beat. "Yes! You can claim your power!"

I wonder out loud if Arisika's sacred movements freed observers from the self-hatred that can make women easy prey for gender and racial discrimination. I ask her to address social justice and spirituality, and she responds that they are inseparable. "One of the things that social justice means is that you have a choice of how you address Creator. Native Americans and enslaved African Americans couldn't even worship, and that's so, so important. If we were put here by Creator, and we each have a mission, anything that makes us doubt ourselves and our spiritual directions and our essential holiness as children of Spirit, anything that teaches us that we are unlovable and that there's something fundamentally flawed about us, and that takes away from our ability to hear the voice of the Divine, and to find our essence of being here, is wasted time." She talks about today's media and its diversionary effect on women, keeping us from finding our true gifts.

"I think about my enslaved ancestors who were called to sing, or to serve beauty, who couldn't do that. Alice [Walker] writes about it in *In Search of Our Mothers' Gardens*.[2] These women, the only thing that they could do for beauty was to maintain a garden, to sew, to repair, to do the upholstery in the church. But if they could have written, if they could have painted, they would have been great artists. So social justice means that we have a world in which all our gifts and talents can be seen and that we can love in the way that we're called to love. Because loving is also how we are nourished, how the Divine replenishes us. So if you are called as a man to love men, or as a woman to love women, if that is how the Divine replenishes you and speaks to your heart, and if you're told you can't do that, we lose. We waste so much time and energy. Social justice is simply a way that we can be seen for who we are."

Arisika adds, "If we have bodies that are different, we will be seen as sacred regardless. For me, I come through the body, so that means I need to stretch to figure out the people who are differently abled—those who have cerebral palsy, who are quadriplegic, who have different mental abilities—that I have to stretch as an able-bodied person to make sure they're in the circle too." Her arms reach outward. "The people with mental illness, they're in the circle too. We have to hold everybody." She clasps her hands and forms a circle with her arms. "The Creator put everybody here. Our task is to make a way that we hold everybody. And to heal the broken. Because I think that it's out of our brokenness that we do these horrible acts. So how do we hold the world that includes everybody? And doesn't do harm?"

I ask Arisika how she brings in the earth as part of this sacred wholeness.

"In my classes, I often talk about the earth and gratitude to the earth, that she didn't shrug us off in the night. There's a proverb I read once: 'Earth is the mother at whose breast we suck always.' I'll bring that out, how the earth is the body. Sometimes in opening my talks, I use Alice Walker's *Her Blue Body Everything We Know*."[3]

Because my community occasionally uses the title poem, "Her Blue Body," in our Sunday liturgies, the last stanza of the poem jumps to mind:

> We have a beautiful
> mother
> Her green lap
> immense
> Her brown embrace
> eternal
> Her blue body
> everything
> we know.

As our interview nears its ending time, I ask Arisika to share her words of wisdom for young women. I specifically ask her to talk about faith.

"I can't impart a faith to someone else. For maybe about ten years, I had a series of roommates who were lesbians who were incest survivors. So what could I say to them? They had to find their own faith. I had a very severe and brutal experience of child abuse in terms of physical abuse, beatings, you know, being whipped with a shoe heel and wooden hangers and all those kind of things, and being locked out of the house, but I didn't have early sexual abuse. I wasn't raped at five or at seven. And so how I come to faith in the Divine and in the generosity of the world is different from someone who finds their faith out of their experience.

"What can I say to a young woman? In my forties, I believed that the most important thing was to know yourself. In my fifties,

I began to believe that, for me, the most important thing was to forgive yourself. Forgive your shortcomings. Know who you are. Know what you strive for. In my fifties, I found myself in Mexico on the beach at six in the morning doing a spontaneous ritual. I had read that both Aphrodite and Oshun[4] were supposed to have renewed their virginity once a year. They took a bath, and they renewed their virginity. Virginity in the old sense was not about an intact hymen; it was about a woman who belonged to herself. And I found myself washing away everything that had been done to this body that I had not asked to be done to it. Everything that had been put on it, against my will, without my choice. And then, I washed away everything that I had chosen, but, with the wisdom of hindsight, I would not choose again. And then I called into this body what I wanted for the next decades of my life. And now I think I would add another thing: I would wash away any regret I have for the changes that are coming to the body and call it sur-render to the changes of age.

"And in that way, in the faith I have, [here's] what I would say to a young woman: I would encourage you, as an act of faith, to believe that your life has meaning. To believe that there is some innate intelligence and goodness in the world. You can look at the world and you can say, 'It is all going to hell in a handbasket. It is getting worse: the maltreatment of women, the degradation, the total pollution of the earth, the fouling of our nest, when it is the only place we have to live.'" Arisika's eyes carry a look of profound sorrow as she lifts up her palms in surrender. "You can look at it, and you can say, 'I give up. There is nothing.' And it is an act of faith to believe that your life has meaning, that your actions, small as they seem, are part of what can tilt the planet to come back to virtue, and that, as an act of faith, we accept that our life and our choices and our services to the good are meaningful.

"Alice [Walker] says something like, 'absolute trust in the goodness of the earth.' Given all the evidence that we have to the contrary, all the genocides of this century that we are living, all the misogyny, all of that, I take heart that so far every year, the flowers still bloom, and in the city, the trees still consent to put out leaves for us. I believe that our goodness matters. I believe that, given the ways that we can react, our choice to heal and to do good and to help others absolutely matters, no matter what else is going on." She cups her hands then moves them toward her heart. "And that's all we have as humans. Whether we have a habitable planet or not, what we do matters.

"And," Arisika adds, noting that we live in a culture where women are encouraged to make their lives dependent on their relationships, "You have to understand that you are whole, whether you are in relationship or not. Every person has to believe that. It's critical. Your true soul mate is Spirit. That is the only mate to your soul. That part of you is your connection to Essence, Source, Divinity, and that is not in the body."

She paraphrases her friend Marge Piercy, author of *Woman on the Edge of Time*: "Hand friend, heart friend, pillow friend, Spirit friend.[5] We need the friends of our hands. We need the people who walk the picket line with us. We need the people who sit with us at the kitchen table and listen to our stories. Some of those are our hand friends. Some are our heart friends. Who is it who will listen to your deep grief when you're disappointed in your children, when your best friend has betrayed you, when you wake up in the night weeping and afraid? Who is it who will bring you the gift of touch? Hand friend, heart friend, pillow friend, and Spirit friend. We need our ritual sisters and brothers. And we need our connection to the Divine, however we language that and know it."

Going Deeper

1. How did Arisika's childhood and her choice of profession influence her spiritual experiences?

2. What do you think about interpreting the word "virgin" to mean a woman who belongs to herself? How do you practice that concept in your own life?

3. Arisika suggests that telling our stories invites a rebirthing— an honoring and valuing of ourselves and our life experiences. How might you rebirth yourself through the sharing of your story? How might your communion with Spirit be revitalized through the telling and valuing of your faith journey?

Try This

Set aside at least twenty minutes. Prepare for meditating by using the "Greeting Silence Meditation" in the section "Meditations and Guided Visualizations" (page 269), either prerecording it for yourself or having a friend read it out loud for you as you relax. Sit or lie comfortably, with a notebook and pen at the ready. Close your eyes and begin the guided visualization. Afterward, continue the deep-breathing exercises on your own for several minutes.

When you feel ready, open your eyes and answer the first question below. It's best if you respond immediately and write whatever pops into your head before reading the second question. Likewise, as soon as you've read the second question, answer it without hesitation. Just jump in; no censorship allowed. Continue in this way, writing with great compassion for yourself, until you have answered all three questions. For any of the questions, substitute the name of the Divine that works best for you.

- What is your most memorable experience of the Divine? Write your response now.

- What do you know of your mother's or grandmother's experience of the Divine?

- What thoughts, feelings, or images does the word "birthing" bring up for you?

Rachel

The Sacred within Me

Christianity, at its core, is an earthly, embodied
religion. It's something I hope we can reclaim.
RACHEL BRUNNS, LUTHERAN VOLUNTEER CORPS

Rachel's chestnut hair drapes her shoulders. She
came to the Bay Area as part of the Lutheran
Volunteer Corps shortly after she graduated from college. I ask Rachel about her experience of the Divine,
and she puts her hand to her chin and thinks for a
moment before describing the profound impact that
the Mel Gibson movie *The Passion of the Christ* had on
her when she saw it as a fourteen-year-old girl.

"I'm kind of horrified about it now because it's
so violent. There are so many things wrong with that
depiction of God." She casts her hand down as if
brushing off this embarrassing memory. "But I think
that image of God as someone who is vulnerable and
open and refuses to back down on a message of love
and caring, even if there are consequences, really spoke
to me and continues to speak to me. All the worries
and fears I had about random things disappeared with
that energy that I felt, that connection and love."

When Rachel describes a more recent spiritual experience, she again talks about connection and energy. Prior to graduating from college, she studied abroad in Peru, and she felt the ineffable presence of Pachamama[1] at Machu Picchu. "It was a spiritual experience to go to this intersection of ancient history and beauty and spirituality and to soak up the presence of Pachamama." She sighs, reminiscing. "It's such a cool space, one of the Seven Wonders of the World, but it's so accessible. You can go and lie down in the grass of these terraces and just be in it. It was the first time I experienced the Divine Feminine."

Rachel explains that she'd grown up with male images of God in the Lutheran Church. "My dad's a Lutheran pastor. I was really immersed in the church, biblically literate, and connected with God from a young age, feeling a spiritual meaning to my life."

At the same time, she wishes she hadn't grown up in a patriarchal religious tradition where God was ingrained in her as male. "But I did grow up in that, so it's been very powerful to have the experience at Machu Picchu, where it was like a feminine thing."

"How was it feminine?" I ask.

Rachel straightens her spine and sweeps back her hair from her face. "It was more like an embodied experience. I was feeling my body as more connected to the Divine and feeling divine energy in myself and in what makes me female and feeling that it was a sacred thing and not just something that made me different from men. It was like I could see the Divine in myself a little and in the creative process of rebirth."

Rachel explains that she was in the Peruvian highlands during Holy Week and that the Incan history impacted her in a profound way also. "It was death and rebirth celebrating Easter in Cusco, connecting with the Divine Feminine at Machu Picchu. All the [Inca] people built this city, and now they're gone, but I'm here, connecting with this divine force of nature. It's like this continuity of birth and death and rebirth. I'm just one piece of this larger cycle of life. It wasn't just my personal relationship with God. It was this relationship with humanity and creation as a whole."

When asked how the spiritual experience in Peru changed her life, Rachel said that it linked her spiritual values and her feminist values. "Before, there was always a disconnect. When I became a feminist in college, I reconciled it with my faith by thinking, 'Yeah, Christianity's a patriarchal religion, but I don't have to agree to those patriarchal standards.' But it's a system that shapes you whether you want it to or not. So having that experience [in Peru] was a moment when it clicked that there are other ways of looking at God. I think I knew that, but it was the first time I'd experienced it. Because God is really beyond anything that we can name or know or see, obviously God is whatever we want God to be, but that was the first time when God was for me a woman. And that allowed me to change, because I couldn't just change by willing it. I had to experience it."

After finishing college, Rachel applied to the Lutheran Volunteer Corps, which placed Rachel with the East Bay Law Center, where she handles intake for its low-income clientele. "I'd felt that I'd gone as far as I could with academic learning—talking and reading—and that it was time to go into the world and see what was really happening and how what I'd learned and experienced connected with realities like poverty and racism and police brutality."

I ask Rachel to tell me about her work at the law center.

"Ninety-five percent of the people we work with are people of color, and we only help people who are below a certain income, and that's really poor. So I'm sitting behind a desk, I'm talking with this person, and I'm so aware of the fact that I'm young—I'm twenty-two—and I'm white, and I'm an outsider, from the Midwest, and what am I doing 'helping' this person?" Rachel frowns. "It's good to grapple with that tension.... I try to think of my work in terms of mutual liberation, because anytime you have oppression, it hurts both the oppressor and the oppressed because it destroys relationship."

She elaborates further on the link between spirituality and justice and credits her parents and her college for instilling these values. "I always understood faith as being rooted in action. So much of my college experience was talking about ethics and developing values, how they connect to the real world and what we do with our theology and our experiences with God. To me it's clear in the Gospels and the accounts we have of Jesus's life that faith is connected to social justice. An absence of social justice just totally strips away the essence of Christianity."

Asked her advice to women younger than herself, Rachel responds, "I would say two things. Really listen to yourself. That's hard to do when you're young. With Christianity, if you fall to the side of the beliefs that have been given to you, you feel like a bad Christian, or at least that's how I felt. But it's okay to find your path. It's okay to disagree. It's okay to doubt. It's a good thing to question, to learn, to grow. At the same time, it's important to value where you are. Go where you find God, and let it develop."

When I ask Rachel about how she cares for the earth, we end up talking about vegetarianism. "It's important to me because growing food to feed cattle is wasteful. Vegetarianism is being in solidarity with people who can't afford to eat meat and takes into consideration the animals themselves. But ..." Rachel masks a grin and admits, "I come from a hunting family. I still remember the duck I killed! Yet I also appreciate that my family doesn't really buy beef, because we have deer meat."

I screw up my face at the thought of gutting a deer, but Rachel tells me that connecting to where their food comes from is a good thing. "It's important to think about what we put in our bodies and our connection to other living beings, with those who are hungry, with the earth."

Rachel explains that this is part of an embodied spirituality. "One of the reasons I stayed a Christian is that Christ as a human being is embodied. That's so important and it relates to the Divine

Feminine and the earth and the idea that bodies matter and that God experiences life on earth because God cares about the earth. God cares about our bodies. God cares about the cycle of life and death and is present in that. That image of God as a person, vulnerable, embodied, connected, is essential to Christianity, and ..." Rachel sighs. "I just wish it was more prevalent, because I think it's so important. Christianity, at its core, is an earthly, embodied religion. It's something I hope we can reclaim."

Going Deeper

1. What experiences brought about changes in Rachel's spirituality?

2. How would you characterize Rachel's moment at Machu Picchu? How do you relate what she experienced to your own life?

3. How, for Rachel, is Christianity an embodied religion? How does her experience and point of view relate to your faith experience(s)?

Try This

Find an open place that has a bit of human history to it. If you can, try to discover the indigenous history, as well as Western civilization's history, of the place. Lie down or sit in a secluded spot on that site. Breathe deeply, possibly using one of the meditations at the end of this book to help you do that. Write down your thoughts when you are done.

Anna

Circling into the Womb
of the Mother

The circle of the labyrinth is like going into the
womb of the Mother. Whenever I walk the labyrinth, I feel like I'm being held.

ANNA YANG, RETIRED NURSE

When asked about the Divine, Anna Yang tips
back her head and closes her eyes. Her billowy
white hair graces her shoulders as she reflects. "There
have been times at night when I was upset or afraid
about something, and I imagined sleeping in the heart
of the Divine: being held in that loving presence, in
the arms of Quan Yin. When I'm in the heart of the
Divine, I feel I'm safe and that all is going to be well. I
feel very peaceful and secure and loved."

Quan Yin, she explains, is an ancient Chinese
goddess providing unconditional love and comfort.
"Quan Yin listens to all your cries. She collects the
tears of the world and pours them out. She is a goddess
of wisdom and compassion."

At the time that Anna first envisioned herself resting in the heart of Quan Yin, she was in her late thirties

and dealing with multiple challenges, like the childhood traumas of "growing up in an alcoholic family." She was also experiencing problems with her physical health. "I just kind of fell apart, and I didn't have any energy to do anything. Traditional Western medicine didn't have anything for me to utilize that would be helpful, so I started working with acupuncture and different healers that I trusted. I'm a nurse so it was interesting for me to experience the healing, because my nurse brain was going crazy, saying, 'This is so weird!' But my body was saying, 'Yeah, but I feel a whole lot better!'"

Energetic healing methods—the laying on of hands and healing prayers—helped Anna connect with the Divine for the first time. "When I grew up, I knew about God and Jesus, but I didn't necessarily feel close to that. When I started learning different healing modalities, I opened up to allowing myself to be a conduit for the Divine Energy to flow through me. It was clear that I wasn't doing [the healing]. I was allowing that Energy to come through me. So that's what really opened me to having a relationship with the Divine."

Anna adds that she experiences the Divine in nature, too. "When I'm walking in nature, I feel very connected to the Divine. When I lie on the earth and spread my arms, I feel very close to the Divine."

When I ask what she is doing *for* nature and the earth, Anna replies, "I realize that I am one with all around me and what I do impacts others. I say sacred earth prayers. I give gratitude to all plants, minerals, water, animals, and people on the earth." In her daily life, Anna recycles, reuses, and composts. She refrains from using petroleum-based items. She shares her resources with environmental organizations. Acting out of a recognition of our essential oneness enables Anna to become a clearer channel for this energy to flow through her and "lighten the area wherever I am."

Anna gradually began to see the interconnections a few years ago when she undertook a graduate program in women's spirituality at the California Institute of Integral Studies. "That's when I really got a sense of the Divine, when I opened up to what has been missing in traditional Western patriarchal religion, and it was really amazing to me." As with her previous healing experiences, Anna found her relationship to the Divine expanding and changing. "I love cross-cultural studies, and it was fascinating for me to look at different religions and all the different goddesses and what they really mean. At some point, I felt that there was just the Divine Mother and that the goddesses were simply different aspects of the Divine."

When asked about her current relationship with the Divine, Anna again closes her eyes and inclines against her chair. By now I am used to her pauses. They imbue each moment with a sustained and unruffled peace. She opens her eyes to say, "My relationship definitely has deepened, and I feel the Divine much more present now. I feel more in partnership with the Divine. I feel my divine-ness. The Divine is without, and the Divine is within, and I really have a sense of that in myself. Like it says in the Our Mother prayer, the Divine is within."

The prayer, penned by Miriam Therese Winter, begins, "Our Mother who is within us, we celebrate your many names. Your wisdom come. Your will be done, unfolding from the depths within us." It goes on to say, "Each day you give us all that we need. You remind us of our limits, and we let go. You support us in our power, and we act with courage. For you are the dwelling place within us, the empowerment around us, and the celebration among us, now and forever, Amen."[1]

Anna muses, "'Each day we're given all that we need.' I really feel that in my life. When I feel uncertain about something, I'll repeat that piece of the Our Mother prayer: 'Each day I'm given all that I need.' And it happens. I'll go to do something, and the answer will be there for me or the support or the supply—whatever I need—shows up, and I think, 'O yeah, I'm given all that

I need.' That happens because the Our Mother prayer acknowledges the Divine within."

Anna explains that every morning, before journaling or meditating, she repeats the Our Mother prayer and a second prayer, "A prayer that is a kind of a hello to the world: 'This morning I greet Mother Earth and Father Sky and the life force in all creation. This morning I greet the seen world in its beauty and the unseen world in its mystery.' It ends with 'This morning I welcome the breath that breathes me, the compassion that surrounds me, and the love in my heart.'[2]

"I love the idea of the breath that breathes me," Anna emphasizes, smiling, and I remember that the Hebrew for Yahweh imitates the sounds of respiration and that the universe, from the micro to the macro, is continually contracting and expanding like the lungs that keep us alive. Anna expanded her morning prayer to add in all the elements and realms, including those represented by the labyrinth: "At the center of the Chartres labyrinth,[3] there are six petals, each one dedicated to the mineral, the animal, the plant, the human, the angelic, and the universe."

I am reminded of the huge labyrinth tarp that Anna has brought during Lent to herchurch. It unfolds to reveal the Chartres labyrinth swirling in pathways outlined in purple on the heavy canvas. On several occasions, including Good Friday, Anna has carefully spread it out over the sanctuary floor at herchurch. I ask Anna to say more about the labyrinth.

"The circle of the labyrinth is like going into the womb of the Mother. Whenever I walk the labyrinth, I feel like I'm being held. It can hold anything I'm thinking about or worried about. Sometimes I walk it wondering about a question I have in my life: 'What should I do about …?' Sometimes I just walk it to see what's there for me, what comes up while I'm walking. When I sit in the center of the labyrinth, I feel very connected to the universe. I always feel more centered when I come out.

"Grace Cathedral used to have the carpet labyrinth [inside the sanctuary], and after dropping my kids off at school on Friday, I would go in, walk the labyrinth, and lay in the center of it. Sometimes the school's boys choir would be singing above me. That was an amazing experience: to hear these voices just wafting around the cathedral. I could just feel the notes of the music flow around me."

Anna has taken her portable cloth labyrinth to churches, colleges, centers for people with disabilities, and medical sites like University of California at San Francisco. She loves standing at the entrance to the labyrinth and welcoming people in. "I feel like I'm welcoming them into a special sacred time—a time out of ordinary life, a time out of rushing. Just a time of quiet walking and being with yourself and the Divine." Anna even invited people to walk the labyrinth for her fiftieth birthday party. But for her sixtieth birthday party, she wanted something different. She participated in the croning ceremony[4] at herchurch, where she attends whenever she has the chance. She also had a croning ceremony with friends. "I didn't know I wanted a croning ceremony until a friend asked me. Then I said, 'Yes, that's what it is. That's what I want.' With my croning ceremony, I made a statement: 'I am here. I am willing to show up. I am willing to foster gifts and talents that have lain latent within me. I'm willing to grow into the person that I am.' And it's a gift to offer that because the universe will say, 'Okay then!'"

As an example, Anna tells how she has sensed the Divine's urging that she develop writing as one of her unused talents. "Finally I said 'yes' to being a writer, and I don't know what that's going to look like. I always got nudges about writing, but I kept saying, 'I'm not a writer! I'm not a writer!' That's part of the croning ceremony: being willing to open up to the untapped talents that I have—deepening and increasing my capacity for being *me*."

When asked what she would say to a young woman about living a spiritual life, Anna responds, "I'd say: Stay in your authentic self. Set limits and boundaries that are good for you. Listen to what has heart and meaning for *you*. But also know that you're a part of a collective. You can be in the center of yourself—*self*-centered—*and* you can be available to be part of a larger community in a good way. You're both giving and receiving." Anna smiles and turns up her palms like the scales of justice. "It's a balance."

Going Deeper

1. How did Anna's ailments affect her spirituality? How were they labor pains for birthing a new understanding of the Divine?

2. How is Anna's sense of the Divine different from yours? How is it similar?

3. Where do you see labor pains of birthing new understandings—of yourself, God, community, or vocation—in your life?

Try This

Google "labyrinth" and find one near you. Before walking it, find a place nearby to sit quietly and focus on your breathing. After a few minutes of calm, centered breathing, approach the labyrinth and stand at its entrance. Notice what sounds in your heart. Walk the labyrinth slowly and meditatively. Once you arrive at its center, stop for a minute to observe your emotions and your state of being. Turn to retrace your path. Continue walking slowly with your heart focused on your inner prayers as you return to the labyrinth's entrance. In your notebook, jot down what it felt like to walk the labyrinth.

You can also "walk" the labyrinth at your computer. Just go to www.gratefulness.org/labyrinth/chartres.htm to begin.

Alice

Resonating like Home

It felt like this light on me, this golden glow, and this connection to the Source, the Divine. So many times I've been struggling against my own feelings of unworthiness and the sense of being oppressed as a woman, as a minority. You have those everyday pressures, and then there's your own emotional baggage that kicks you down and keeps you down, and the task is to dismantle that. But this was just such a moment of "I'm of worth. I have value. I have a place."

ALICE MARTIN, COMPUTER PROGRAMMER AND
OWNER, HERHEALING ENERGY READINGS

Alice Martin's smile is shy and her black eyes observant. When asked to characterize her experience of the Divine, she begins with a story about herchurch. "It was during last year's croning ceremony.[1] Oh, how can I describe it?" Searching for words, Alice looks toward the altar, allowing me a partial view of her tucked-in crown of hair. She depicts the older women sitting up front in chairs like thrones, how they were honored for their wisdom, how she was moved to tears. "It's like the floodgates just opened, and I was in this experience of joy. I really felt the presence of God, of Goddess. It was like a down-pouring."

Alice reaches up with both hands as if parting a curtain. "It felt like this light on me, this golden glow, and this connection to the Source, the Divine. So many times I've been struggling against my own feelings of unworthiness and the sense of being oppressed as a woman, as a minority. You have those everyday pressures and then there's your own emotional baggage that kicks you down and keeps you down, and the task is to dismantle that. But this was just such a moment of 'I'm of worth. I have value. I have a place.'"

Alice recalls the experience as "Two-way. It wasn't just me receiving. It was about my reaching out and saying, 'I'm connecting to this greater Whole.'" Minutes afterward, she questioned her experience. "I was like, 'What the hell? What was that? Was that good or bad? Am I crazy, or what?'" She wasn't sure how it squared with the real world, where one needs to earn an income and put food on the table. At the time, she'd just gone on disability.

Alice had worked as a software programmer for the same company for almost twenty years. She recounts how a close friend of hers had risen through the ranks to become the CEO because "he was a visionary with really excellent ideas. But he was not a good manager." She qualifies their longtime friendship as brother-sisterly but adds that she was never allowed to have a better idea than him, and he always had to be one up. "I went through a lot of things under his so-called leadership that were pretty horrific, really emotionally abusive, but I stuck with the company. I thought it was all my fault, that I wasn't good enough still, but I got to the point where I couldn't even understand the code that I'd written. I'd gotten to a mental and emotional state where I was basically getting to be not functional, and I was suicidal. One thing led to another, and I ended up going on disability.

"It was at this particularly low, really toxic mental time that I found herchurch. And it's funny how I was able to come into herchurch. I grew up Catholic, went to a Catholic high school, but I'd renounced Christianity when I was in my teens even though I sort of appreciated and valued the parables and teachings of the Gospels. I was like, 'Why can't we follow *this* instead of all the other garbage and nonsense surrounding it? Even though I read a lot about other religions, none of what I read resonated like home, where I could put my whole spirit."

When the work problems began, some of Alice's friends suggested that she check out the goddess rosary at herchurch to see if it would relieve her stress. Months later, while on disability, she tried it. "The first night I walked into herchurch for the goddess rosary, I remember steeling myself. 'Okay I'm walking into a church. I can walk out. They can't keep me here. I don't have listen to their message.' It's like I was steeling myself for this onslaught of Christianity and still hoping for some kind of comfort or salvation. And the moment I walked in, I just felt okay, almost like I was waiting for a punch that never happened. Pastor Stacy got up, said hello. Gave me a piece of paper with the prayers on it. Gave me a rosary. Said I was welcome to come into the sanctuary and sit down. It was like the perfect sense of acknowledgement and giving me my own space. Absolutely perfect for me in that moment. I felt so welcomed."

Alice remembers feeling safe and welcomed. In addition to the rosary at herchurch, she also started meditations that were spiritually based. "The meditations really helped me ground myself. Up until that moment, I was scattered. I didn't feel like I had a right to exist. But then I began the process of accepting myself and accepting this body and being here, being present."

Soon after, Alice was invited to attend herchurch's Faith and Feminism Womanist Mujerista Conference. Just as she'd done when she'd first walked into the church, she gave herself the option to leave. But she was surprised. "I was listening to this woman who was speaking with authority and enlightenment. There was such strength in it, and I was like, 'This is my people!'"

Alice still hadn't attended a Sunday service at herchurch, and during the conference she went to her first one. Speaking of the Sunday morning service, she reflects, "Even though I don't consider myself a Christian per se, the framework is familiar enough that I feel very comfortable. It's like an old shoe, yet it doesn't have the old baggage, you know, like Catholicism. Also, it's not so rigid that if I'm going in a different way spiritually, there's not an obvious clash or even a conflict. This place allows my own worth to be, allows the growth to happen, and doesn't try to eradicate it or change it, as if I were a weed in the garden that's not conforming to the rest of the flowers. Even though people are in different places and have different views of the Goddess or God or Christianity or whatever, it's very free-flowing. It's a beautiful place for me. And this is the ongoing nurturing of my spirituality, just being in this place."

In terms of her current spirituality, Alice says, "I'm in a process of learning. In order to begin healing anything else, to be really active in that, I need to heal myself first. I need to learn how to be in a better place in regard to myself: a neutral, loving, compassionate, non-judging place. If I can't do that for myself, how can I do that for anybody else?"

When I ask Alice if she feels she has a community in which she feels supported in her connection to the Divine, particularly the Divine Feminine, she says, "I'm still getting used to being in the community. Throughout my entire life I'm so used to being alone and being outside of the community for one reason or another. With herchurch and with my school, I've found these outlets, these ways to feel okay. Sometimes I'm wanting more of an intimate connection, but then, in a lot of ways, I'm still not really ready."

Asked what one thing she might contribute, Alice responds, "If I could affect or contribute one thing, it's just giving people the ability to be open-minded and to have better access to their own neutrality. I want to help them get to that core of openness in their mind. Because when people are open, even though they have differences of opinion, they can find ways to compromise. It's not like it's 'all your way and none of my way' kind of thing. It's like, 'Well, I'll move on this if you move on that, and we're both in a place where we're trying to help each other.' That can only happen when people are trying to be as neutral as possible and not judging, but respecting, their differences."

Alice has decided that she's not going to go back to her previous job. "I kept getting the message, 'Keep doing what you're doing. Money will come. Your path will keep going. Just keep having faith, doing what you can.' I guess it's the power of prayer, of spirituality, because I'm on the edge a lot with my own personal bills, but amazingly enough I've still been able to maintain, and for me that's because of this opening up and acceptance, being okay with where my path is. Now I'm starting to do some odd programming jobs, contracting, and I plan on going to school in the fall. It's like everything's lining up for me."

Alice's last response is a story prompted by my question about the Divine Feminine. But it is also a story about belonging. "Since the early 2000s, I started having this yearning, and even though I did not consider myself Christian, I kept getting drawn to the Virgin Mary, to the Mother. The company I worked for was a Filipino company, so I would travel to the Philippines every once in a while, and they're very Catholic, with a penchant for the Virgin Mary. That's how I was able to open up to come here to herchurch, because that was what I was wanting, this incorporating of the Virgin Mary back into my life without all the Christian hullabaloo, because I wanted this female face, this mother face. Being at home here I feel like, 'Yes! Exactly! This is what I'm looking for: this female, mothering kind of thing that I can glom onto and be a part of!'"

Alice beams, and her earlier comments come back to me: "I'm of worth. I have value. I have a place.... I'm connecting to this greater Whole."

Going Deeper

1. Which experiences led to Alice's revelations?

2. What would you characterize as an epiphany of "I'm of worth" in your own life? In what ways is that epiphany a rebirthing of yourself?

3. What actions or reflections can you undertake on a daily basis to open up your mind and heart to the experience of divine love for yourself in both body and soul?

Try This

Take a few minutes to close your eyes and breathe deeply, using one of the meditations in the section "Meditations and Visualizations." Breathe quietly until your breaths take on a natural rhythm of their own, and then, with your eyes still closed, focus on your inner eyelids for a few minutes. Watch the darkness. Notice the muted changes in the texture of the darkness. If anything else changes, track it with your inner eye. When you are done, write down what you experienced.

Sarah

Hanging Out the Wash like Prayer Flags

My spiritual connection with God has changed. It's becoming more these practical ways of connecting.... When I'm hanging out the wash, the experience is all about these different textures and colors that I'm touching and hanging up like prayer flags in the wind.

SARAH COZZI, OWNER, CELEBRATE LIVING:
ENHANCING CHRISTIAN COMMUNITIES

Sarah Cozzi radiates energy and youthfulness. In conversation, she focuses that energy intensely. Her brown eyes, accented by dark hair and frames, zero in on me as I ask her about her experience of the Divine. Sarah says she often feels God's presence when people come together for sharing meaningful discussion, and she portrays it as "transformational love and insight."

She especially felt "a clarity, a deep knowing" in a conversation that occurred with her first spouse, Brant, twelve years earlier when they were living in Minnesota. They'd been married a few years and were discussing a move to California. Brant was talking about going to the Pacific Lutheran Theological Seminary (PLTS) in

Berkeley to become a pastor. When it came to options for Sarah to pursue in Berkeley, Sarah told Brant she knew she was good with the small group ministries at their church. She'd had leadership training and knew how to foster group sharing and bonding, but she'd never thought of it as a vocation.

"I remember Brant and I got in the car—we were leaving a ministry meeting—and I was just so energetic and excited about what we were doing with the small group ministry. I'm a verbal processor so I was expressing my love and passion for the work." By way of demonstration, Sarah makes spirals with her hands and speeds up her diction. "And I realized I could make this my life work. I could get a degree! I felt all of this excitement and passion just knowing that this could really work out. And it was so clear, just so clear. So often in life we can barely see the step ahead of us, much less the path ahead."

Sarah portrays this clarity, this deep knowing, as both rooted and open to the heavens. She stretches down and then up above her head. "The deep knowing was like a tree coming up through the center of me and extending beyond myself, with its roots going down into the ground, that's what it felt like."

They decided that Brant would start seminary and that Sarah would get a job first and then enroll later. But two months after Sarah and Brant moved to Berkeley and settled into seminary housing, Brant died. He'd already had two heart transplants (one when he was sixteen and the other right after they were married), and shortly after moving to California, he had open-heart surgery again. "He didn't do well in surgery," Sarah says softly. "And I ended up having to make the decision to take him off life support. It was pretty awful. I wouldn't want anyone to go through it. I was just twenty-eight."

After a brief pause and a grab for the tissue box, Sarah continues. "That was twelve years ago. Although everyone expected me to move back to Minnesota, I stayed." In the midst of tremendous grief, Sarah held onto her vision for a degree in small group ministries. Her employer—Jewish Family and Children's Services—and the seminary apartment complex became the communities that helped her survive the period following her husband's death. "God for me was the community. The people in the seminary housing just cared for me. I always had the option of knocking on someone's door, dinner plate in hand: 'I don't want to eat dinner alone, can I sit with you?' I had as much alone time or community as I wanted and needed." Sarah's employers were equally supportive, giving her two weeks of bereavement after only ten days of employment. They also gave her vacation time she hadn't yet earned so she could make frequent trips back to Minnesota.

Sarah enrolled in seminary the following fall and completed her studies for a master's degree in Christian ministry with an emphasis in adult faith formation and retreat ministry. After graduation, she took the position of alumni coordinator at PLTS. When the position was eliminated, she felt adrift. "It'd been so perfect for me. And now what was I going to do?" She explains that she and her second spouse, Eric, were talking about this when he suggested that she could contract her services. Sarah initially rejected the idea. "I felt a ton of pushback. And then over the next three days, it was the only thing I could think about, dreaming about the possibilities and how exciting and dynamic it could be. Again I felt this deep knowing: I *can* do this. It *is* possible. I felt excitement and energy and had lots of conversations: 'What about this, and what about that?' I felt a deep sense of knowing: I *can* do this. I can."

In addition to directing church liturgy and her small business, Celebrate Living: Enhancing Christian Communities,[1] Sarah is now a mother. Her son, Aidan, is two years old, and because she often literally has her hands full, she talks about experiencing God at practical, daily moments. "During different phases in our life, we have different spiritual needs. Right now, with Aidan, I've got a commercial-length spot of time to myself. So right now, things like hanging out the laundry and working in my garden are spiritual experiences.

"My garden is a great place for prayer and connecting with God. There's this deeper connectedness to the earth and the world where we live: knowing where our food comes from, knowing how our decisions affect the earth. And when I'm hanging out the wash, the experience is all about these different textures and colors that I'm touching and hanging up like prayer flags in the wind. It becomes very spiritual. I like to talk about our underwear as prayer flags, as a spiritual experience!" Sarah laughs. "Because that's what it turns out to be!"

Sarah goes on to explain that her "go-to image of God is masculine." Still, she loves acquiring images and language to think about the Divine that aren't limited by gender. "I think we should think about God in the fullest, biggest, most expansive way. If we simply keep God as only masculine, we tremendously limit God. My hope is that the language and images that I've learned through the Faith and Feminism Conference and through seminary will continue to expand my capacity for envisioning God, and that I don't settle on any one image but allow this expansion to continue, like the expanding universe. God is bigger and closer than our human brains can imagine, articulate, or verbalize. As far as we think we can reach, it's not as much as God is."

Sarah opens her arms to embody divine infinitude, and I am reminded of her earlier description of hanging out the wash, her toddler's T-shirts waving like prayer flags in the breeze.

Going Deeper

1. How does Sarah describe the sense of God within her as she faced vocational decisions?

2. How did Sarah's experiences of God change with loss and motherhood? How has your experience of the Divine changed?

3. What is your go-to image for God? How has it changed over the course of your life?

Try This

The next time you are working outdoors (gardening, trimming back hedges, or similar tasks), turn your thoughts to the Divine. Converse. Experience the grace of the elements that surround you and your connection.

Ann

Seeing Ourselves with Love

The Divine is the ability to see ourselves with absolute and complete love. There's an ability to have a relationship with ourselves internally because we are divine. It resides within us. Like Jiyu-Kennett said, "The eyes with which I see God, God sees me."

ANN DANNELLY, PROGRAM AND EVENTS
MANAGER, STILLHEART INSTITUTE

When Ann Dannelly sits down, her posture remains gracefully erect, treelike. Her forest green sweater picks up a lighter hue in her eyes, and I remark on this. "But, my eyes are blue!" she protests, laughing. "Don't you remember?"

The truth is I don't. I haven't seen Ann in two decades because she's been living in a Zen Buddhist monastery in the foothills of the Sierra Nevada and has left only recently to accompany her elderly mother.

I ask Ann to describe a time when she felt the Divine palpably, but she doesn't talk about Zen Buddhism or meditation. Instead, she recalls a wooded hill near her childhood home in Paso Robles, California. "Across the street from our house was this hill. It was like a forest. It was one of my favorite things to do. That was like my little retreat. I'd go up there and just be in nature. It was wonderful. Nature has always been calming, very centering."

When asked why, Ann explains, "Nature is a way of realizing that there's more to this existence than what meets the eye. In nature there's a certain sense of feeling connected. Humans generally tend to live a life out of balance. Going back to nature is a way to reconnect with that calm, that center, with all that animates life."

Even though Ann's earliest spiritual experiences were in nature, as a child she was instructed to believe otherwise. She explains, "When I was a kid, I got the impression that there was God the Father. He sits on a throne and has a long white beard and he judges you: Are you doing good things or are you doing bad things?" Again, she laughs. She tells me about her father, a Methodist minister, and how, after his passing, she felt his presence one crystalline moment as she sat on a bench in the sun. "Like he was checking out my life in the monastery, just seeing it for himself."

I ask Ann to tell the story of how she came to be a practitioner of Zen Buddhism. Ann responds, "I think I was twenty-seven. I was in a lot of pain. Life just wasn't working the way I was taught it should, and I wondered what I was doing wrong. I had this friend, Lynne, and she did this thing that I call 'spiritual shopping.' She went to all these different teachers, and she'd invite me to go along with her. So she'd take me to these places, and we'd get to this point where she'd turn to me and ask, 'Well, Ann, what was wrong with it?' And I'd tell her. Because I just thought they were all totally off the wall and weird." Ann cackles, slapping her thigh. "It happened so often that it got to be a joke between us."

"And then one Saturday night Lynne calls me. She says, 'I'm in the middle of a weekend workshop and you should come tomorrow.' I said 'Okay,' and I walked into the Mountain View Zen Center, where Cheri Huber was leading this workshop.[1] I sat down, and Cheri did this meditation, and I just started sobbing and sobbing. I was still sobbing at the end, and I told Cheri, 'I feel like I could just sob forever.' And she said, 'Be my guest. You can go out in the garden. I think the record's about an hour.' She was just so calm and so centered and not disturbed in the least with my reaction. So then Lynne and I left, and we're sitting in the car, and we did our little ritual. Lynne asked, 'What was wrong with it?' And I said, 'Nothing. Absolutely nothing.' And I've been a student ever since."

"Why did the teaching at the Mountain View Zen Center impact you?"

"Because it was just so clear. And there was no fear. And the teachings were so sound. There weren't any beliefs being taught, like if you're going to be in this religion, this is what you have to believe. None of that. In fact, I found out later that one of the things the Buddha taught is, 'Believe nothing.' There are actually three instructions: 'Pay attention; believe nothing; and don't take anything personally.' It's all about discovering what our beliefs and assumptions are, seeing through them, and letting them go. That's what I was getting from Cheri that day. Plus, I've stuck with my practice, and I've really gone deep with it."

Ann meditates three times a day, and I ask her to give me a sense of what meditation is like for her. "Meditation is like finding that still place in the lake, underneath. On the surface you can skip a pebble on it, and it gets all crazy—that's the mind—but when you meditate, there's a dropping down into the stillness, that still space underneath."

I wonder out loud if meditating is meeting divinity within oneself.

"Interesting that you should ask this. I was just talking to a friend about this. I was telling her that I thought that the Divine is the ability to see ourselves with absolute and complete love. There's an ability to have a relationship with ourselves internally because we are divine. It resides within us. Like Jiyu-Kennett said, 'The eyes with which I see God, God sees me.'[2] They talk about removing the veil in most religions. It's so true. We just don't see. Like one year, I sent a birthday card to my sister. It read, 'I wish you could see the magnificence of your own being.' I mean, human beings are phenomenal, we really are. Each human is a spark of divinity."

Still talking a mile a minute, Ann says, "But we're conditioned not to see this. We're conditioned to hate ourselves. If we can get beyond that feeling of 'There's something wrong with me, I lack in some way,' then we find that innate wisdom that's there inside us. The work we have to do is to clean up all the gunk we're carrying emotionally. To be willing to be open and to see everything that we encounter in life every single day as a gift that's created specifically for us to see through our stuff and really be present, because it all happens in *this moment*. If we're really present, everything's a miracle, and we're so blessed. Life is constantly giving to us all the time. The question is, can we say, 'Yes'?

Ann rests her arms on the table. "Just the other day I had this sense of how perfectly my life has unfolded. I was relaxing at Stillheart,[3] and I just had overwhelming gratitude for everything that's happened in my life and my ability to work with it and respond to it, and to me. Now, that's the Divine."

When I ask how she's helping to heal the planet, Ann responds, "By living from a place of knowing that I'm intrinsically good. I wish everyone would wake up and realize, 'Who I am is authentic goodness,' because the most radical act you can do to save the planet is to stop believing in the voices of self-hate. We have the power to save the planet, but as long as we're thinking, 'I'm not a nice enough person, my legs are too fat,' etcetera, we can't do anything. The important thing is dropping down into your authentic self, because that's how you'll be able to save the planet.

"We have to bring it back to ourselves. There is no 'other,' so the world is me. In our Daily Recollection[4] we say, 'There is no self and other [because] the awareness of pure undisturbed consciousness slips into all consciousness.' So what am I doing to heal me? What am I doing to be in a place where healing can happen? No matter where I am, my practice is to be in the present moment with whatever needs to be healed. I'm fortunate to work in a place like Stillheart where spiritual practice is important. It provides me with that sense of community. And of course, there's *sangha*."

Ann describes sitting with the Mountain View Zen Center twice a week. As an experienced practitioner, she often leads the sitting sessions. She explains the three jewels of Zen Buddhism: "*Bodhi*, which is the truth; *dharma*, the teaching of that truth; and *sangha*, the people who you practice with. The *sangha* community is really important. It's in relationship that we see the Divine. Because in relationship, we're able to see the places where we're stuck much more clearly than if we're off on our own."

I ask Ann about her remaining family. She talks about her sister and her two nieces, ages eleven and fourteen, and prompts my question on her advice for young women—girls like her nieces—who are on the cusp of womanhood.

Without skipping a beat, Ann responds, "I'd tell young women, 'You have the wisdom inside of you. Do everything you can to honor that. Honor that Light in you, and don't let anybody talk you out of it.'"

Going Deeper

1. What beliefs did Ann examine and why? When have you felt inclined to examine your faith? What changes occurred?

2. Ann states, "Who I am is authentic goodness." What is good within you? Name at least twenty things.

Try This

Ann practices Zen meditation. One form for beginners is to count up from "one." On each inhalation and exhalation, silently count, "One ... two ... " and so on, with the goal of counting to ten. It's important to be seated comfortably, with your spine straight so that you can breathe deeply from your abdomen. Meditate for fifteen minutes. Whenever you notice yourself in a thought, simply release the thought and start with "one" again. Eventually you will be able to just concentrate on the breath and abandon the counting. After meditating, ask yourself later during the day (or week if you continue to meditate daily) if meditation has any impact on the way you see yourself and live your day.

Rhina

The Church of the Open Door

"El reino esta entre ustedes"—we build the
kingdom of God among us—is what someone
explained to me one day: My Christian faith
informs and calls me to the cause of justice,
and justice fuels my faith.

REVEREND RHINA RAMOS,
NORTHERN CALIFORNIA NEVADA CONFERENCE,
UNITED CHURCH OF CHRIST

There is an ampleness to Rhina's warmth, a gentle
humility to her presence. For her, Jesus is a trusted
friend. The Jesus she knew as a teen and a newly con-
verted Baptist is the same Jesus she calls on now.
Alternating from her accented English to Spanish and
back, Rhina explains, "Maybe it's because I chose to be
Baptist that Jesus has a stronger pull on me." She laughs.
"Católica yo nací, pero bautista yo escogí!" [I was born
Catholic, but chose to be Baptist!]

Growing up during El Salvador's civil war years,
before Rhina could go out and play, she had to kneel
and say the rosary. When Rhina was fourteen, she
made the long trek north. Arriving in Long Island,
New York, she looked for a Catholic church to make

the confession she'd promised during her journey. The priest heard her confession (which was that she hadn't attended Mass regularly), but when Rhina started to ask him the existential questions that were troubling her, he brushed her off.

"Maybe I would still be Catholic today," Rhina muses. "But the priest didn't want to talk to me. He just said, 'Come to Mass, and all your doubts will be answered.' I left unsatisfied. We were living next to a Baptist church, and I saw one of my bilingual teachers go in, and I asked her, 'What do you do, in your church?' And she said, 'Just come next Sunday!' I did, and I went there forever, until I came out."

Rhina, with all her youthful enthusiasm, embraced this new faith. She practically lived at the Baptist church, and it was full of Salvadorans, people who looked and talked like her. She became a youth leader and started dating a young man in the church. "We were just fooling around, my boyfriend and I, but we felt we were sinful—*muy enpecados*—so we had to run and get married. *Imaginate* [Imagine], being nineteen years old and running to get married!

Rhina chuckles. "You see, I was not a girl who dreamed about getting married. I dreamed about other girls! My husband Rolando was a good man, *un buen hombre.* Coming out to him was heartrending. "I don't know how I did it. I just said to him, 'When I'm with you, I feel like embracing a woman.' And he said, 'Let's look to God for help. Let's find counseling.' We went to a Methodist Spanish-speaking pastor who was also a clinical psychologist. I saw him individually, too, and though he was conflicted about it, he helped me come out. He asked me if I felt possessed, and I said, 'Yes, I feel that I am possessed. That must be why I feel this way because I don't want to feel this way.' He gave me books to read and asked me to describe the woman I'd fallen in love with, this *profesora* who was wonderful and who was lesbian. He asked me to say why I loved her, and I described all these qualities that were human qualities. He told me that this love was not un-normal. But

I felt tormented. At that time, I believed in the rapture. Sometimes if I was home alone, and Rolando hadn't come home, I would think, 'Could it be that Rolando was taken in the rapture? That I was left to the tribulation?' Oh, how I tortured myself!"

Rhina laughs again. Hers is a rumbling chortle that punctuates most of her sentences, and I wonder out loud how a young woman who was so deeply tortured could emerge so joyful.

"God," she answers. She is emphatic that God was with her in her divorce and crisis of identity. "God was the people who were loving, who accompanied me through this breakup." She says this more than once: the idea that God is also the people she sees around her, the people who minister to her with their presence and kind words. She gives an example: the Methodist pastor-counselor who helped her to accept herself, even though he himself was conflicted about it. She felt God's presence in his open-hearted counseling.

After her divorce, Rhina decided to go to back to school. She already had a law degree in labor rights and had been looking forward to defending immigrants and other blue-collar workers, but after her divorce and subsequent move to California, she enrolled in the Pacific School of Religion in Berkeley. "I loved seminary. But for me it was pure intellectual exploration—nothing about being ordained." She could not envision herself as a pastor. As a defender of her people, yes. As an immigrant organizer, yes. But as a pastor, no. "I even wrote this essay on why I didn't see myself as a pastor. Pastors are persons of faith; they don't lose it. They don't grumble." She chuckles again, an invitation to laugh with her at the constant self-judging belittlement that, for many of us, is the soundtrack of our lives.

To put herself through seminary, Rhina continued to work with the immigrant community in the Bay Area. A seminary advisor suggested that she explore more feminist theology, and she took an ecofeminism class with Rosemary Ruether. "It was about domination of the earth and domination of women." The class helped her to see the impact of environmental degradation on low-income communities and how poor communities are organizing for green-collar jobs, caring for the earth rather than dominating it.

But the female imagery for God was and continues to be less compelling for Rhina than the male imagery. Rhina explains that the Holy Mother, venerated as the Virgin of Guadalupe in Rhina's native El Salvador, feels more removed for her than Jesus. She muses that perhaps her Catholic childhood, where she had to kneel before the saints and *La Virgen*, is why she feels the Holy Virgin is more distanced. You have to approach *La Virgen* with more reverence, ask permission. *La Virgen es especial* [the Virgin is special], for special occasions, like her feast day when you light a little candle and set it before her."

Perhaps the Virgin of Guadalupe's darkness resonates for Rhina, as did the Baptist church full of Salvadorans, but Rhina is clear: "I like her, *la Virgen Morena* [the Dark Virgin], but for me, Jesus is more accessible, more *humano*." She recounts sitting in her apartment studio in the half-light of approaching dusk and feeling his presence *"como un pastor"*—as a shepherd—watching out for her, his little lamb. She describes him as a compassionate leader, always encouraging and enabling Rhina, who has suffered the worst of self-hate, to love who she is and to give back to the community.

"For me, it's very clear. A big part of my spirituality is form-ing community, serving others, finding ways to contribute to a healing society. '*El reino esta entre ustedes*,'—we build the kingdom of God among us—is what someone explained to me one day: My Christian faith informs and calls me to the cause of justice, and justice fuels my faith."

When she finished seminary, Rhina decided to give back by becoming an ordained pastor. Until then she had been working as a community organizer, but when she applied for candidacy in ordained ministry, she was not welcomed, not as her full self. Because she'd heard that the Methodist denomination was looking for Latino pastors, Rhina applied to that denomination for candidacy. "I told this Methodist recruiter that I wanted to be an openly gay *pastora*, and he said the church doesn't need to take care of you; you take care of the church. It was like he was telling me, 'You need to stay closeted.'"

Staying closeted seemed to Rhina like stumbling backward into her tortured years. She attended other churches, feeling most at home in a United Church of Christ church pastored by two women with a long history of involvement in the Oakland community. "I love it there," Rhina says. "Sometimes I am so tired, but once I get there, I feel the sacred energy that everyone brings. It feels good to pray not just by myself but with people, people connected to me."

Seven years after the Methodist recruiter disappointed her, Rhina was ordained on May 26, 2012, in the United Church of Christ. She feels she has been adopted, that she can truly be who she is in this new church. She is full of faith for the ministry she is starting. She characterizes her vocation as "a *pastora* for queer Latinos who suffer rejection in other churches," and she proclaims her vision: "*La Iglesia de la Puerta Abierta* [the Church of the Open Door]!" The UCC of Northern California does not yet have a Spanish-speaking Open and Affirming church to call Rhina as pastor. "But I will start one!" Rhina laughs. "It will be the first Spanish-speaking Open and Affirming ministry of the UCC here in the Bay Area! Just wait and see!"

Going Deeper

1. How did Rhina's discovery about her sexual orientation open up her spiritual experience of God and help her to rebirth herself?

2. How did Rhina experience divine love in moments of pain and transformation? Who was the face of the Divine for her during these moments of transition?

3. Describe when *you* feel God's presence. When have you felt God ministering to you through other people? How have these moments aided self-discovery and self-acceptance?

Try This

Reflect on your religious community (or whatever grouping of people where you feel most supported). Where is God for you in that community? When are you "divine" for others?

DIVINE CONNECTION

Part II

Humanity was born in the yearning of God. We were born to share the earth.

CARTER HEYWARD,
EPISCOPAL PRIEST AND THEOLOGIAN

ell into this project, I decided to ask myself the interview questions. After meditating, I clicked open the file listing the questions and typed in my answers stream-of-consciousness style. My answers surprised me. In response to the first question, "Think of one instance when you felt in a very palpable or otherwise powerful way the presence of the Divine and describe it," I wrote:

> There was a moment in wartime El Salvador when I did the unadvisable: I walked off alone. The group I was leading was waiting for the refugees, about thirty families who were repatriating en masse from the United Nations camps in neighboring Honduras, to arrive in their home territory, which was still disputed in the country's decade-long civil war. It was dangerous to go off hiking alone, because the area could change hands at any moment. But I did. I sought solitude and something that I did not have the words for: a very deep yearning that I breathed out into the warm, damp air.
>
> It was the end of El Salvador's rainy season, and the road was a strip of red mud snaking its way through voluptuously green hills. When I got to the site that the refugees would be returning to, I paused. Others who'd

repatriated earlier had shorn the earth of its thick mane to make room for the newcomers' shacks. The elephant grass lay in heaps next to the stone wall from which the abandoned village took its name: Corral de Piedra.

On the other side of the border, the refugees were fighting for their right to return to this place, yearning, as the prophet Isaiah says of the Israelites exiled in Babylon, for home. But what was I yearning for? What pulled at my heart? Darkness was approaching. I turned to walk back, and the sky turned crimson and then violet, hemorrhaging at the horizon. I will always remember this sunset, this moment, when the yearning within me suddenly leapt into words: "I want a child. I want a baby of my own."

These words, this desire to birth and nurture another life, did not fit with my outer reality, a life of constant travel and exposure to wartime risks and my cross-cultural, transcontinental marriage to a Salvadoran guerilla leader. But the desire arose, a voice from my inside self. The feeling was as intense as experiences I'd had in church when I'd felt God calling me to work in El Salvador. It felt as prayerful as the Sundays when I had stood next to my father as he pronounced the benediction. The yearning I experienced in El Salvador's countryside was like the euphoric oneness I sometimes felt when I'd run cross-country, my feet skimming the dirt roads of Orange County's as yet undeveloped canyons. In the midst of war and great suffering, the spirit by which I heard God, praised God, lived God, spilled out its deepest desire in me: to make room for another, a baby. I wanted to birth and nurture a baby of my own.

I realize now, after hearing other women's stories, that yearning is universal. Whatever its form, whether for children, for belonging, for reunion with loved ones or one's homeland, yearning is our longing to connect. It is a longing for wholeness. And because it is for wholeness—for life in its abundance and infinite expression—it is not limited to humanity.

Carter Heyward, an Episcopal priest and theologian, wrote a marvelous litany that Pastor Stacy Boorn occasionally uses for the rite of Holy Communion at Ebenezer Lutheran (herchurch):

> In the beginning was God
> In the beginning
> the source of all that is
> In the beginning
> God yearning
> God moaning
> God laboring
> God giving birth
> God rejoicing.
>
> And God loved what she had made
> And God said,
> "It is good."
> And God, knowing that all that is good is shared
> held the earth tenderly in her arms
> God yearned for relationship
> God longed to share the good earth
> And humanity was born in the yearning of God
> We were born to share the earth.[1]

For humanity, the Holy One, and all of life, relationship is essential. In the yearning for connection, we open ourselves to Spirit. We invite wholeness. We begin to see our commonalities and our underlying unity instead of the separation and brokenness we have so often assumed as humanity's deepest truth. At some deep level we realize that we are all connected, a profound mystery long experienced by mystics and now studied in the field of quantum physics.[2] I believe our yearning stems from a desire to experience more fully our existence as it really is— that we are each singularly splendid and simultaneously integral to the whole, a spectrum of colors pulsating in life's cosmic kaleidoscope.

The women I interviewed draw from their web of human relationships—parenthood, partnership, community—to describe their experience of God. They exemplify the practice of being in communion with others and the Divine. In ways both ordinary and extraordinary, they embody the divine connection.

Jeanette

Dropping into the Hands of God

My understanding of the Divine is relational. It has to do with accompaniment and with intimacy ... with consolation and resilience. These are key concepts that come to mind when I think of the Divine.

JEANETTE RODRIGUEZ, PhD,
PROFESSOR OF THEOLOGY AND RELIGIOUS
STUDIES, SEATTLE UNIVERSITY

Jeanette Rodriguez responds to my questions with energy ten times her size. She speaks with traces of a New York inflection and a sprinkling of Spanish. "When I was nine years old, I had a dream. I've only remembered two dreams in my whole life, and this is one of them." She describes how, in her dream, she'd lost her sandal and then sighted it some distance away. "I went to get the sandal, and the earth started to move, and almost like quicksand, I started to be pulled down."

Jeanette's eyes widen beneath her dark rectangular glasses. "And at that moment, twelve angels flew out and took hold of me, pulled me out of the quicksand, put me on hard surface, and said, 'We will always be here to protect you.' I believe that. I've experienced that

93

the rest of my life. My friends have a joke: that my angels are working overtime!" She laughs heartily. "Because of the places I've been
and the things I've done. From an early age I had this experience
of these guides watching over me, and it's true. I've been through
two wars, been to some pretty hefty places, and nothing's ever happened to me."

Jeanette, the daughter of Ecuadorian parents, and a theology
and religious studies scholar, has just finished her keynote address
on the Virgin of Guadalupe as the feminine face of God at herchurch's Fifth Annual Faith and Feminism Womanist Mujerista
Conference. Jeanette gave voice to the indigenous Nahuatl experience of Guadalupe, expressing that "to be a devotee of Guadalupe is
to be a defender of all oppressed peoples. Guadalupe is inseparable
from her people. She appeared to them as their Mother, accompany-
ing them, nurturing them, supporting and defending them." In fact,
as Jeanette explains in her talk, *Tonantzin*, the Nahuatl word for
Guadalupe, is actually a title signifying "Our Mother."

I am reminded of Jeanette's story of her own mother, which
she had shared in the plenary session. Jeanette's mother had been
hospitalized, and Jeanette recounted walking home alone to the
housing projects, because her father was working two jobs. She was
ten at the time, she explained, and her younger siblings were sent
to live with others during her mother's long illness. "So I was this
child who needs her mother, walking into the projects by herself,
turning loneliness into solitude by going to the Catholic church.
Our church was so poor it was a Quonset hut, and I would go in
and sit in front of the statue of Mary. For me, the statue was alive.
I went there every day after school to pray. One day the priest asks
me, 'What's going on, *m'ija* [my daughter]?' I didn't tell him, and
I didn't tell him the next time he asked either."

The priest kept asking, day after day, and finally Jeanette told
him of her mother's illness, and he told Jeanette to come to the
convent every day after school from then on. Making sense of this

experience, Jeanette said, "We glimpse the Divine through human relations. I don't even remember the priest's face anymore, but I remember the Oreo cookies and the milk. I remember doing my homework until my father could come and get me." She goes on to describe her mother, once she returned from the hospital. "And I saw the Divine through my mother, through her presence and unconditional love."

Long after Jeanette's mother had passed away, Jeanette experienced her presence and words of encouragement at a time of deep distress when Jeanette was hospitalized multiple times for an acute illness. "By the third time I went into the hospital, people were getting really freaked out. They were giving me antibiotics, and I wasn't getting any better. I was losing my hair. I'd lost thirty pounds. I was in the hospital during Christmas, and my kid sister—who lives in California but had flown up—she walks into my hospital room on Christmas night, and I turn to look at her, and I say, 'Oh geez, am I going to die?' Jeanette laughs. "Of course she says something like, 'You're not dying. I'm going to kick your butt out of that bed!'" Jeanette chuckles and claps her knee. "I laughed—she could always make me laugh—but I was close to death. I had last rites. I had a priest come. I really felt the power of the Spirit in the prayer that night, and in the middle of the night, I felt someone caressing my arm. I looked, and there was nobody there, so I went to that deeper place that I go to, and then I realized that it was my mother. I knew my mother's touch."

Jeanette knew her mother's touch, and not even death was strong enough to sever their relationship. In her mother's caress, Jeanette received a message. "I got the message from her that I was going to recover and that it was going to take a long time. And it did. I was in the hospital for five and a half weeks, with eight months of recovery."

To help me understand her illness, Jeanette describes the stents they put in her stomach ducts and pancreas. "When they did that to the pancreas, the pancreas blew up. It was extremely painful. I looked like I was seven months' pregnant. My stomach was out to here," she gestures. "And it was as hard as a rock. I couldn't eat, and they had to feed me through a port so they wouldn't have to keep sticking me with needles. The good news is that I don't remember a lot of stuff that happened." Because Jeanette was in extreme pain, she was receiving nine cubic centimeters of morphine daily. Perhaps because of the medication, she didn't remember the visits of her colleagues, but they maintained an around-the-clock presence both in the hospital and when she was recovering at home.

"It's funny because the grace that came out of that was really the experience of being very loved. My colleagues in the university all signed up to make sure someone was with me 24–7 until my recovery." She elaborates on this, that for her, accompaniment is the essence of spirituality. She characterizes it as intimacy and openness, vulnerability and surrender—the qualities of receptivity.

"My understanding of the Divine is relational. It has to do with accompaniment and with intimacy. It has to do with consolation and resilience. It has to do with orphanhood. These are key concepts that come to mind when I think of the Divine."

Jeanette is a single mother of two. At that time when she was close to death, her daughter was already away at college, but her son, who was seventeen, was still at home. She says that her long illness and hospitalization were much harder on him than on her daughter because he was still living at home. As evidence, she quotes a poem of his from that period. She says the first line went something like, "I asked her if I could take her earrings off, and she said, 'No, *m'ijo* [my son], I want to look pretty.'" In the poem he offers again, and again she refuses. In the last line of the poem, he notes that even after her earrings are removed by medical staff, "She was still beautiful." Jeanette's dark eyes glisten as she relates this example of filial love. Mother to child, child to mother—it is all about relationship.

In another incident, Jeanette recounts how a relative of hers was kidnapped, causing her great anguish. Afterward, in a keynote talk, she described that period of suffering. Her keynote was sandwiched between two other keynote addresses, both entitled, coincidentally, "Rise Up, Oh People of God." "And mine," Jeanette says, chuckling, "was called 'Wounded by Love: What to Do When You Can't Get Up Anymore.' I was speaking about suffering and evil, and I used the example of the kidnapping. My initial reaction was anger at God. But then I realized that for a person of faith, the only real response is to drop. And when you drop, that's when you drop into the hands of God."

Similarly, Jeanette recalls reading at her mother's funeral a scriptural passage of the death of Jesus's good friend, Lazarus. When she got to the part of Jesus telling Martha to have faith, she says, "I stopped reading, and my throat got like I couldn't swallow. I wanted to cry out, 'No, I do not believe! You really blew it with me on this one!' But I knew that in that moment if I said no, I'd enter an abyss I didn't think I'd recover from. So I said, 'Yes, I believe, Lord. Help my unbelief,' because I was so overcome with grief."

For Jeanette, community is another way in which the Divine holds us. "I have multiple communities. I have my Catholic Christian community that I go to. I have a leadership group that I facilitate, and I am honored to be invited into the Moon Lodge by indigenous women of great faith and courage."

She characterizes her Latin American religious heritage as a syncretism between indigenous practices and Catholicism. "As a Catholic, I celebrate Holy Week. I attend Holy Thursday and Good Friday services. But as a mestiza, I go to church on Holy Saturday to keep Mary, the mother of Jesus, company. We do this because we understand and have experienced her grief. This is why we have a theology of accompaniment. You look at the scriptures, and you have Ruth and her mother-in-law, and Elizabeth and Mary. You know the friendships that have gone on and the accompaniment."

Jeanette's examples portray a divinity who yearns and embraces. They call to mind the comforting words of Our Lady of Guadalupe spoken to Juan Diego and an oppressed people: "Am I not here? I, who am your Mother?" These words are Guadalupe's invitation to faith, and for Jeanette, faith (along with courage and the accompaniment of others) is what enables her to answer, "Yes."

Going Deeper

1. What experiences in Jeanette's culture and childhood influenced her understanding of the Divine?

2. Describe the value of accompaniment for Jeannette and how it affects her spirituality.

3. How does your relationship to family and other people important to you impact your understanding of the Divine?

Try This

Close your eyes and take a few minutes to breathe quietly. Think of your mother (or a person who is like a mother to you). Remember a time when this person did something loving for you. Imagine yourself taking in this gesture or gift from your loving mother or friend. Imagine yourself expressing your gratitude. Stay in that moment as long as you want. When you are ready, write a few words about it.

Irma

A Mother's Embrace

Don't worry. Things will come out well.

THE REVEREND ROSA IRMA GUERRA DE
ALVARADO, RECTOR, SAINT FRANCIS OF ASSISI
ANGLICAN CHURCH, EL SALVADOR

In her pressed jeans and blue blouse with its round clerical collar, Reverend Irma Alvarado is the very essence of calm. As I set out my recorder, she extends her small brown hands on the table. An intricate flower ring graces her finger, a gift, I presume, from her spouse, who is also a Salvadoran Episcopal priest here in El Salvador.

I ask Irma to describe an experience with God, and she responds, "God is always present, but there are moments of greater intensity." She meets my gaze with eyes that are black and thickly lashed as she tells me about a time when her son, Josue, was six years old and diagnosed with leukemia. "The bone marrow exams were very painful, *muy doloroso.*" She describes how her son, curled in a fetal position, received the jab of a thick needle the size of a nail. How hard it was for her to watch his face tense in pain and know that after months of high fevers and swollen glands, it had come to this: leukemia.

"With all the love and hope that one has for one's child," Irma says, "I began to pray." On the eve of the third round of bone marrow tests, after leaving the hospital to put her infant daughter to bed, Irma prayed for her son's life. She lost all sense of time as she wept, wrestling with God. Suddenly, she felt an intense calm enter her heart. "I felt within my heart this certainty, this tranquility, that everything would be okay. So strong was her feeling of certainty that she was able to sleep peacefully.

"The next day, when I went to the hospital, I told my husband, 'Everything is going to be okay.' That third round of tests came back clear, and there was the miracle of God—*el milagro de Dios.*" While Irma and her husband continued to bring Josue back to the hospital for continued monitoring, he remained healthy and is now twenty-six years old.

More recently, Irma felt immense calm and certitude after praying for her grandson, who was born two months premature. Irma's own mother, watching the infant struggle for oxygen, commented that he would surely die. Irma describes how his little ribbed chest heaved, how his throat emitted a sound like a mewing kitten, even as he slept. "He was so very fragile—*tan indefenso, tan fragil*—especially his lungs. His tiny chest shuddered with each breath." Irma says she laid her hands gently on his chest and began to pray, weeping.

Recalling this moment, Irma's eyes gleam with the mist of tears. "I don't know how long I knelt there, praying over him—maybe for an hour or two—but then his little chest calmed. Again I felt the power and that certainty that everything would be all right. When my daughter came home from her classes, I told her that her son would no longer have difficulty breathing. I felt that certain. 'He might have other illnesses,' I told her. 'But his lungs are healed.' And now he's five and attending kindergarten. It is another of God's miracles." Irma wipes her eyes. "Because God is merciful."

When I ask Irma if she sees feminine aspects to God, she answers emphatically, "Yes. God's attributes of love, compassion, forgiveness are like those of a mother. I'm a mother to my two children. As bad as my children behave, I love them—*por muy mal que se porten, los amo.* I can't say, 'No, I don't love them because they disobeyed me or didn't tell me where they were going. They're my children. I love them. God is like that. That's the feminine part of God."

She lowers her voice and explains that women are often more open than men, especially when it comes to difficult situations like those with disobedient children. A mother's heart, she says, is always open. By way of example, she tells me of her husband's reaction to their sixteen-year-old daughter's pregnancy—how her husband wanted their daughter to live with the unborn baby's father, even though their daughter didn't want to. Irma recounts, "My position was that if she wanted to stay in our home, she should be able to. She was so young, I explained to him. She needed our love. Same with my son, when we had problems with him. I said to my spouse, 'If I don't love them with my whole heart, who will?' That is a mother's love. I love them completely and totally, no matter what.

"For me, that is the feminine part of God. When my children have problems, they come to me, and I help them as best I can, offering my embrace, even if I have nothing else. I hug them, and I tell them, 'Don't worry. *Las cosas van a salir bien.* Things will come out well.'" And for me, that is God: like a mother. Jesus himself compares his love to that of a mother hen, how he wanted to comfort his people, to bring them under his wings."

I thank her for sharing this story with me, and she responds that hers is not a docile or dormant faith. "God," she asserts, "gives us opportunities to practice."

Irma's family was of scant resources, but they blessed her with a trade: making pottery. Growing up in Ilobasco, El Salvador, she learned the art of shaping, firing, glazing, and finishing all kinds of ceramics, from vases and figurines to tea sets and wall ornaments. At age sixteen, she left her family home and went to work and pursue higher educational studies in San Salvador. After studying and working for a few years, she met her future husband, David, and he introduced her to the Anglican faith. Irma's family was very active in the Roman Catholic Church, but she liked the community feel of the Anglican Church and the fellowships that they had after the service. After four years of dating, she and David married in an Anglican ceremony, a blow to her parents because they had expected her to marry within the Roman Catholic Church. Even though her parents initially rejected her marriage, Irma felt deep trust in her convictions, and she and David became missionaries.

After she bore their children—first a son and then a daughter—Irma worked at a ceramics studio in their home while raising the children. Soon she began volunteering with the church's youth movement. The Anglican bishop in El Salvador, the Right Reverend Martin Barahona, recognized her talents and helped her to enroll in lay theology classes at the country's Anglican seminary. Since the seminary required that all students have vestments, she had one sewn to fit her. A remarkable feeling came over her the first day she donned it. It was a simple vestment, black and straight, but she felt awakened as soon as she slipped it on.

She looked at herself in the mirror, and an intense inner confidence took over. Irma compares it to the feeling she got when she put on her softball uniform. "As a young woman and mother, I played [for] various teams and federations, and it didn't matter how tired I was from studying nights and child rearing and working all day. When I put on my softball uniform to play ball, I felt the energy of an athlete! The first time I put on my vestments, I felt that same feeling. I looked at myself in the mirror, and I felt good. I was no longer the Irma who was studying theology for lay ministry. Instead, I was the Irma studying for the priesthood!"

Irma shared this feeling with her husband and later Bishop Barahona. "I said that I was feeling the calling to the priesthood. With the bishop's support, I began studying for ordained ministry.

It's been two years now since I've been ordained. I'm the first Salvadoran woman ordained and serving in El Salvador."

During her studies, one priest discouraged her, grousing, "I don't think you'll make it. Women are good for laying the altar clothes and for teaching Sunday school, but they will never be accepted as priests."

Irma smiles mischievously as she recounts her response. "I asked him, does this come from you or from higher up?" Since she herself felt certain of her vocation, Irma chose to ignore his dismissive words. "If I were not a strong woman—strong in my faith, strong in my sense of self—I might have said to myself, 'Maybe he's right.' But I felt firm in my convictions. I valued myself."

She convenes a group of young women called Jovenes Unidas. "I'm always telling them that they should support one another, unite. Sometimes there's competition among them, for various things. I tell them that women are not second-class citizens. In the eyes of God, women and men are equal. 'Don't ever think,' I tell them, 'that a woman is not as capable as a man. She should be as equally respected and valued.' And I tell them, 'Never put down another woman.'

"Three things are most important." Irma counts on her fingers. "*Uno*: women are *hijas de Dios*, equally valued. *Dos*: women have equal abilities, equally capable as men. *Y tres*"—she touches her third finger—"we must always stand up for other women! We need to stand together, to be united." She closes her fingers to form a solid wedge of warm brown flesh.

When I ask Irma about spirituality and social justice, Irma asserts that, as believers, we are called to protect the defenseless: women and children abused in the home, those who live in poverty. Her ministry is both rural and urban, among very poor people, and some of the youth have found kinship in gangs. The area where her parishes are located is besieged by crime and violence, and yet Irma's ministry on behalf of the defenseless is respected.

"I tell my parishioners that I, like them, have problems: economic troubles, emotional and physical problems, challenges with my children. But I see it as an opportunity to be polished, to allow, in these situations, for God to burnish me to a brighter hue."

I ask Irma about the earth, and she responds, "The earth is our mother, a gift for our nurture and sustenance. We are called to care for the earth, but we're not taking care of it. I often speak out against the boys who are killing birds for sport. I wouldn't protest if they killed them out of need, to feed their family, but when they kill them for sport, I denounce it. They just say, "What's a bird? It's nothing." And I answer, 'It's life, and we have to protect it."

In similar fashion, she tries to teach the people of her parishes that the trees give life, that they cannot continue to cut them down without great harm to themselves and the rest of the ecosystem.

The last story Irma shares with me is also a testament of faith—and of persistence—and reminds me of the hemorrhaging woman who reached out to brush the hem of Jesus's garments, eliciting Jesus's commendation that her faith had made her well.[1] "A few years ago, I was entering menopause and was bleeding profusely. I had an operation. They scraped the inside of my womb, the damaged part. After that, I didn't have my period for two years, that is, until I was asked to represent the bishop by preaching at a very important service. On Saturday, I was at my little table writing my sermon, and I felt that the bleeding, which had begun the day before, was only getting heavier. At the rate I was going, I wouldn't be able to able to preside or preach because I was bleeding through the pads much too quickly. I couldn't last even an hour without a change of pads—and I was doubling them up! So I prayed to God, '*Dios Bendito*, blessed God, here I am. I need your help. You know that I need to be well for tomorrow. Like the hemorrhaging woman of the Bible, I need your touch, I need your healing.'

"God told me, '*Tranquila*. All will be well.' And again, I felt that sensation of security, of certainty. I went to bed still bleeding heavily, but the next morning when I got up, the bleeding had stopped. And I haven't had any more problems with it."

It strikes me that Irma has communicated the essence of the compassionate Mother-Christ described by Julian of Norwich, the great female mystic of fourteenth-century England. The visionary words Julian received in the midst of the Black Plague and her own debilitating illness were, "All shall be well. All shall be well. All manner of things shall be well."

Like Saint Julian of Norwich, Irma incarnates the love of the divinity she reveres. The divine message that Irma receives both echoes and inspires her own words uttered to console her children in times of distress: "Don't worry. Things will come out well."

Going Deeper

1. What is Irma's experience of faith? What do the worship vestments do for Irma and why?

2. How do the words Irma receives in prayer reinforce the words she shares as a mother to her children and vice versa?

3. What do you gain from Irma's experience of prayer? What do you experience in prayer?

Try This

Close your eyes and breathe deeply to release the labors of the day. Allow your body to relax, releasing whatever tensions remain. Imagine a Divine Being holding you, and exhale deeply into this moment of embrace. Continue to breathe in this manner, exhaling all fears and inhaling the depths of Divine Love. Stay here as long as you like. Afterward, take note of images or words that come your way.

Kimberly

Welcoming Occasions
to Know God

To me, Guadalupe is the comforting, embracing, reassuring mother who welcomes whatever comes into her life as a gift from God. No matter how inscrutable and terrifying it can be, you can still see God in it and know that you can be comforted in it. Even if something brings pain, it's still an occasion to know God.

KIMBERLY RAE CONNOR, PhD, ASSOCIATE
PROFESSOR, UNIVERSITY OF SAN FRANCISCO

When asked how she understands the Divine, Professor Kimberly Rae Connor relates two compelling stories. She speaks quickly, punctuating the slightly Southern cadence of her sentences with light-hearted laughter. The first story she tells is a memory of an incident that occurred when she was twelve, shortly after her mom remarried. This memory was prompted by a question put to Kimberly when she was on spiritual retreat. "A nun, someone I'd never met before, asked when I was most afraid. Somehow she was able to elicit something from me so powerful and so compelling that it's how I think of God now. It's a silly little story but it's very hard for me to tell without crying. Not long after my mom married my stepdad, we went on our first family vacation together."

Kimberly describes a creek where she and her stepfather, who has a paralyzed left arm, were playing a game in the water. "The water would rush me down, and he'd be at the end, and he'd catch me. But one time he didn't catch me, and I'm going downstream with this current, and it's freaking me out. But worse than that, he's lost his footing and is afraid that he's in trouble because he has a paralyzed left arm, and he can't really swim very well. He's worried about me, but he has to take of himself. Meanwhile I'm way down, still going with the water, and I'm scared to death, and finally I get to the other edge, and I'm hysterical, just sobbing. I'm too terrified to cross that water again. And out of nowhere this old fisherman comes, and he says, 'Do you want me to carry you over the water?' And he puts me on his shoulders. My spiritual director said that's God, and so now I always think of God as this guy who puts me on his shoulders and carries me over the scary river. It's so corny." Kimberly dabs at her eyes with a tissue and laughs self-consciously. "But it's amazing, too.

"And then I have this thing for Guadalupe," Kimberly continues, explaining how she originally came across the Virgin of Guadalupe, the apparition of Mary the Mother of God, as she was conducting research for a course she was preparing to teach. But Guadalupe quickly moved beyond the intellectual realm to that of the heart. "The reason I love Guadalupe is because of the Magnificat, because she responds the way I want to respond. Think about Mary's life. She's this young girl who finds herself pregnant. Can you imagine if that were us? And how does she respond? Does she say, 'Screw you, God! I can't frickin' believe you did this to me!'? No, she's saying, 'My soul magnifies the Lord ...' (Luke 1:46).

"To me Guadalupe is the comforting, embracing, reassuring mother who welcomes whatever comes into her life as a gift from God. No matter how inscrutable and terrifying it can be, you can still see God in it and know that you can be comforted in it. Even if something brings pain, it's still an occasion to know God."

In the chapel of the university where Kimberly teaches stands an image of La Virgin Guadalupe with her star-speckled cape. "Next to it, in beautiful gold-leaf lettering, is Guadalupe speaking to the peasant Juan Diego, saying, 'Why are you afraid? Don't you know your Mother is always with you?'" These words are important to Kimberly. "I've lived a good part of my life in fear. The only thing that challenges fear is love, and the only place to go for constant love is God. So the combination of the broad-shouldered fisherman who's going to carry me through danger, and the image of Mary who accepts in faith and joy whatever her life brings her because she knows it's from God—those are the two things that keep me going and make me feel close to God."

Kimberly acknowledges that her images of God are very parental. "I think it's because of my parents and their strong faith. The way my parents loved me is my best model for how God loves me. That's why my faith is still salient to me to this day, even though, as an academic, I'm troubled by the direction the church takes in a lot of ways. In fact, one of the things that troubles me about current iterations of religious faith is the emphasis on certainty. I think that mystery is essential for faith. I think the challenge for me is to see the mystery as something beautiful and not as something fearful. For me, God is most operative in my life when I can see God as a sanctuary, away from my inadequacies and fear.

"There are the two things we want in life: to be loved and to be in companionship. If you have God in your life, however you discern God, you've resolved the big existential human trauma. If you can keep that relationship going with God, then you can handle everything else because you're not out in the world looking for things you can only get from God: unconditional love and unconditional presence."

Kimberly believes that faith is most vital when it looks to right the injustices that others suffer. This is part of what she likes about

Guadalupe. "Guadalupe wasn't concerned about the bishop in his basilica but about the lonely and scared peasant. The religious life is very connected to a life of witness and justice. There is no point in being a religious person unless you try to be Christ in the world. I don't do that as well as I should, but I think it's one important role that the church plays—to model Jesus in the world and to use our institutions not so that we can have places to have potlucks but so that we can do good and be good in the world."

I ask Kimberly what she does to nourish her faith. Her use of metaphors and the lyric pulse of her words should have prepared me, but I am surprised when she tells me that her principal devotional practice is reading poetry.

"I'm finding more spiritual nourishment in reading poetry, even more than religious literature and scripture. I love poetry—all kinds. It forces my mind to break out of customary ways of ordering information and knowledge. I'm an academic, and I'm trained to do research and write discursive prose and to give lectures and interpret and explain things in very clear and precise ways. Poetry allows my mind to explore in other ways that are also necessary for a full understanding."

Kimberly chooses her devotional poetry books the way people let a Bible fall open to the page they're meant to read. She goes to the poetry section of the used-book store (Green Apple Books is her favorite) and chooses whichever one draws her attention first.

"So this one time I pull off a book, and it's by a guy I went to graduate school with, and I'm like, 'No way! So-and-so wrote a book of poetry?'" Kimberly contacted her former classmate to invite him to join her in writing about a mentor-professor of theirs who'd died. At the funeral, another of Kimberly's favorite professors did the eulogy and called her mentor-professor "the boundary walker." "He picked this image for him that I would use to describe myself a little bit: on the periphery, but always moving, always walking, never still. Like my mama says, 'On the walk.'"

Going Deeper

1. When you are fearful, how does your relationship to God or understanding of God help you to address fear?

2. Think about Kimberly's words, "Mystery is essential for faith. The challenge is to see the mystery as something beautiful and not as something fearful." How would you apply her words to your own life?

3. What does your understanding of mystery say about your relationship with the Divine and with yourself?

Try This

If you have a book of poems handy, read one of your favorites. Or read the poems in this book. The poetry of Mary Oliver or Denise Levertov also works well for reflection. Read your selected poem slowly, closing your eyes periodically to savor the images and rhythms. Try reading it out loud to a friend or family member. Reflect on the poem with others or write a poem or two yourself.

> **Mother God**
> God to me
> Is my dark-haired mother,
> Stroking my forehead
> As she lullabies me to sleep.
>
> My Mother is the earth
> And all her creatures,
> The web that brings us into relationship
> With one another.
>
> God to me
> Is the Mother
> Who spills Her essence into the world,
> Creating and calling us to create
> From the wombs of our being.

God to me
Is the Mother
Whose voice was drowned out
For most of history,

And yet,
I find Her in my deepest wisdom.
Alone, I feel Her touch
Upon my brow,

Mothering me still,
Mothering us all.
LANA DALBERG

Elena

Celebrating the Mother's Diversity

[I want] to open the eyes of everyone to see the diversity that the Divine Mother has created in this world, and to be able to celebrate that diversity, not just accept it or tolerate it, but welcome it with open arms and open minds.

SISTER REVEREND ELENA KELLY, ORDER OF
SAINT HILDEGARD, STOCKON, CALIFORNIA

Sister Elena Kelly is tall and broad-shouldered. She takes a seat and drapes her dark floral-print skirt over black suede boots. Elena is not your ordinary woman religious. She is starting a convent for transgender women. She made her own transition several years earlier, after serving in the U.S. Navy, raising six kids, becoming ordained in two religious traditions, and founding a nondenominational church in Colorado.

These facts spill from her with ease, with laughter, but her life has been anything but facile. She points to the Divine Mother as the one who sustained her. "My first experience of the Divine Mother," Elena recalls, "was a long time ago. I wasn't even five years old yet. My mother was an alcoholic, and my dad was a farmer and gone all day. One day my mom and dad get in this terrible fight, and I'm horrified. I remember running back to my room, getting down on my knees, and saying, 'Dear Heavenly Mother, the Heavenly Father is not paying attention when I pray. Would you please do something about my parents and make them stop fighting?' No sooner had I said those words when the house went silent. And I thought to myself, 'So there is a Divine Mother. I thought so. If there's a Father, there has to be a Mother.'"

Elena did not agree with the theology of her parents' ultraconservative Church of Christ (which she hastens to clarify is not to be mistaken for the better known, more liberal United Church of Christ). At the age of nine, Elena told her father that she wanted to attend a Roman Catholic church in their little prairie town because she'd gone there with her Italian friends, and one of the nuns had taught her to pray to Mary. "I never felt so right as when I started praying to Mary. That was my introduction to the Divine Mother."

When Elena was still very young, she dreamed, "An angel from heaven—I like to call her Divine Mother—came down from heaven with this big white robe and feathery wings, and she wrapped her arms around me and took me away from that horrible life I had."

When asked to elaborate, Elena responds with a brutal story of public shaming. "When I was in first grade, I only liked to play with the girls. I didn't want to play with the boys. They were rough, nasty, mean, and had cooties. I don't know what my teachers were thinking—at the time I just thought they hated me—but they said I was no longer allowed to play with the girls at all. I remember there was one little girl who lived close to me, and we were best buddies. We knew we weren't supposed to play together, but we didn't care. We snuck behind this wall in the school yard, and we were sitting in the dirt playing when my teacher—who was also the principal—comes around the wall and sees us there. She grabs me by the ear and lifts me up off the ground. She tells everyone else to get back in the classroom. She drags me up in front of the classroom and chews me out about playing with girls. She spanks me and sends me back to my chair, shouting, 'You've been told not to play with girls. Don't you know the difference between boys and girls?' Of course I could tell the difference. They were beautiful, and I wasn't. This was the beginning of my understanding that it was not okay to be a girl.

"From then on I pretended to be a boy because it didn't hurt as much. But they called me sissy. The boy's locker room was horrible for me because I was different. They called me perverted. I cried a lot. I did not fit into that little country school at all."

Elena also discovered that she was the only adopted child in the whole school. "I didn't know who my real parents were. I thought that if I found my birth mother, she could set it all straight. She could explain to everyone why I was the way I was. And it would all be okay, and everybody would be fine with it instead of beating me up for who I was. I had to find her. I was eleven years old when I ran away for the first time. I was gone for two months. I cannot imagine what my parents must have gone through, now having had children of my own. But I'd dreamt that my adoptive parents and I were in Denver. In my dream, this huge crowd of people was on the sidewalk in front of the Ogden Theater on East Colfax. I looked up through the crowd, and a woman's face was looking at me and smiling at me. I knew that she was my birth mother and that I was her son. I tried to reach out for her, and that was when the dream ended. I grew up believing that I would find my birth mother in front of the Ogden Theater, so every time I ran away from home, that's where I was headed."

Elena ran away two more times. The second time, "when they found me they had me committed to a mental hospital. That's when I gave up hope of ever finding my birth mother, and that's why I got into drugs." At the mental hospital, Elena quickly discovered that she could get special privileges, including drugs of her choice, if she said whatever they wanted her to say. Her diagnosis? "Acute adolescent maladjustment," she states with a wry smile.

The last time Elena ran away, she sought refuge with the Hare Krishnas. Previously, on a rare family vacation, she had encountered a Hare Krishna group chanting in the airport. "Us being country folk and not understanding these things, my family thought the Hare Krishnas were entertainment provided by the airport." Elena chuckles. "There was one woman among them, and she had her head shaved with a little ponytail in the back. I couldn't understand why on earth a woman would shave her head, and I was just fascinated."

The woman gave Elena the Bhagavad Gita to read. "I loved that book. A year later, I ran away to join the Hare Krishnas in Denver. I lied and told them I was eighteen when I was only fourteen." Elena studied with them for two years, until her deep identification with the Divine Feminine gave her problems, and she left.

A year later, at age seventeen, Elena entered the U.S. Navy. She had just fathered a child with her girlfriend, and she needed health insurance and an income to support their new family. Once married, their family grew, with more children being born after Elena left the military and relocated the family in South Carolina. There she enrolled in seminary. She graduated, was ordained, and moved her family to Denver to start a nondenominational church. But no matter how busy her outer life, deep down Elena felt torn up by the secret she was guarding: "I always knew that I was a female inside a male body."

Covering up this self-knowledge was destructive. As a teenager, Elena attempted suicide twice. "In the mental hospital I tied a pillowcase around my neck as tight as I could. When they found me, I had no vital signs. I remember waking up in the ER with all the nurses around me. Another time I was super depressed about not fitting in anywhere, and I felt hopeless. I downed a bunch of pills with wine and took my dog on a walk. I took him off the leash and told him, 'You're free and so am I.' Next thing I knew, I'm waking up in ER. Someone had found me facedown in the street and called the paramedics, who pumped my stomach and God knows what else to bring me back.

"Mother Mary, the Divine Mother, saved me from killing myself," Elena asserts. "She's been there every step of the way. Things happen to me every day that She has ordered and put into place."

Elena devotes every morning to prayer and reading sacred scriptures. She describes her home altar. "In the middle of my altar I have a statue of the Divine Mother Mary from Italy. I searched over the entire country before I found the right one. I also have other images of the Divine Mother. I have Isis. I have Durga. I have Kali."[1]

Since Elena so strongly identifies with the Divine Mother, I ask her if she feels more like a mother to her children. I want to know if she feels like a mother to the transgender women in her convent.

"I didn't transition until my kids were grown. When I came out, my two eldest sons rejected it, but my daughters' reaction was, 'You were always like a mother to us.' I had both a mom relationship and a father relationship with them. When they were getting ready for dates, I'd sit next to them and help them. 'Are you sure you want to go with that eye shadow? It's kind of loud. Might clash with your dress.' I was like their girlfriend, especially in high school. But it wasn't like I dressed up in a pink tutu and danced around the house with them. I also taught them how to change the oil in their car, how to change the tire when it goes flat. I took them hunting, taught them how to shoot.

"Family life was wonderful, for me and for them. They have a perfectly wonderful mother, still a dear friend of mine. And I got to be a girl and a boy without them being too suspicious of it. I was terrified that if anyone found out I was a girl on the inside that I would be killed. That's exactly what I expected: to be tortured and killed."

Empathetically, I blurt, "It used to happen all the time."

Elena corrects me. "It still does. In fact, the number one murder rate for transgender people in the world is here in San Francisco, right now. This is a mecca for transgender people, but also a mecca for weird people who want to come kill them. People pick them up downtown in the Tenderloin, where they're desperately trying to eke out a life, selling drugs, selling their bodies because they can't get a job.

"My heart breaks every time I go through the Tenderloin. I get in a conversation with one, and pretty soon we're joined by two or three more. They're desperate people, and they're vulnerable people. That's part of why I'm forming this convent: to help them get off the streets. To help them get work, get an education, get out of that horrendous situation. Like I said, my heart breaks every time I see them. I just want to give them everything I have."

I ask Elena if she could contribute only one thing to this world what it might be. "To open the eyes of everyone to see the diversity that the Divine Mother has created in this world, and to be able to celebrate that diversity, not just accept it or tolerate it, but welcome it with open arms and open minds."

Going Deeper

1. What experiences in Elena's childhood stand out to you? How do you feel you would have responded in her situation?

2. What is your experience of the Divine in moments of profound stress?

3. In your view, how does a Divine Mother differ (if at all) from a Divine Father?

Try This

Set aside fifteen or twenty minutes for people watching. Choose an area with lots of foot traffic, and allow yourself to observe others without judgment. Sit or walk slowly, breathing a few cycles of relaxed and easy inhalations and exhalations. As you breathe, experiment with the following Buddhist loving-kindness meditation, holding each person that you observe with compassion. On each in-breath, surround that person with loving compassion. On the next out-breath, repeat in your mind a series of simple phrases for that person. Examples: "May you be happy. May you be healthy. May you be safe." On the next inhalation, hold a different person with compassion, and exhale with the same three phrases. You can also do the loving-kindness meditation at home or in transit. If you are meditating with your eyes closed, bring a close friend to mind for each inhalation and bless him/her on the exhalation, moving onto another person with each breath cycle. This form of meditation derives from the Buddhist loving-kindness (*metta bhavana*) meditation and is practiced worldwide.

Belvie

Who Can We Become Together?

To the extent that we can understand our interconnectedness and interdependence, [we see] there is no 'other.' There's justice for all, or there's justice for none. There's justice for the planet.

BELVIE ROOKS, EDUCATOR,
AUTHOR, PRODUCER, AND COFOUNDER OF
GROWING A GLOBAL HEART

Belvie Rooks, a multitalented educator and producer, meets with me by phone. In answer to my first question about a spiritual moment, she remembers an incident that occurred when she was twelve or thirteen. Speaking in a strong and emphatic voice, Belvie explains that her adopted family was from the South and went back often. "I grew up in San Francisco, and I was visiting relatives in Texas. Nearby there was a creosol plant with lots of creosol logs, you know, crossties." She describes how the railroad crossties were treated in the plant and stacked to dry, up to twenty or thirty feet high, and how she'd been warned never to take the shortcut through the plant. But she loved walking through it because of the horses at the house where the foreman stayed. "I just loved the horses. I would stop and talk with them, and they always would come over to the fence to nuzzle and be petted.

"So on that day I was walking through and visiting with the horses. And waaaaay in the distance I heard a train whistle because there was a railroad track on the other side of the creosol plant. The trains were very long, so in my head I thought, 'Should I make a run for it? Am I going to be stuck while the train goes by?' I'd always been told that you never try to beat the train, so I decided that I should just let the train go. I kept petting the horses, but I felt a nudging. Something was saying, 'Run! Run!' I felt that the urge to run was to beat the train, which didn't make sense because it was a no-no. I could hear the train getting closer. I could hear the whistle blowing. Finally, when the train was really much too close, I decided, 'To heck with it.' I was actually going to try and beat the train, and I'd never done that. So I left the horse that I was petting, and I turned around, and I proceeded to run to beat the train. I'd run maybe about twenty or thirty steps, and that entire one-story block of creosol lumber fell. The place where I'd been standing was completely covered by a mound of crossties. The horse was injured, and I think it had to be put to death.

"I was shaking because standing there, looking at an injured horse and a pile several feet high of crossties, each weighing ten pounds, I knew that I could have been buried there. I felt delivered from death. After I responded to that inner urging that was so powerful, I felt that it had saved my life. I felt deeply, deeply grateful and moved and shaken and opened."

In reflecting on how that experience changed her, Belvie says, "It created a space of awareness of some Guidance that I had no language for. I was raised in a Methodist church, and in my grandmother's tradition, that was God speaking very clearly. But in my awareness as a teenager, it just was this profound urging that captured my attention and that I responded to, so the lesson for me was deep gratitude that there'd been this urging—this still, small voice that was totally inner. It created an awareness of the reality that there was Something out there larger than me that when listened to and honored was protective."

In response to my question about what was happening at the time of the experience, Belvie explains, "I was adopted into a family that was not my family of birth, and I always felt like the odd person out. I was in that space of trying to figure out where I belonged and who I belonged to [when the event happened at the creosol plant]. The reason that I was sooooo reluctant to leave was that I was talking to the horses. I felt really drawn to share with the animals when the family space that I was in was not safe."

Belvie clarifies that her adopted family was Christian Methodist Episcopal (CME). "CME tended to be much more conservative [than African Methodist Episcopal, or AME]. But that was the religious tradition I was raised in and I was a Sunday school teacher at the time."

Shortly after the creosol plant incident, Belvie became involved with the Quaker's American Friends Service Committee (AFSC) near her home in San Francisco. "With the AFSC, there was an emphasis on peace and on [stopping] nuclear energy. All this had not been part of the CME tradition, and it was very engaging to me. Around that time, I ended up being selected by my CME church to go to a youth gathering in Chicago and just the level of ..." Belvie laughs, and I imagine her shaking her head at the memory. Instead of detailing what happened, she summarizes the conference's impact. "I just had this profoundly negative experience there. So when I came back to California, I realized that I was no longer comfortable in that tradition. I wanted something else, and I was very excited about the AFSC."

Belvie recounts how she embarked upon her spiritual journey, trying to finding her own personal connection "that was visceral and real." With the Quakers, she learned to sit in silence. She meditated. She explored various paths, all rooted in the connection to Spirit that transcends religious denomination. Nature was especially Spirit-filled to her. "When I went into a redwood forest, it felt holy to me. It felt sacred."

On Sunday mornings she listened to gospel music. "Even though I'd stepped away from the kind of fundamental Christian tradition that I'd come out of, I felt that what I *loved* about the black church was the music, so for many years while I was on this personal search, *that* was my relationship with the Divine. *Music* was really my spirituality. That, in addition to nature, was the place where I felt the greatest connection, a *real* connection to the Divine, except [that] what I also loved—even when I was rejecting the theology—was the community."

We laugh because Belvie has a knack for anticipating my next question, which this time is about community. "The black church was the most diverse community that I'd ever been in. In the pre-desegregation South, it had rich black people and poor black people—*everybody* in the community." Belvie missed that community when she left it. "But for many years I could not embrace the patriarchal Christian tradition that I'd been raised in. It was pre–Dr. King so there was no emphasis on social justice. And I realized that I wanted very much to be in a community where women were really acknowledged and held up."

Eventually Belvie discovered the East Bay Church of Religious Science (EBCRS) in Oakland, a community founded by Reverend Eloise Oliver. "Reverend Eloise embodied a lot of the tradition that I'd come out of because she had come from the southern black church out of a lineage of fundamentalist preachers. [Because] her presence as a daughter 'defiled' the holy space of the pulpit, she began her own rethinking and movement away from that tradition into metaphysics."

Belvie is deeply grateful for the community of EBCRS. She can sing the music she loves because the androcentric words have been changed. She loves Reverend Eloise's sermons, which "are rooted in women's ways of knowing, so finding her and being a part of the community that was drawn to her has been very liberating, very powerful."

Belvie herself is a powerful and visionary woman. Prior to our interview, I had heard that she had cofounded an organization working collaboratively to plant trees along the slave trade routes. I ask Belvie about how she came to envision this work, and she tells me about a deep spiritual awakening using holotropic breath work and how she'd experienced a past-life connection with an ancient African woman ancestor imprisoned in a slave castle on the coast of West Africa.

"In that moment of deep breath work, my embodying of the spirit of that woman put me in touch with her suffering on that journey and where it would take her. I held that vision and that place of suffering when I was physically in Africa and in one of the slave dungeons, the women's dungeon in Elmina in Ghana, on the west coast of Africa. You're sitting in a space where, for over three hundred years without interruption, people were bought and sold. It's palpable because it's a dungeon and not much has changed. You're on hallowed ground, ground that holds tears. Being in that space of deep suffering, like people who made the journey to Auschwitz and people who made the journey to Wounded Knee, you feel an overwhelming capturing of the soul, of the spirits that have resided there.

"There's a space where women were brought out into the air every now and then, and it is just beneath the governor's residence, and there is a back stairway up into the governor's bedroom. And we actually walked up those back stairs and into the governor's chamber and were hearing about how the governor periodically looked out and had all the women paraded below him and how he would choose a woman to come up into his chamber that night, usually a young woman, usually a virgin. Sitting in that dungeon and in that cramped, dark space with its tears, I was weeping, just imagining what it would have been like to have been a woman in that circle, preparing one of the young women to go up that stairway, to be washing her and preparing her since she had been selected, with no power to alter the course of what the governor had ordained. I was just sitting there and weeping, knowing that once the governor had raped her, on her way down, all of the guards had the privilege of raping her as well. I was feeling the sadness, what it would have been like in the circle of women preparing that young woman and more importantly, what it would have been like to have welcomed that broken spirit back into the community the next morning. The part that I could not imagine was being the woman going up those stairs.

"So what do you do when you have sat in that space with the women who were very real?" Belvie asks. "I was in such a heartbreak that I just curled up in a fetal position on the bed. After I'd been sobbing for three days, when my heart would not be anything but broken, my husband asked me, 'In the midst of this kind of suffering that you're feeling, what would healing look like?' It was not a question I was prepared for at the time, but it turned out to be profoundly insightful. And when I went down to the river to wash my feet as the elders told us—that after being in those slave dungeons you have to go down to the river or to the ocean and you have to ritually wash your feet to get rid of that suffering—and down there I recalled a poem of Alice Walker called "Torture." The refrains kept coming to me: "When they torture your mother, plant a tree. When they torture your father, plant a tree." So when I was thinking on the question, 'What would healing look like?' this ritual and these refrains of planting a tree gave life to the vision of honoring the men and the women and the children and the grandmothers who had been lost and who were erased.

"We know how many tons of flour the slave ships carried; we know everything except the names of the people on those ships.

That's heartbreaking, this complete erasure of people. They were mothers and fathers, uncles and aunts, potters and weavers and healers. Calling people slaves is a way of erasing them. So my husband and I embodied this vision of growing a global heart."

Shea, baobab, and other cultivated trees are all that remain of many of the abductees' villages, and Belvie and her husband envisioned the planting of trees as a way to give meaning to lost lives in this time of catastrophic climate change. In Africa, they spoke with environmentalists and women from tree-planting collectives. They "seeded the vision" by talking at churches and green festivals in the United States, and they are going back to Africa to launch the project in a major way. But they planted the first tree in Alabama.

"We had the first tree planting in Selma at the tip of the Edmund Pettus Bridge where, in 1968, the world watched Dr. King as civil rights marchers were trying to march from Selma to Montgomery. It was that image of carnage that shocked the world and the nation and pushed a reluctant Lyndon Johnson to sign the Voting Rights Act, and we were really honored to be invited by the Voting Rights Museum for the jubilee enactment of that march. We planted the first tree there as a way of commemorating all of the people who'd given their lives both in the civil rights movement and on the underground railroad."

My next question is about how one's spirituality relates to social and environmental justice, which Belvie, once again, has already begun to address. When I pose the question, Belvie takes a deep breath. "When we cut down trees that are the lungs of the earth, there is a relationship between that and the asthma issues of children in South Central Los Angeles, where there are no trees.[1] For me the relationship seems to be the ways in which we are interconnected and interdependent not just on each other as humans but on the larger environment, the totality of all there is. Alice Walker has a book, *Her Blue Body Everything We Know*.[2] Everything we know as humans emerges and is rooted in that small blue planet: her blue body. The clear-cutting of the trees and the wholesale raping of the earth, we do that to our own demise in the sense that we do not just walk on top of the earth, we are integral to it, to her. I talk about slavery, but I could be talking about the clear-cutting of trees or the burning of women at the stake as witches. The shift in social justice is the shift in our consciousness. To the extent that we can understand our interconnectedness and interdependence, [we see] there is no 'other.' There's justice for all, or there's justice for none. There's justice for the planet."

Belvie also talks about pointing the finger back at herself, at her own heart. "Where am I in this? How am I in this? I am not exempt from the things that I am describing that contribute to what is not working in the world, in the country and on the planet. I am not exempt. Constantly, with humility and kindness both for myself and for others, I'm hoping to be supported as I make the shift, just as I am supportive of others who are also attempting to make the shift. I think about my own journey, that once I had greater understanding about the impact of what I do and how it affected the climate, then I could make other kinds of choices. I feel that even with the urgency, there is a level of kindness and compassion in acknowledging and recognizing that everybody has the possibility of shifting. As Reverend Eloise says, 'When we know better, we do better.'"

Beyond Belvie's voice, I hear a doorbell ring and a woman calling, "Belvie! They're here!" I know our interview is coming to an end, and I thank Belvie for her time. Visiting her website, I read about Growing a Global Heart's threefold vision: "To help plant a million trees along the transatlantic slave route and the underground railroad to honor and remember the millions of unnamed, unheralded and unremembered souls who were lost during the slave trade; to help combat the ravaging effects of global warming and catastrophic climate change; and to actively highlight and support African-inspired sustainable solutions."[3]

I am reminded of Belvie's words, "Where am I in this? How am I in this?" Her words both encourage and challenge me, especially her query, "The question that I feel is important that we embrace at this point in human history is, 'Who can we become together?'"

Going Deeper

1. What elements of Belvie's childhood shaped her sense of self and the Divine?

2. How does Belvie see humanity? How does she see the relationship of humanity to the earth?

3. How do you see your relationships, both with other humans and other species? How does your understanding of the Divine enhance your relationship with others (including other species) and the earth?

Try This

Sit or lie down for this meditation. Either prerecord it or have a friend read it to you. Get comfortable and breathe deeply for several minutes, until your breathing lengthens into a natural, calm rhythm. Imagine stepping into and sitting down in a comfortable train that takes you to another place. The train has no windows, but the doors will open soon. You count down: 10, 9, 8, 7, 6, 5, 4, 3, 2, 1. The doors open, and you step into a garden. Take in the sights and sounds of the garden around you. If there is sunshine, feel it on your face. Feel the solidity of the ground beneath your feet. Reach down to run your hand over its textures. Breathe deeply. What do you smell? If you turn your head, what else do you see? Observe everything around you. Remain in this place as long as you want. When you are done, slowly open your eyes and write down what you experienced.

Malisa

Seeing the Divine in Each Other
(*Namaste*)[1]

> For me, it's all about relationship. The Divine is
> relationship.
>
> MALISA YOUNG, TUTOR

Malisa sets a glass of water before me and grins. I thank her as she sits down Indian-style on the couch across from me, her twin braids gracing her shoulders.

When I ask Malisa about her spiritual experiences, she smiles and announces that her deceased grandmother and great-grandmother come to her as guardian angels. She describes her great-grandmother, who died shortly after Malisa was born. "In the only photograph I've ever seen of my great-grandmother Emma, she is lying on her deathbed. She was the daughter of slaves. She still has the head-wrap on her head, and she's wearing all white. She's dying, but she looks very serene and very calm. She's got her hands in the *Namaste* position [palms together, over the heart]. So when I was learning yoga and such, I would always think of her when I saw that position because she sort of embodied that to me, the peacefulness of just being. And the feeling I have with her, when she comes to me, is really that of a calm being.

"That's not what I get from my grandma Mary. From her I get a doting-ness, which is what I got from her when she was alive—this encouraging, nudging, stroking"—Malisa smooths her braid—"kind of thing. But with my great-grandmother Emma, I feel more of a strong, quiet being-ness. Obviously I'm lucky to have both!" Malisa laughs and raises her shoulders in a gleeful, bashful way.

I encourage her to say more, and she depicts her deceased grandmothers as energy. "Sometimes I feel them as though another person is in the room, and sometimes I see them without their actually being visible, without the color and substance of a person in front of me."

As a child, Malisa didn't regularly attend any particular congregation or tradition, but she always had a strong sense of the Divine. Her family moved around a lot, at least once a year. She says she felt that she never belonged anywhere, partly because she couldn't understand why her peers questioned the existence of God when she felt God around her everywhere.

"I always felt much more spiritually connected than the people my age. So my problem with religion wasn't religion itself; it was the lack of spirituality that I experienced in religion, the lack of connectedness that I *knew* from personal experience to be there. Like when I was in high school, and all the smart people talked about philosophy, whether or not there was a God, I just always knew from personal experience that of course there was. Of course there's this Being. And I thought it was so absurd when people said, 'Well, if there's a God, why can't I see him?' I'm like, what do you think this world *is*?" Her eyes widen as she gestures all around us. "*This* is God! God is a larger being that we are part of. We're cells of God. Sometimes, just for fun, I ponder the limits of God. For me, it's everything that is. But then, what is everything that is? Where does God end?

"Sometimes I find it more interesting to think of God as relationship. I'm a big fan of *Namaste*, this reminder that I see the Divine in you. If I have any religious practice, that's it: *Namaste*, seeing the Divine in others, even the people who really piss me off." She leans forward. "I have to tell this story that Joseph Campbell tells. There's a man walking down the street and another man riding on an elephant. The man on the elephant is screaming at him, 'Get out of the way! Get out of the way!' And the man on the street is saying, 'My teacher told me that there is a God in me and that I am part of the Divine, so I'm not going to get out of the way.' He doesn't get out of the way, and the elephant picks him up and throws him to the side of the road and keeps on going. The [thrown] man gets up and goes back to his teacher and says, 'You told me that God is inside of me and that I'm part of God, and look what happened to me!' And the teacher says, 'Why didn't you listen to God telling you to get out of the way?'"

Malisa punctuates the story with bubbly laughter. "I tell that story, and some are annoyed because they really want to believe in their godliness, but there's a responsibility of believing also in the divinity of all the others. Some people don't know how sacred they are, and others hold onto the idea that they're part of the Divine, [saying] 'I'm the chosen, I'm one of God's people,' however they choose to say it, and they miss the point that so is everyone else. Everyone is part of the Divine.

"For example, people don't respect kids. It really upsets me to see people treating kids like they're less than human because they're smaller. They talk to them like they're idiots or tell them that their opinion doesn't matter, or they completely ignore them like they don't exist. Or they're violent and take advantage of kids because they can't defend themselves."

Malisa's long fingers quietly curl into fists. The lack of respect for children goads her because she sees their gifts. "I like kids more than I like adults because they're closer to understanding how amazing the world is. And I'm very conscious of speaking and interacting with children in a loving and kind way, because some of them don't get that. Some have never experienced kindness or respect, and they don't know that it exists. I go out of my way to share that with them. I like being a person that they can trust and interact with. I love that."

Malisa talks about tutoring at a continuation high school in San Francisco, where she helped the youth with their online research, senior theses, and other writing projects. "All of them had dropped out of regular high school. Almost all of them had arrest records, a large percentage with felony-arrest records. A number of them had children already. And these were eighteen-, nineteen-year-olds, some sixteen-year-olds, most from the Bayview-Hunters Point [ghetto] area. I spent a good couple of months getting them not to hate me. They didn't trust anything I said. They took offense to my questions and my requests that they turn down their headphones out of respect to the other students. It wasn't a power trip I had; I was getting them to respect their classmates. They tested me, used profanity all the time. Finally they realized that I wasn't going to make them do something just to fill their time. So when I asked them to do something, they would do it. They trusted that I was asking for a good reason. And they *all* graduated!" Malisa claps her knees in delight.

"Just before they graduated I found this copy of *Oh, The Places You'll Go* by Dr. Seuss.[2] I asked them if I could read them a section. They looked at me like I was crazy. 'This is a great graduation gift!' I told them. 'Just let me read a part of it.' They all quieted down and were completely attentive. When I stopped reading halfway through, all of them wanted to hear the end of the story. They were stunned by it because the book is about how amazing life is except when it's not. Sometimes life is just going to suck, but you realize you have what you need to get through the hard parts." The story resonated with Malisa's students. "Some of their friends were dead. Three of the students were pregnant. They were going to graduate and then have babies. And they trusted me enough to ask questions and to talk about these things."

Respecting and honoring children and youth is a gift of Malisa's. Several years back, she took on parenting her nephew when her brother and the boy's mother were unable to do so. She is still very connected to her nephew, although he now lives with his mother. Malisa knows that she can love others' children as if they were her own. In answer to my question about what her heart would say to young women, she says that she desires love and respect for every young person in the world.

When I ask Malisa's opinion of the relationship of spirituality to social and environmental justice, she puts her hand to her chin. The tiny medallions on her bracelet shimmer in the late afternoon light. "I think the lack of social justice is people not recognizing the interconnectedness of the world. I think that if people understood how connected we really are, we wouldn't even have to suggest social justice or environmental justice. I think that that disconnection is really the biggest, saddest thing." She sighs. "I live my life in a way that I see those things. For me, it's all about relationship. The Divine is relationship."

I ask Malisa if she has a spirituality community. At first she talks about the wonderful community she found at her college several years back. Now her community is a church in San Francisco she recently started attending. "When you walk in, you feel it," she says, referring to the Spirit in relationship. It's no mistake that the church is named the Church for the *Fellowship* of All Peoples," she adds, emphasizing the word "fellowship."

When I ask her if she has anything else to add, she nods toward my glass of water and says that for her, water is sacred. "The Ganges River is an embodiment of the dynamic life force of the Goddess Ganga.[3] Even if you don't believe in the Goddess Ganga, we all have this understanding that water is the most fundamental nourishment. The idea of trying to take ownership of water through bottling it and commodifying it is just ..." She shakes her head as if to say unfathomable. Malisa explains that her undergraduate work focused on the relationship between water sustainability and gender equity in education. "Historically women are responsible for providing water to the family. The less accessible the water becomes, the more time and energy it takes women and girls to get the water and the farther they have to go from home. The girls are younger and younger when they have to do this, and they are getting raped along the way." She explains that as water becomes less accessible, so does education for girls and women. Women's power as water bearers diminishes, domestic violence increases, and the health of the family declines. "Women and water. You can't talk about one without talking about the other."

I nod in agreement and lift my glass to polish off the water. When I thank Malisa, she raises her shoulders in her bashful, giggly way. In my mind's eye, I recall her other signature gesture, the *Namaste* pose she attributes to her great-grandmother Emma. I practice it now. Hands at the heart, head slightly bowed, I acknowledge the Divine in Malisa.

Going Deeper

Malisa talks about seeing the Divine in relationship, and often it's in relationship that we grow the most spiritually. Think of at least one instance of a relationship in your life where this is true.

Try This

Meditate for at least twenty minutes. If helpful, use the meditation exercises at the back of the book. After the meditation, be more mindful of your next conversation or interaction. Write about it later, possibly incorporating questions like the following: What am I learning about myself and the Divine through my interactions with others, especially those close to me?

Sadaya

The Womb of God through Which We All Come

It's like my whole being remembers that fundamental essence, that true purpose to be resonating with the Divine, to be part of the Divine. We're not separate at all.

SADAYA ZIMMERLE,
PSYCHIATRIC SOCIAL WORKER

Sadaya Zimmerle transmits both lightness and spark over the phone, reminding me of her high-energy step as she led the Dances of Universal Peace[1] I'd attended. "At the Mendocino Sufi camp," she says, "we get to do the dances for days. Tears come to my eyes, and I feel deeply held and loved and fully accepted. In the midst of dancing and also in chanting, I feel a deep clarity like I'm on the right track, and a deep well of joy. I might come to the Sufi dancing with all kinds of things on my chest, and it's like that stuff gets sloughed off. Whatever pain I have gets gradually shed toward the surface, and I get down into joy."

I ask her to describe a specific moment in her Sufi dancing when she feels the Divine.

"Well, there's the *Bismillah*, which means, 'In the name of God who is mercy and compassion.' You bow on the chanting of '*Bismillah*,' and then you do a bouncy walk-turn and bow again, and then you walk again. And before you start a new phrase, you pause extra long just before you bow. You are allowing yourself to catch up to that beginning, when you are beginning in the name of God again, kind of like, 'Wait 'til you're lined up with God, then go.'"

Even through the phone, I hear her smile as she repeats the Arabic, "'*Bismillah ir rahman ir rahim*: In the name of God, who is mercy and compassion.' The word for compassion, transliterated *rahim*," she explains, "is the same as for womb. So when you say, 'God of mercy and compassion,' it's like saying, 'Through the womb of God through which we all come.'

"This [the *Bismillah*] is at the beginning of almost every chapter of the Qu'ran, and it is one of the Sufi practices. And there is something about bowing to the Divine, about taking that breath to be in sync with the Divine, that brings tears to my eyes. That's why we call it remembrance. It's like my whole being remembers that fundamental essence, that true purpose to be resonating with the Divine, to be part of the Divine. We're not separate at all."

I ask Sadaya if she has always been a Sufi, and she answers that she was part of the Baha'i faith for many years, from the time her fifteen-year-old son was a baby. "Before that I wasn't associated much with any religion except that my stepfather was Jewish. He was a secular Jew when I was growing up, and then he became more and more Jewish as we went along. So over time we started celebrating Shabbat every week and Passover, and I went to a few Jewish Renewal services. But even though we did prayers, he didn't talk about what his religion meant to him. No one mentioned God when I was growing up. It was more taboo than sex!" She laughs.

"But I was always the kind of person who wanted to be connected to something beyond myself, and so I did service. I felt connected by helping other people. In college, my first summer job was working with developmentally and physically disabled people. Just that experience of serving and caring for someone made me want to help heal the world." Sadaya became a psychiatric social worker. But she didn't know how to connect outside of that work, and it depleted her. "My clients were often experiencing the worst possible moments of their lives, and I was painfully bogged down by all that. I needed deeper roots from which to get replenished. The Baha'i faith gave that to me. Baha'i's writings would almost shimmer on the page. I gobbled them up. I felt like I was soaring from his writings, and I lived by that scripture for many years.

"But then I discovered the Sufi dances. And I was like, oh my gosh! You mean you can pray, sing, and dance all at the same time? I had always been the one trying to enliven things with singing and theater. When I discovered the Sufi dances, it was this new form of meditation and prayer for me.

"For three years I did both the Baha'i faith and Sufi dancing. Then I became really ill, and I couldn't do both anymore." Sadaya's voice becomes more hushed. "On my first mammogram, I got a breast cancer scare, and I had to get a lumpectomy. That was incredibly difficult. To make matters worse, I was really hard on myself. I felt terrible about being so attached to a body part, because I'd hoped to be a spiritual person!" She laughs softly. "It was just a brutal test for me. When I was starting to get better and recover from the lumpectomy, I got hyperthyroid, which brought me to my knees. I mean literally, I'd get up from a chair, and my heart would be pounding. My liver got affected. I could barely move, and I was just absolutely exhausted. It took months to get better. I got my thyroid irradiated, and then it took months for the hormones to go down, and then they went down too low, and then I had to do thyroid replacement therapy, which took months to kick in.

"During this time I was terribly torn because I had this whole list of "shoulds" I should be doing because I was on the local spiritual assembly for the Baha'i faith." Sadaya explains that as a leader she felt obliged to attend the Baha'i activities, but the Sufi dancing drew her at a very deep level. "So when I had to choose, I found that I always went to the Sufi dancing. Even if I couldn't dance, I wanted to be there, with the prayers and the music."

A dream helped Sadaya decide. For continuing education credits, she attended a caregivers' day at Spirit Rock Meditation Center. "My mom, who is mostly Buddhist now, invited me to go. I had to meditate for a day, just sitting there with my quandaries and pain about choosing between the Baha'i faith and Sufism. To stay there all day, sitting and meditating, was really important, because I think that cleared the way for this amazing powerful dream I had that night."

Sadaya's voice gathers in volume and speed as she describes her dream. "I was on an organic farming commune. I was eating purple broccoli, plowing the land, and there were these beautiful gardens all around me." She recounts the dream's crisis moment, when she realizes that she has to call her employer to explain why she's not at work. With a laugh, she repeats the explanation she gave to her boss in her dream: "'Apparently, I'm now an organic farmer!' And even though I was reprimanded in the dream, when I awoke, I felt elated. I felt like I'd been transplanted, like I'd been given permission to serve God in this different field." She adds that just as the world needs both social workers and organic farmers, the world needs many ways that people can love and live in God. "And even though I thought I'd be in the Baha'i faith until I died, I felt called to a different path."

Shortly thereafter, Sadaya attended the Mendocino Sufi camp. "*Ruh* means 'spirit' or 'breath,'" she says, expanding on the name of the order that runs the camp, the Sufi Ruhaniat International Order. The Arabic's similarity with the Hebrew *Ruah*, a feminine expression of the Divine that also means "spirit" or "breath," pleases me, and I share this with Sadaya.

As is the tradition in Sufism, Sadaya requested and received a spiritual guide. "For my guide, I picked the leader of a dance circle that I'd been attending for three years, someone I knew pretty well." She explains the central concept of a guide. "A lot of the way we grow spiritually on this planet is through relationships. Just having a designated spiritual friendship and just by being willing to have some guidance, we open ourselves to the larger Guidance. It's like the bowing of the dance I mentioned earlier: bowing to the Divine and being willing to receive input from somebody. But you are also free to do what you think is best."

The Sufi dances are a special time of rejuvenation for Sadaya. "When I go to the dances, I feel so at home. When I arrive, my heart is open and ready, and everyone I meet is in that state also. It's like we're meeting inside the *Namaste*. I meet you in that place where I see the Divine in you and you see the Divine in me. We are both at that place of seeing the Divine, and so it's like we're one.

"Being in that place is very beautiful—energizing and relaxing at the same time. It's love-filled praise. And it's also the ultimate climate for me to grow in. I find that when I go to the Sufi camp for a week, I flourish. Any things I'm working on—to increase my consciousness, to be more effective or more resilient—happen there because I get everything I need." She describes the Sufi camp as a gathering of 150 to 250 people, with spiritual class offerings, the Dances of Universal Peace, and the *Zikr* or Sufi-specific dances and chants. "It's like one continuous prayer of singing from the heart."

I ask a quick question about caring for the earth, and Sadaya answers, "We have an incredible diversity of gifts on the planet, and only through working together will we be able to do what we need to do. She says addressing climate change is one example of how we could do things differently. "People are not willing to face the science, people are not willing to make the sacrifices required, and greed and materialism have been allowed to run rampant at the expense of life. If, instead, facts and fundamental values were driving the equation," she posits, "it wouldn't be a question of *whether* we would address climate change. We would just do it."

When I ask Sadaya about her current relationship with the Divine, she answers, "The Divine is the whole point of my existence. When I work at my job for the county serving people with chronic mental health conditions, everything I do or practice is some kind of manifestation of love. All love comes from God. I am a conduit for that love, serving God by loving and caring for other human beings and helping them shine their light. For me, that's resonating with the Divine, serving the Divine. The same thing with my family, when I'm doing the best I can with my husband, son, my loved ones. It's all connected.

"God," she adds in one of Sufism's most beautiful analogies, "is love and lover and beloved, all at the same time."

Going Deeper

1. For Sadaya, how do movement and chanting lend themselves to prayer and connecting with the Divine?

2. How do dreams impact Sadaya's life and decision making? How do dreams factor into your daily living?

3. In your experience, how is God both lover and beloved, as well as love, all at the same time?

Try This

Put on a selection of sacred music—whatever combination of sound and words that you find holy and healing—and move to it, putting your whole heart into your movements as you paint with your body what you hear and feel with your entire being.

Carolina

Light and Love in All Beings

For me, divinity is present in everything: in the
whole universe, in the planet, and in each being.
It is light and love projected into all beings.

CAROLINA CASTRILLO

Carolina's face is heart-shaped, like an exquisite dark chocolate. In a sweetly pitched voice, she asserts that the Divine dazzles in the perfection of nature. "For me, divinity is present in everything: in the whole universe, in the planet, and in each being. It is light and love projected into all beings."

In her small backyard flower garden in San Salvador, where she has returned after years of living abroad, she gestures to the flaming "ginger plant" and then places her hands over her heart. "I think that the Divine guides us so that we know how to find it deep within ourselves and also through contemplation of nature and beauty in the world.

"Contemplating nature, you feel small and humble. You feel reverence for this great divinity that is present in nature." Carolina recalls standing at the lip of the Grand Canyon and taking in its astounding depths. "It's something so impactful, so strong, that you feel this Presence there, an incredible energy. There are other places, such as the Volcán Irazú in Costa Rica. Standing there at the edge of that misty summit, you feel this sensation of wow!—this sense of the energy and strength of the Absolute. You feel a desire to revere and respect the divinity that's there, that's integral to this perfect universe."

With an endearing smile, Carolina adds, "But it's not necessary to go to faraway places. You can also experience the greatness of creation simply by looking around you, wherever you are—admiring a flower, a girl or a boy playing nearby. A flowering tree is enough to put you in contact with the greatness in nature and its essence of love and harmony."

Carolina stresses that we need to bring the God that we glimpse in nature into our daily lives. "The challenge is to deepen this connection, with other human beings, with everyone, but also with all of the plants and animals and the universe in its entirety, because we are part of it."

I feel profoundly grateful that Carolina, whom I have known for over twenty-five years, can share these insights with me. Born and raised in San Salvador, Carolina was forced to flee El Salvador's brutal military dictatorship on two occasions. When she was a girl and her father was persecuted for his work, her family escaped into neighboring Guatemala. Later, when Carolina was a university student married to a fellow student activist, her husband and his brother-in-law were killed, and she fled with her infant daughter to Costa Rica and later to the United States, where she survived thanks to the goodwill and graciousness of others. Later, she began assisting others fleeing persecution, leading one of the many Central American Refugee Centers that emerged.

Travel, albeit in exile, opened Carolina's consciousness of God. "God has given me this great opportunity to know people from cultures of different countries. When I had to leave my country, going originally to Costa Rica, then Canada, then to the United States, my stays in these countries helped me to open my perspective. When you live in just one country, you have a very provincial perspective; you see your context as the absolute." Carolina explains that she had been raised Roman Catholic but had come to embrace a more universal faith. "Meeting people of other faiths in the United States helped me a lot. I had the pleasure of being part of a human rights movement where persons of many churches participated: Methodist, Anglican, Lutheran, Unitarian Universalist, and other faiths. I particularly like the Unitarian Universalists. In their meeting places, they didn't have any symbols; their space was plain. It appealed to me that they could include people from many faiths, as long as they respected certain universal principles, and for me this was like, wow, how beautiful!"

Carolina has also met people of different faith traditions in the various positions she's held with Catholic Relief Services, Lutheran World Relief, and most recently, Oxfam. "My work has given me the opportunity to know places like Indonesia, Bangladesh, and the Mindanao Island of the Philippines, and in these places I had a great thirst to observe and learn how they practice their Islamic faith. I was also in India, and I could share with my coworkers there some of their Hindu traditions and get to know a little about their faith. This attracted me. I started to read more and more about yoga, about Hinduism, and Deepak Chopra's beautiful books. When I returned to El Salvador, I looked to connect myself in this direction, with this philosophy.

"In the last two years I've been participating in a Buddhist group here in El Salvador. My work sometimes prohibits me from participating regularly in the group's *sangha*, but at least, I am gaining a little from the practice of sitting and also from yoga. Being silent deep within yourself, listening to this great interior silence, you connect with the Divine. And it's beautiful to gather together with others who are also in this spiritual search."

I ask Carolina how her spirituality relates to the earth, and she acknowledges that humanity's sense of separation and superiority has wreaked havoc on the planet. She attributes much of this destruction to the social construct of masculinity and Western men's domination of other species, other peoples, and of course, women.

Carolina puts her hands on her hips. "If women were in more positions of power, where they made decisions that affected large numbers of people and species, the world would not be in the desperate condition it is in now." Carolina is concerned about climate change, water and food shortages, and the contamination of our planet. In response to my question about her advice for young women, she emphasizes that today's adults have mortgaged their children's future.

"We have left them with the great debt and challenges of environmental destruction, social inequity, and poverty, when clearly the earth provides abundance for all. We have mortgaged the future of our youth, because their living conditions are going to get even more critical, with water shortages, climate change, and scarcities as time progresses. Our youth have the challenge of confronting these difficult realities and taking action to stop environmental degradation and to love and rescue nature."

At the same time, Carolina attests that youth are more capable of breaking through stereotypes. "They can disrupt these engrained stereotypes—for example, the patterns of violence toward women that are so deeply entrenched in our society. The very characteristics of youth—to rebel, to break with the dominant pattern, to take a fresh look—all contribute to breaking stereotypes. The youth are the future of our societies."

In contrast, for much of her life, Carolina says that she behaved as she was taught, swallowing her own thoughts and renovating ideas. "As women, we have been formed [with] this social construct, and we are inculcated with certain behaviors and attitudes that many times put us at a disadvantage in society and with respect to men. For example, characteristics such as remaining quiet, meek, humble, submissive, subordinated to others, and not saying what we think or not seeing ourselves as equal to others. This affected me a great deal in my life because my way of being is very quiet. If I knew things, I didn't say them, and sooner or later a man would say them. And later I would say to myself, 'Well, if I knew those things, why didn't I say them? Why didn't I take that step?' It's like we restrict ourselves, put limits on ourselves."

As Carolina became conscious of the restrictions she imposed on herself, she learned to trust her ideas and to assert herself. She feels that today's young women are better equipped to disrupt stereotypical thought and to enter into more equitable relationships. Indeed, Carolina's oldest daughter is an outspoken leader in international cooperation, working on behalf of the Salvadoran government to create harmonious relationships with other countries and regions.

"As women, we need to draw from this inner certitude, this trust and confidence in ourselves, whether that might be in the workforce or in our personal, political, or social lives. In whatever field, we need to value our dignity and rights as equal to everyone else's. We need to act on this inner courage to continue forward.

"Many women in El Salvador are very courageous because during the civil war they suffered a great deal and confronted very difficult situations. Personally, I experienced very hard moments of persecution and the deaths of my first husband and other relatives. Yet many women lived horrendous situations even worse than mine. For example, my family fled in a car to Guatemala that first time, and later, as an adult, I fled by plane. But many women had to flee through the mountains by foot, carrying their children on their backs. They had to find within themselves an inner strength to confront a whole series of difficult situations. We women have to arm ourselves with this *valentía*, this inner courage and strength, to value our rights, and to increase our dignity and self-esteem. If we are able to do this a little bit more, the world would be better."

Carolina hopes that each of us finds inner peace and connection to the Source, that Blessed Light that unites us all. "Spirituality is essential for each person, and each person needs to look for his or her own path. I am very respectful of different paths that people can take. We need to appreciate this diversity and base our lives on these universal principles of love, peace, and compassion. We also need to create a practice that makes what we think, talk, and do coherent. Otherwise, a person is split, saying one thing but doing something completely different. And secondly, we need to have this inner peace. This is fundamental. Many people look outside for what they already have inside. We tend to look outside for satisfaction, for happiness in external things when we really need to deepen our inner gaze."

I thank Carolina for the interview, and she beams, her face radiant beneath its cap of dark curls.

Going Deeper

1. How did Carolina's experience of exile influence her faith?
2. In what ways did meeting and engaging with people of different faiths influence Carolina's own faith?
3. What are some universal values that you identify in the faith traditions you have encountered?
4. Which value resonates most for you?

Try This

Next time you are in a relatively secluded or quiet outdoor setting (a park, beach, lakeshore, or neighborhood park at a time of low usage), sit comfortably. Focus on your breath, inhaling and exhaling calmly while sensing your body and its surroundings. If your eyes have been closed, open them and gaze intently at a natural object in your surroundings (e.g., a canopy of tree leaves, a nearby rose) and notice the quality of light on or around it. While remaining seated, admire this object's colors, textures, scent—whatever you can take in with your senses. With your heart, express gratitude for this gift of nature and for its presence in your day. Expand your gratitude and allow your eyes to take in other creatures or aspects of nature, thoroughly admiring their qualities and gifts to the world. Allow their beauty to speak to you, to impress upon you some aspect of the divinity you worship in your life. Be sure to whisper or gesture your gratitude before moving on with your day.

Debbie

Experiencing the Divine
in the Multitude

Spirituality is *why* we do social justice. It's what
makes social justice work.

REVEREND DEBBIE LEE, DIRECTOR OF
INTERFAITH COALITION FOR IMMIGRANT RIGHTS

Debbie, a second-generation Chinese American
and a United Church of Christ (UCC) minister,
describes marching with tens of thousands to protest the
wars in Central America. "I experience the Divine in the
multitude," she says, grinning in her black clergy shirt.
"There's something about being with the sea of people
who are moving together with a common purpose and
something about the physicality, the vulnerability, and
the diversity of humanity that gives me goose bumps!
Those have been the moments when I really felt, 'This
is what it means to be part of humanity, and here we are
on this planet, and God has made this all possible.'

"The marches protesting the wars in Central
America were my first experience of that sense of mass
humanity being very purpose-driven and very inten-
tional. Being with all sorts of people united in a message

was very powerful to me. I remember seeing books about Martin Luther King Jr. and the civil rights movement, and it always looked like the sea of people coming out of Egypt, on the move and guided by God. So that's what I felt like being part of the marches in the late eighties, calling for an end to funding the Salvadoran military, and then some fifteen years later, marching down Market Street again, this time with my kids as part of the movement trying to stop the Iraq war."

Debbie rests her hands on the table. "And also after Prop 8 passed,[1] when the courts were hearing the case, I was marching with the faith community coming from the Lutheran church in the Castro. That was such a joyful experience. I remember a lot of singing, a lot of joy. We were escorted by the cops, many of whom had requested that shift because maybe they were gay or lesbian themselves and wanted to be there to ease the [civil disobedience] arrests that were going to happen."

Debbie explains that the marches were significant for her because she came from a small town in Ohio that was primarily white. "Being a minority in the community where I grew up, I didn't have a sense of peoplehood. I came from an immigrant family. Both sides had converted to Christianity in Asia, one side in Indonesia and the other side in China." Before Debbie's grandparents converted, they were Taoist and Confucians. "So while there was a lot of devout piety in the family, the tradition wasn't that deep," she clarifies, adding, "At one point, as a young adult, I asked myself, is this really the faith I want? I grew up with it, but is this the faith I choose? I considered going down another path—Buddhism—but I also felt that I could find something liberating in my [Christian] faith despite my struggles with its history of gender oppression and colonialism. I felt (and still do!) that Christianity has a radical and subversive message of liberation, love, crossing boundaries, and finding truth and the sacred in the other."

The community that helped Debbie to deepen her sense of Christian spirituality was a UCC house church. "A lot of people were Asian or Pacific Islander in the congregation, and that really fit. I'm kind of international in my perspective, and they had been looking at the models of Christian community in other countries, at the relevance of Christian faith and theology in the context of struggle, and I felt like that was the journey I was on. I was trying to ask the same questions."

The UCC house church, she says, was a wonderful community for reflecting, growing, and trying out new ways of being church. "We didn't want to reproduce the hierarchy of church, so we didn't have a pastor. There were ordained UCC people in the congregation, but we took turns sharing the leadership. I really liked that model, and its critique of power, how everybody could lead reflection." Debbie decided to enroll in seminary. However, several years passed before Debbie decided to pursue ordination. Working with teenaged immigrant girls helped sway her in that direction. "I was working with high school–aged immigrant girls, many of whom were coming from churches that hadn't ordained women. In conversation, they would ask me, 'Why don't you get ordained? Many of them wanted to consider it, so for me, seeking ordination was partly saying 'yes' to my desire to exercise leadership, but it wasn't just for myself. It was symbolic for these young women. Because of the patriarchy within religion, it can often be so alienating, so my message for young women is to trust that they will find a space and an articulation that works for them, and that it belongs to them."

Debbie mentions that her community now is a group of women clergy who gather together to share their experiences and, of course, her women friends. "I feel most connected sharing my spirituality with women," she adds. When I ask about her current relationship with the Divine, she pauses and looks toward the window. Even though she is due to colead a press conference in less than twenty minutes, her face is serene when she turns back to me. She explains that she has a syncretic or "blended" faith. "For the last eighteen years, I've been a Tai Chi practitioner, and so that's been my strongest connection with the Divine in terms of breath and energy, even more than traditional praying." Tai Chi helps Debbie to be more present and aware that she's connected to the Divine at all times, not just when she's practicing Tai Chi.

She tents her fingers on the table. "I'm a body person. I do Tai Chi. I play soccer. I like the nonverbal aspect of the body stuff." She gestures outward. "Tai Chi, awareness, intuition, being able to connect easily with the Divine through beauty, all of that's spiritual. Sometimes I'm just walking, and I see"—her hands branch out like a tree—"that beauty's right there, all around me!"

Debbie's ability to see the Divine in nature came from her parents. "They loved nature. And guess what—it's free!" She laughs. "We went to a lot of parks and did a lot of camping. The love of the outdoors, that part I really got from them."

When I ask about social justice, Debbie takes a deep breath and lets it out slowly. "Spirituality is *why* we do social justice. It's what makes social justice work."

For the last several years, Reverend Debbie has worked as the director for Interfaith Coalition on Immigrant Rights. A true organizer, a person who finds the Divine in the great human mix, she is at the helm of the immigrant movement, which is as diverse as any movement can be, involving peoples from all over the globe who now reside in the United States. Within a few minutes of our interview, she will be speaking at a press conference, blessing immigrant students who have courageously pressed for the passage of the Dream Act.[2]

But before Debbie leaves for the press conference, I ask my last question, which is about the health of our planet earth. She answers, "To safeguard the health of the earth, I want an end to militarism: to end military bases, conflict, and occupation. I was recently in Puerto Rico for a women's conference against militarism. One of women answered a question about why they are against militarism with the statement, '*Militarismo es contra maternidad.*' Yes, I thought, that's one of the reasons I do this work. Militarism is counter to motherhood; it's counter to everything sacred. I don't know how we can continue to bleed billions of dollars every day toward that end. So ending militarism would be my life's goal." She laughs heartily at the vastness of this endeavor, one into which she throws her full being, like a slender Tai Chi student in the slow-motion wave of fellow practitioners or like one of many sign bearers in a river of marching people.

Going Deeper

1. Debbie describes feeling the Divine in a sea of people moving together with a common purpose. Have you ever felt the presence of God in this way?

2. How did Debbie see her spiritual choices in relation to young women around her? How do you see your faith-related decisions in the context of your friendships, family, and other relationships?

3. How does Debbie express Tai Chi's effect on her faith?

Try This

Google "Tai Chi class" or "Tai Chi teacher" to find a class offering near you and/or obtain a book on Tai Chi to learn more about it. Foundational to Tai Chi is the deep abdominal breathing practiced in meditation, as well as attunement to nature, including the nature within one's self.

Teresa

God among Us

Encountering the poor, you encounter yourself
with God in a totally different way.

SISTER TERESA

Dressed in light cotton and sandals, Sister Teresa motions for me to take a seat in the tiny adobe-style house she shares with four other women religious in San Jose Las Flores, El Salvador. For nearly four decades, she tells me, she has lived and worked among Latin American's impoverished communities. "For me, vocation has been very much defined as living my life among the poor."

Still it was a big shock for Teresa—"*un choque grande*"—to arrive at the nearly destroyed community of San Jose Las Flores in the midst of El Salvador's civil war. For Teresa, "the shock was to realize how far I was from the great suffering that so many people were living." Yet one day, during her contemplation time, she heard God speaking to her inwardly. "It was a crisis, but also a great revelation. God told me clearly in the words spoken to Moisés: 'Take off your sandals, because this place, the place you are entering, is holy ground' [Exodus 3:5]." At another time, Teresa recounts, "In a state of prayer, I felt Jesús come and take hold of my shoulder. 'This is your place,' he said. 'I want you right here.'"

God was telling her in no uncertain terms that this community she was serving in the midst of extreme poverty, isolation, and war was holy, the dwelling place of the Almighty. "After that experience, each day I felt more dedicated, with greater commitment—*entrega*—because to me it was clear that the people were the face of the suffering, crucified Christ, with their willingness to give their lives for the good of all, and at the same time, they also exemplified the resurrected Christ with their vitality, solidarity, and courage."

Sister Teresa describes the constant shelling in the surrounding hills, the periodic military incursions and occupations of their small village, the strafing of helicopters flying overhead, and the fear that these acts generated. "During the war," Teresa says, "the Armed Forces High Command required that I and the other sisters with me report to them every two weeks. When we left the community to go report ourselves, the people entered into a state of fear. When we returned, they shouted, 'Ay! The sisters have returned!'" Teresa laughs. "We didn't feel that it was really about us, but rather that the people felt this presence of God that for them was tangible with our reappearance." The people also perceived God's accompaniment, Teresa says, in the miracles they witnessed as they survived attack after attack on their community.

She stretches out her hand and places it on the flower-dappled tablecloth. "This is my experience of God, in the people who are an expression of the incarnate Christ. In the midst of the war, the people here showed joy, solidarity, and compassion. They were available to one another. When terrible things happened, they were afraid; they wept and trembled, but nothing stopped them from having faith and moving forward. It was an experience that changed my way of being."

Teresa ducks her gray head slightly before revealing her afflu-ent background. "See, I am from the bourgeoisie in my coun-try, and I was able to study. But my greatest education has been the poor, to see their living conditions, to feel how everything is denied them, to feel how much they are underestimated, how much they are despised. I feel their condition in my being"—her hand moves to her chest—"and their reality changed me, con-verted me. Encountering the poor, you encounter yourself with God in a totally different way."

She explains that she was a restless novitiate—*inquieta*. "My restlessness, my inconformity generated its own problems, but I didn't change route, I kept following my heart. I kept after what I felt was my calling. After I finished my formation in my religious vocation, I came to Latin America."

In 1980, Teresa was impacted by a letter that Salvadoran Archbishop Oscar Romero sent to then-president Jimmy Carter, which was widely circulated. In the letter, Archbishop Romero clearly delineated the consequences of U.S. aid to the Salvadoran military regime and requested that Carter refrain from sending it. A month later, Romero was assassinated while consecrating the Eucharist during Mass. Teresa recounts, "The letter Romero sent to Carter impacted me greatly. Romero and his commitment—his courageous, prophetic stance—sent shivers up my spine." She raises her hand as if to hold the letter before her once again. "And there was another letter, one circulated among my congregation. That letter said that the situation in Central America was very grave and that many women religious were exhausted and living in fear. In 1983, I responded to this second letter, saying I would be willing to serve in Central America." In 1983, massacres were occurring almost weekly, and tortured bodies were visible in San Salvador's streets. Four U.S. churchwomen and a dozen Salvadoran priests and nuns had been killed, and yet Sister Teresa arrived in El Salvador, ready to serve. "I came in '84. Finally I felt like I was really getting into it, like I'd dived in!" With her long arms, she imitates a plunge. "I threw myself into the water here in El Salvador. *Me meti* [I dived in], and I went in deep, which made me very happy!"

When I ask Teresa if she has a community that enriches and deepens her understanding of the Divine, she talks about the people of San Jose Las Flores, where she has resided for twenty-seven years. She also talks about her sisters. "We bring together contemplative life, community, and mission. And this is a great experience of God, because contemplation is not separate from life. When we sisters gather to express what we dream and think and experience, we create this model that God wants, that we *are* a community and an expression of the Kingdom of God." In their collaborative style of leadership, Teresa says they support the community rather than imposing a direction. "It's the Kingdom of God among us," she states emphatically. "We have to look for it and create it among us: this faith and love, solidarity and justice. Our task is to unite faith and spirituality with life: *unir la fe y la vida*. For life is a river, always changing, fluid. Nothing is stable."

And on this note our interview comes to an abrupt end, for we are both summoned into another meeting with this people in whom God is clearly manifest and for whom we are also, on occasion, vessels of God's abiding presence.

Going Deeper

1. What does Teresa describe as important factors in her spiritual life? What, in your life, is most nourishing and stimulating to your faith?

2. In what ways are you, like Teresa, diving into life and diving into faith? How do you find your spiritual aspirations and desires strengthened in working with others? How do these activities build your happiness and your faith?

3. In what ways are you a vessel for the Divine Spirit?

Try This

Get into a comfortable space and read "Meditation on Being a Vessel" in the section "Meditations and Visualizations" (page 274). Prerecord it to allow yourself to experience the guided visualization more fully as you breathe deeply, imagining your entire being filled with grace and goodness, a blessed container for the Divine.

Susan

Appreciating the Sacredness of Life

Compassion is at the heart of my spiritual beliefs. Compassion asks us to care for one another, to be stewards of the earth, and to insist on justice for all.

SUSAN SOLSTICE, HOMEMAKER AND
HOME-SCHOOL EDUCATOR

When I ask Susan about her experience of God, she cocks her head to the side before answering. Often she is this way in church: slow-moving and deliberate. Smiling, she says, "One of my earliest senses of God happened when we were on a camping trip when I was four or five. One morning I got up before everyone else in the family, and I went out to collect firewood, and I heard this music—kind of like the sounds a forest makes, but it felt like music." She describes listening to the forest's hum of creature song and feeling immensely happy as she picked up sticks. "Then my father got up and was very angry at me that I'd left the tent, adding I wasn't even picking up the right kind of sticks."

I ask Susan to say a little more about her religious upbringing. She responds bluntly. "It was repressive. I always felt that I had been brainwashed as to what God was, but when I tapped into what God felt like for me, God felt like an appreciation of the sacredness of life." She recounts hiking solo through a section of Sequoia National Park at age twenty-two, how the same childhood sense of exuberance and wonder at the beauty of creation, of feeling right with the world, surrounded her.

Susan now lives near the ocean, raising her family together with her partner, Andrea, in the town of Pacifica. "Now I like to go the beach because I tune into that Presence. Actually I can kind of feel it anywhere. Like a month ago I was driving to church, and I felt this sense of peace and love come into my heart." She feels this when her daughters are in a good mood and playing together. "It's like they're part of the Sacred Divine, and I'll feel this intense love for them, but then if they start fighting with one another, it breaks up."

She laughs and a bit of gold winks from a back molar. She is completely at home with recounting these Spirit-filled moments, but she admits that the Divine is elusive. "The hard thing for me is that I can't control the feeling. It just seems to happen, and then it seems to go away. I don't know how to bring it about. When it happens, I feel like a little baby who's waving her hand in front of her eyes before she knows it's a part of herself."

I appreciate the power of her metaphor. Very young infants do not yet possess the capacity to distinguish themselves from their surroundings, and for them, everything in life—the mother, the sibling, the puppy, the flower—is still all wondrously connected.

Susan points out that Ebenezer Lutheran (herchurch) is a spiritual community that honors what she calls the female values of "compassion, kindness, and being good stewards of the earth." Because of herchurch's emphasis on female worth and values, herchurch helps Susan to feel connected to the Divine Presence. "I spent so many years trying to un-brainwash myself—telling myself *not* to focus on the oppressive Christian ideas that I grew up with—that I have difficulty praying by myself. That's why I come to church every week. When the choir was singing last Sunday, I felt this peaceful, joyful feeling. I was totally happy to be in church."

Straightening up a little in her chair, Susan proclaims that "herchurch celebrates women and celebrates their strengths." But herchurch is not just women. It is women and men, children and crones, people in wheelchairs and people who dance. It is an inclusive community, leaving out no one who desires to participate. "Getting together once a week to celebrate these values is very important. Most people don't have a group that comes together to share these inclusive values," which, Susan adds, are crucial for humanity's well-being. "We wouldn't have most of our societal problems like war and crime if people had grown up with these kinds of loving values."

When I ask Susan to say more about this, she responds, "Compassion is at the heart of my spiritual beliefs. Compassion asks us to care for one another, to be stewards of the earth, and to insist on justice for all." Susan believes that she and her wife are passing on these values of "kindness, caring, and self-expression" to their daughters. Asked what she would consider her greatest contribution to the world, Susan responds, "That my children grow up to be happy and make positive contributions to the world."

For Susan, safeguarding the planet is a way of honoring the Divine. Susan details her family's conservation and food-growing efforts. "We raise chickens to produce our own food and save the energy involved in shipping and selling eggs commercially. Our chickens are fertilizing the yard. My goal is to change our backyard into a model urban farm. The chickens are the first step."

I love hearing how Susan integrates caring for the earth, valuing women, and creating sustainable communities. For Susan, the feminine principles emphasized at herchurch are central to these efforts. She describes the various images of herchurch—the statue of Our Lady of Guadalupe, the painting of the woman-tree of life, the various goddess figurines—and shares what they mean to her. "Female imagery is an intermediary step to the concept of what I believe is the true concept of God, which is amorphous, beyond sexual roles—this vast, positive, loving Presence that permeates everything. We can tune into this Presence. The gateway for me is the nurturing female presence much more than the father presence. For me, the nurturing female imagery makes the Divine much more accessible."

This does not mean that Jesus is out of the picture.

"Jesus," Susan attests, "was able to access God in a very fundamental way. He was able to see through the rules and oppressions of his society and get to the basic core of what the sacred is. The fact that he referred to God as a mother hen makes me think that he honored the Feminine Divine as much as anyone could in those days."

Susan is glad that her daughters can hear the message of the resurrected Christ, often referred to as Wisdom or Sophia[1] at herchurch. The female imagery at herchurch also enables her daughters to be empowered by Christ's central message of compassion. "They don't have to fight with this oppressive idea that God is a man and that men are in charge."

Because God is imaged as female, Susan's daughters can experience innate goodness in themselves, which rarely happens for girls when God is equated with maleness. According to Susan, when a girl values herself, she is empowered to care about herself and, from that place of self-love, to care about others in ways that enhance and reinforce her core goodness.

"Lena," Susan says of her rambunctious eight-year-old, "was watching this cartoon when she shouted, 'Look there's the Goddess!' It was a female superhero, a sort of very powerful being, and I thought, 'Isn't that wonderful that she thinks of God as the Goddess?'"

Going Deeper

1. What factors in Susan's given family informed her spirituality?

2. Why was it important to Susan to create new ways of being family?

3. What are Susan's values? What are your values, and how do they influence your relationships? How does your relationship with the Divine influence how you relate to others in the world?

Try This

Breathe deeply. See your home in your mind's eye. Imagine doing one small thing that connects it to the ecosystem of the place on earth that you inhabit. It could be planting "bee bushes" or plants native to your area. It could be watering the neighbors' trees during a dry stretch or—thinking big—organizing a community garden. Write down your imaginings, however tentative or far-fetched they seem.

Marci

Like Family

I don't know if it's some Holy Other presence
that's making things easier for me or if it's the
uplifting of a mental burden that I had before—
how I just kept wondering about things all the
time, and now I stopped.

MARCI CHALA, MOLECULAR BIOLOGIST

As Marci sets a cup of peppermint tea before me, she comments that she is feeling the beginnings of an ear infection. I tell her we could reschedule, but she shakes her head no and tucks a couple of brown tendrils behind her left ear. She steeps her tea in a tall infusion mug, recounting her studies in molecular biology and her job at a company that analyzes the health of individuals with heart transplants to make sure their autoimmune systems are accepting the transplant.

When I ask Marci to relay her experience of the Divine, and she giggles nervously and briefly covers her face with her hands. "One time I went to the goddess rosary at herchurch, and I distinctly remember feeling something different, that something else was there. I don't know how to explain it but to think of it as maybe a good energy of sort. I just felt this peace."

Marci fidgets with her cup as she tells me about the doubts and anxiety that had plagued her before that moment. "I've always been a skeptic. The fact that my parents couldn't agree, just between the two of them, when Christmas was, put some skepticism in me." Marci explains that she is half-Arabic and grew up in a home with two different Christian calendars. "My dad and his family were associated with the Antiochian Orthodox church. The women weren't supposed to show their elbows or their ankles, and the men were the breadwinners, usually businessmen." Her mother's side of her family was "Bulgarian Russian Orthodox, also very conservative. They have a different calendar." She shakes her head remembering. "So Christmas was on the twenty-fifth for one and seven days later for the other. It was really hard to trick myself into believing. Even my parents couldn't agree on when things were supposed to happen. Their Easters were a week or two apart, and it just seemed really silly to me, and I thought it couldn't be true. I felt like I was being lied to by my parents." She laughs. "I said to myself, 'I'm not going to believe any of this nonsense!'"

From her early years forward, Marci questioned everything. "I've always been analyzing everything, wondering if there's any proof. In my chemistry class we studied Einstein's equation that $E = MC^2$, which is a way of saying that light and matter are the same thing. Another thing a teacher mentioned during a lecture that I'll always remember is called the de Broglie wavelength [equation]. You can take a huge molecule and find its own unique wavelength. For instance, you can take a salt and put it in this equation and come out with just a number, but it's in light units, which means that salt has its own equivalent wavelength. Each piece of matter has its own equivalent of light wavelength. I don't think anybody has been capable of extrapolating that to something as complicated as an animal or a human. But it's our equivalent to a soul. To me that's my proof."

Marci has doubts about anything that can't be scientifically proved. But even Marci's skepticism could not dissuade her from her sense of improved well-being when she started attending her-church. Marci has rheumatoid arthritis, a disease in which one's immune system attacks one's own joint tissues, but she felt much better when she started participating in the goddess rosary, community prayer, and other herchurch activities. "With the simple act of just going to church every Sunday, it does feel like things have gotten easier in my life. I don't know if it's some Holy Other presence that's making things easier for me or if it's the uplifting of a mental burden that I had before—how I just kept wondering about things all the time, and now I stopped.

"I like being part of a community." She laughs again, this time with more ease and fluidity. "I'm really glad I found her-church. It's made my life a lot more peaceful and meaningful. It's kind of like a family away from home."

Going Deeper

1. What factors in Marci's religious upbringing contributed to her skepticism?

2. What qualities did she find in the community of herchurch that allowed her to address her doubts? How did relationships with others in her church community impact her well-being?

3. How would you characterize your own doubts? How do they impact your actions and your relationships? How do they impact your view of yourself?

Try This

Think for a moment until you find a doubt that keeps recurring in your life. Let it surface, and notice all the aspects of the doubt. As you sit with it, see if there are any ways in which it shifts. Imagine how this doubt could become fertile ground for new beliefs.

Emily

Seeing the Glory

God is not separate from life. God is in life and in all of us.

EMILY ZIMMERMAN, PROFESSIONAL EDITOR

Emily was raised by scientists. Her sensible attire (trousers, which make it easy for her to sit with me on an inside staircase at herchurch) and her engaged demeanor reinforce my perception of her as a practical and thoughtful woman. She tells me her childhood was like that of most people: "A mixture of blessing and terrible stuff. I had it rough in certain ways. The science thing was a real mixed blessing. On the one hand, my parents were very inclined to see the wonder of the natural world. But on the other hand, a lot of life cannot be measured by scientific tools, so that became the dark side."

Emily levels her gaze at me. "The other dark side was that my dad had worked on the Manhattan Project as a young man, so I grew up with this feeling that the atomic bomb was supposedly this huge achievement. That 'achievement' of being able to destroy life felt like a mushroom cloud hanging over my family morally, emotionally, and spiritually, and it was attached to what science can do."

Emily recalls that, when she was four, her parents took her to Japan and Korea (her mother is Korean, born and raised during the Japanese occupation), as well as England, France, and Israel. "When we were in Japan, we went to see the memorial site at Hiroshima, so [the impact of the atomic bomb] was in my consciousness from the very beginning."

At the same time, Emily's scientist parents instilled in her an appreciation for the natural world. Her father, a chemistry professor, knew the names of all the plants and wildlife in the various habitats they visited. "He could look up at the stars, and he could explain what was going on up there. I felt that it was in a way accessing that spiritual experience of life, by having that wonder in looking at it." Likewise, Emily's mother, a molecular biologist, would describe in fascinating detail the miraculous process of intercellular communication. But Emily was warned to avoid religious traps and to always apply scientific measures. "Anything that couldn't be measured by scientific method just got wiped off the radar screen. Things like poetry." She gestures dismissively. "And all religion went into that category."

She describes one instance when she was eight and attending a private elementary school that happened to be Protestant. She recalls returning home one day all excited about conveying a Bible story to her mother. "I came home from Bible class, which I loved, and told my mother this amazing story—about Moses, I think it was—and my mom just looked at me." Emily shakes her head slowly. "And she sat me down. She said, 'Let me explain to you: These are just stories. They're not true. They're stories that people made up to try and explain something about the world so that they would feel better. But there's no such thing as God, not really.'"

Emily's eyes widen, and a sadness pulls at her voice. "That was a bad moment for me! I had all that enthusiasm about wanting to tell her. I'd been so happy, and she set me straight. Inside I felt, 'Oh, no!' because the way a child sees, and the way I sometimes see as an adult, you see more than just the sensory impression of things.

"Take this window behind us, with the light streaming through," she says, pointing to a muted fan of sunlight. "Sometimes you can see more than just the sensory impression; you can see the glory behind it. I think children tend to see the world that way. So when my mother was talking to me, I was looking at the surface of her chest of drawers and thinking, 'That's all there is.' It was this moment of existential horror. I mean, I'm laughing now as I tell you this, but back then I felt as if all the life got sucked out of experience. I thought, 'There's only this physical world, that's all there is. There's only this chest of drawers, which is dead wood.'

"That was my Jean-Paul Sartre moment of despair!" Emily's laugh is bittersweet as she describes how the negation of everything that could not be measured by the scientific method circumscribed her childhood. "It was extremely oppressive, because it reduced everything to that one way of looking at things. It was almost as extreme as fundamentalism in its own way, because it didn't allow for any other view."

Later, when Emily was in her twenties, she began to feel a telepathic-like urgency about her younger brother. The urging, which she characterizes as an unprecedented and inexplicable worry, was in that category she'd been trained to dismiss as "what stupid people believe." By then she'd moved to the West Coast and was living on her own, and her little brother was in college back on the East Coast. They had not been in touch. But out of the blue, Emily began to feel intense concern for him. "I felt the need to pray for David, and I didn't have a reason to feel that way, I didn't have any info, any reports of what he was doing. At first I was just worrying. And then I realized that worry wasn't going to do anything, so I decided to pray just to relieve my worrying and my own suffering.

"I felt that of all the people in the world, I loved David the most. I didn't have a church or any religious affiliation, but I decided to pray to Something for help. I prayed that David would be safe, and I was really emotional about it. I prayed a lot. One night I woke up in a cold sweat. I'd had a very vivid nightmare that he had gone to prison and that the whole family was so ashamed of him that they didn't want to have anything to do with him anymore. I was the one person who was concerned about him. When I woke up, I felt compelled to call David and to find out what was going on. It was still the middle of the night, but on the East Coast it was almost morning, and my mom gets up early. Even though I felt like an idiot for being concerned over a dream, I called her and asked her for my brother's number. She gave his dorm number, and I called him. I said, 'David, this may seem really strange, but I had this dream.' He was surprised. 'What was it?' he asked, and I told him the dream. He was really silent on the other end of the phone. And then he said, 'You're kidding,' and he talked nonstop for three hours about what was going on in his life. He talked a lot about his plans to get involved in illegal activity—let me just say it involved some chemical substances that go on the black market for very high prices. Finally after he'd spewed out all the details about his life, he said, 'What do you think that I should do?' And I said to him, 'Well, you're an adult. You've got to make your choices about what you should do. If you were me, and I could tell you what to do, I'd tell you to run away from that situation as quickly as possible, but I can't say that because I know you're an adult.'" Emily chuckles, adding that she'd managed to slip in her advice while outwardly discounting it.

"So, he called me back a week later and he said, 'I talked to all my friends who were involved. The night before you called, we were so excited about how much money we were going to make, but everyone got spooked out, and we all decided to back off from the business.'"

Emily opens her palms. "I felt like, how can I say it? It was like one of those things in Ripley's Believe It or Not that I would not have believed! But it felt like a divine intervention in my life in some way that I could not explain. I certainly couldn't have predicted or controlled the outcome.

"My brother's now in his late forties, and he's a very successful high school teacher and a very charismatic coach. He's got this fantastic life where he's contributing a lot to young people, and so I think, well, maybe that would have happened anyway, but then again, he could have been heading toward prison.

"So for me, that's the Divine. It was rather unpleasant, and it shook up my whole sense of reality. See, I wasn't raised to be inclined to suspend my disbelief, so it really upset my worldview in a major way. I felt, 'From now on, I'm praying!' After that incident with my brother, I prayed for others, that whatever was best for them would happen for them."

Emily glances toward the window again. "I got into this imagery of praying with light. So I would imagine light coming down into my head and going down into my body and reaching other people. Only in the last couple of years did I realize I could pray for myself. I didn't think you were allowed to do that for some reason. In praying for myself, I kept it simple: that my basic trust in life would get stronger. Basic trust in God, basic trust in life—I see those as related, as the same. God is not separate from life. God is in life and in all of us. So I just pray for the trust to get stronger, deeper, and more real. And I feel like if I keep praying for that, everything else will fall into place. That's the thing I most need. If I can gain more basic trust, I'll be more relaxed. Everything will go easier. I'll be more available for others."

Emily prays in the morning, at night, and when she's driving. "Whenever I drive my car I can talk out loud to what I would call God or Goddess or Higher Power or Creator. Praying while driving is a good metaphor because I know I'm driving the

car"—Emily's hands grip and turn an imaginary steering wheel—
"but there's something else that's guiding my life. I know I'm not
always in control. I try to balance my ability to steer and make
choices with the much larger Force or forces that are at work where
I'm not in control."

Straightening out her legs—we have been sitting on the staircase for nearly an hour—Emily clarifies, "I don't see faith as something where you have to suspend your faculties or your intuition or
your senses or your intelligence. And you shouldn't believe something simply because someone else tells you to. Faith is an attitude
of trust. You don't know everything, and you can't control what
other people are going to do. However, you can have basic trust
that there's some kind of bigger Wisdom at work that's benevo-
lent, and it's a better bet to put some trust in that—with optimism
and gratitude and openness—than to face the future not knowing.
That attitude is what I would consider faith. It makes life easier to
live than living in fear."

Having finished all my questions, I ask Emily if she'd like to
add anything. She pauses and says, "I want to say something about
the Divine Feminine. Earlier you asked about my upbringing.
In my upbringing, women were mean to other women; women
were mean to girls. That comes from Confucianism. I found that
problem echoed in fundamentalism, in Christian fundamentalism, which I wasn't raised in but in this way it's similar to the
Confucianism that I was raised in.

"What I want say is this: When women are in systemic
oppression, where their roles are constricted in systems that are
very patriarchal and authoritarian, one of the negative results is
that women end up being very cruel to other women [and girls],
because other women [and girls] are the only people that they have
power over. So coming from that experience, it's been very hard
for me to trust the notion of the Divine Feminine. I used to not
feel safe in groups of all women. Even coming here to herchurch's

Friday Night Group for Women, it has taken me years to feel safe. For those of us who are raised in that type of authoritarianism that results in women being cruel to other women, it's a challenge to reframe God as a she. That might just be me. But I want to say that what's being done here in herchurch is not so easy. It's not so easy for women to affirm themselves. I can speak for myself. I can say that it's been something very difficult for me to even begin to see myself as something to be affirmed as divine. [Pastor] Stacy and this community are up against something that's huge, so it's amazing that it's getting stronger." Emily smiles. "And I think that's a really good sign."

Going Deeper

1. What experience helped Emily to "suspend her disbelief"? What experiences in your life do you attribute to divine influence?

2. How are you present to other women in your life? How do you exemplify the Divine to them or allow yourself to see the Divine in them?

Try This

After several minutes of deep abdominal breathing, pray a simple prayer for the first person who pops into your mind. If you like, you can do the "Meditation on Divine Love" found on page 270. Or if you feel more comfortable with intercessory prayer, say whatever is in your heart for that person. Do not stay with that person too long, but allow another to come into your mind and pray a short blessing for that person, and continue on to the next person.

Alison

Restoring Our Sense of Interconnectedness

> If I could contribute one thing to the world, it would be to restore our sense of interconnect-edness.... We don't know how much we need each other, especially in this culture where we're programmed that we should be able to do everything on our own and if we don't, there's something wrong with us.
>
> ALISON NEWVINE, KUNDALINI YOGA
> INSTRUCTOR AND CAREGIVER

Alison Newvine graciously brings me yogi chai and fresh almonds as I sit waiting in the living room of her San Franciscan Victorian flat. It is like the one I lived in during my student days: chipped moldings, beveled-glass cabinetry, and mismatched furniture all around. I feel very much at home.

Alison sets the teacups onto a crate-like table. Her head is wrapped in an orange and beige scarf that accents the golden brown of her eyes. Her voice is soft but animated as she responds to my question about her spiritual experiences by describing one of her first Kundalini yoga classes. "I went to the class with my sister, who was visiting me, and we'd had a lot of heavy discussion, a lot of stuff coming up about our relationship and our family structure. And at the end of the class, we all just sat in a circle and did a healing chant, and I felt all this heaviness and sadness leave. I felt the weight coming off of my heart area."

She touches her chest. "I felt lighter and just so much gratitude. There was all this space in me now for loving and for creativity that hadn't been there before. After that, things changed. I started to become more open to other people, whereas before I'd been closed off. So that was profound."

I ask what had been happening in her life at that time. "It was one of the lowest points in my life. I was feeling isolated, wasn't happy with my work, wasn't happy with my relationships, wasn't happy with myself. I also started seeing a somatic psychotherapist."

She shares, "The body-oriented therapy in combination with the yoga practice really worked together to give me this experience of myself as a spiritual being, as a good person—to actually be able to believe that and to feel that. From there, I've been able to experience a genuine loving connection with other people, which, for me, is one of the definitions of spirituality or divinity."

Alison describes her Kundalini instructor as amazing. "She chanted mantras, and everyone tuned in. Her voice was so strong, and she was very, very centered and very open. I felt something, and I kept coming back because I wanted to get more."

Alison, who was raised Roman Catholic, had sought out the Divine before. "When I was around thirteen, I started to feel God powerfully. I really felt that connection and wanted to feel it more. But as I became more aware of the things in the church that I didn't agree with—the role of women and attitudes toward sexuality—I kind of rejected all religion."

I ask Alison about her ongoing relationship with the Divine. She pauses, and her beaded earrings sway. "It's feeling like I'm not alone and experiencing that I'm seen and valued and accepted by all that is, by the most powerful Force that is. And through it, I'm able to find acceptance and forgiveness for my shortcomings and also able to tap into my own creativity and the ways I can connect with other people."

When asked to identify one thing she can contribute to the world, she says, "To restore our sense of interconnectedness. I hope that I am helping to heal little bits of the world through the work I do, caring for others and teaching people how to take care of themselves."

I ask Alison if this perspective helps in her caregiving work. She often comes to church with Moji, a young woman in a wheelchair. Alison smiles. "Yes, definitely. When you're working with people with disabilities, there's a lot of frustration and anger that can come at you. I used to take that in a lot more, but now I don't as much. I just have more compassion for it and don't feel like I'm doing something wrong or that I should be able to fix it. Now I'm able to hold the space, allow the person to experience what they're experiencing and just allow the emotions."

"Do you bring Moji to church, or does she bring you?" I ask.

Alison grins. "Moji likes to try different things. So I said, 'Do you want to try this?' I wasn't sure if I would like herchurch or if she would like it, but we both loved it, and we keep coming back. Like once when I wasn't working, she came with another caregiver, and I came, and we saw each other there at herchurch." Alison chuckles. "Moji's very enthusiastic and very vocal, and she appreciates the community and feels very excited. She likes the music and being around people." Allison laughs again because we both know that Moji can be effusive and high-spirited in church despite her language impairments.

Alison takes a quick sip of yogi tea before describing her community of yoga friends. When I ask about a community that supports her experience of a spirituality that includes the Divine Feminine, Alison's eyes grow large and her voice swells with enthusiasm. "That's where herchurch played an important role, because among the yoga teachers, although they don't say that God is a father, you hear more about the masculine. You don't hear Goddess; you hear God. And the teachers and the gurus are male, so it is an almost patriarchal feeling in the way that they talk about the Divine. So I was just really craving the Divine Feminine, and I found it at herchurch. It came into my life when I really needed it, when I was just starved for that affirmation of the female, of the divinity of the female.

"At herchurch I participate in things like Sunday services and the drumming circle. I read a lot about drumming and women's circles, about the power of women coming together in drumming and how we've been doing this for thousands of years. I tried drumming on my own and hadn't really felt anything, but when I'm with the drumming group at church, it really is something that defies description. I feel like there's this way that we're all connected that's very, very deep and very, very old. You just feel it through your whole body, and it feels very loving and warm and kind of overpowering."

Alison needs to head off to yoga class, but we talk a bit about the illusion of separateness as we finish our tea. Alison muses, "We don't know how much we need each other, especially in this culture where we're programmed that we should be able to do everything on our own and if we don't, there's something wrong with us. I think that the more we can rely on each other and see the strengths of other people in ourselves, and likewise, see the things that can annoy us about other people in ourselves, we can reconcile this feeling of separateness and differentness. It sounds kind of corny but"—she laughs and her earrings swing—"just come together and love one another. I think that's what it's all about."

Going Deeper

1. What does chanting do for Alison? How do you regard chanting as a spiritual practice?

2. What happens for you when you sing with others?

3. What examples of interconnectedness can you draw from your own life?

Try This

Sit still for a few moments. Hum. Or, if you don't like to sing or hum, ring a chime or a bell or tap on a bowl. Repeat your sounding or humming with a sense of devotion for two minutes or more. See what comes up for you. Write down what you noticed about the experience. If you like, next time you are in a place of communal singing, join in and notice what it feels like to be singing with others.

Judith

Swirling in the Mandala
That Connects Us All

The tree is divine. I am divine. For me, the Divine is not separate…. It's like a giant mandala that connects all.

JUDITH LAVENDER DANCER,
SOMATIC MOVEMENT PRACTITIONER

Judith Lavender Dancer has been the minister of embodiment at herchurch for the last three years. On Pentecost, the day of our interview, she dresses in a red scarf skirt and red shirt. Her lithe body arches and bends, leaps and twirls as she exhibits the fire and wind and breath at the church's birth, that long-ago baptism.

She herself was baptized six years ago. "When I became a Christian, I realized I couldn't do the traditional church. I've been a dancer all my life, and I realized that I had to bring the dance into the church, because if I can't dance, then it's not my church!" Judith cackles. Her red glass earrings glint beneath her short-cropped hair.

"For me, the spiritual and the creative are so intertwined," she says, lacing her fingers together. "Sometimes I don't even know which one is which!"

Part of Judith's dance this Pentecost Sunday came from the mother crane she'd observed on her walks at Lake Merced. "To show the wind at Pentecost, I was actually dancing out seeing the birds," she explains. "Nature inspires me to feel the Divine. It all comes out in movement: the Divine in the bird, the Divine in me."

Judith elaborates on this, how she sees the Divine infused in all things. "For me, the Divine is not separate. We're all part of the same cosmic soup, and we all kind of swirl in the same energy somehow." She circles the space above her head. "It's like a giant mandala that connects us all."

She sees a link between one's personal faith and community and between faith and one's responsibility to act in the world. Judith describes the journey as solitary but also communal, connecting us back to other people. She talks about how community is really about contributing your gifts, your divinity—all that you have discovered in solitude—back into the world.

As part of her action in the world, Judith is developing and integrating more work with seniors. "Right now, working with elders is expressing my godliness in the world." She smiles and touches the area over her heart. "I feel like each elder has something within them that they've forgotten, and I want to remind them of that and help them bring it forward so it can be honored. Just like stopping to watch the crane is a way of honoring it."

Honoring nature creates soul-moving experiences for Judith. When she visited Sea Ranch on California's northern coast for a short retreat, she found a volcanic black rock by the ocean. "It had this big arch coming over it and was literally right next to the ocean." She had been longing to lie down on such a rock. "I just curled my back and my butt and my head into this rock," she explains, tucking her head in toward her shoulder and folding her hands up next to her chin so that she appears to be nestling into the rock she is describing. "I just lay there, and it was so satisfying to feel the womb of the rock holding me. It felt so comforting and soothing and alive. And right next to me, the waves were crashing." She fists her hand and sweeps it toward me. Mid-swing, she splays her fingers wide and slaps them against her other palm. In the shock of that single clap, I hear the waves she is emulating reverberate around us, and I realize that Judith carries the movement of the waves, the trees, and the birds in her own body, flowing with "the giant mandala that connects us all."

Going Deeper

1. What interconnections do you see around you? How does your body and spirit respond when you encounter them?

2. How are you influenced by sensory experiences, and how do you express your response?

3. Are there new ways in which you can conceive of the Divine, particularly in the areas of movement and sensory perception?

Try This

Draw and color a mandala. Or dance! If you've never seen a mandala, search "mandala" or "mandala design" under the image category of your Internet search engine. If you choose to dance, you have permission to put on your favorite music and kick up your heels, even if you are by yourself!

DIVINE CHANGE

Part III

At the unmanifest level, at what the human senses cannot perceive but only the heart can intuit, the landscape is one massive, restless flow of energy.

DIARMUID O'MURCHU[1]

She changes everything she touches, and everything she touches, changes.

CAROL P. CHRIST[2]

f anything certain can be stated about the Divine, it is that the Divine brings change: death, birth, growth, illness, loss, and other events we do not control. Put another way, according to quantum scientists, at a subatomic level all energy is in a constant flow; to think that we can control all outcomes is an illusion.

When we let intuition and our deepest connection to Spirit guide us, we let go of the timeline set by our minds and acclimate to the shifts that herald the Divine at play in our lives. We release false notions of superiority or control. Like Mary, we make room for the unexpected.

My answer to the interview's fifth question elucidates the ways in which Spirit opens us to the advent of change in our lives even when we cannot yet visualize or conceive of it. Answering the question, "Tell me about your ongoing relationship with the Divine and what the Divine means to you today," I wrote:

When I meditate, I feel a guiding presence. I feel my spirit entwined with the larger Spirit of all life. The visions are examples of this. In that waking but deeply meditative place, I sometimes see images that guide and shape me and stories that are like parables, that I can interpret from different vantage points in my life. They'll mean one thing to me the day of the meditation and a different thing to me five or ten years later. Take, for example, the vision of the midwife who helped me birth five children. Their names were given to me in the vision like the names in a story are already given—Anger, Pride, Nobility, and Stubbornness—and I did not want them. They were scrawny and red. But I learned to love them as my children, to care for them and play with them, even though I'd wanted a child with a name like Kindness. The fifth child I birthed in my vision was a bubbly black baby girl. I loved her instantly, and I identified her with my writing.

At the time of this vision, the memoir I was writing focused on the successes of my cross-cultural marriage with a curly-haired Salvadoran revolutionary, so the dark, curly-haired baby made sense to me. But I struggled with the significance of the other children: Anger, Pride, Nobility, and Stubbornness. I didn't want to nurture or own up to these children. But three years after this vision, I was not celebrating the completion of a memoir about a successful cross-cultural marriage—I was raging. I was stubbornly holding to my worth and rejecting my husband's unrepentant betrayals and deceits: taking funds from a joint retirement account; seducing his teenaged niece in El Salvador; and bringing her to live in our household as his secret mistress. Three years after I received the birthing vision, I understood it differently, how anger, tenacity, pride, and nobility (or inherent dignity as I later interpreted it) were precisely the children I needed to gather around me as I fought this injustice. The memoir that I eventually wrote was not the one I'd conceived of years earlier, but it was my book, and I celebrated her arrival. The day I finished it, I dreamed I had given birth and caught the baby with my own hands.

In response to question five's prompting to describe my experience of the Divine, I essentially told the end of one story—that of my marriage—and the beginning of another—my writing life. The writing I employed was stream of consciousness, which often departs from a rational route. Like dreaming or meditation, it navigates the constantly shifting energy currents where constructs of past and future and here and there do not apply.

Although my meditation practice is more Christian than Buddhist, the Buddhist emphasis on impermanence appeals to me. Buddhist thought stresses the need to let go of our desire for immutable constants because grasping after them induces suffering. Life *is* change, and we are more in the flow of life if we acknowledge this and open ourselves to the beginnings that emerge from the endings, even if we cannot yet see them.

The women in the next set of stories exhibit a mind-set of welcoming change. They show that by placing our spirit within the greater Spirit that surrounds us, we allow one phase to conclude and a new one to begin. They exemplify ways of opening ourselves to the spiral of loss and inspiration, death and creativity. They show that by having confidence in our deepest selves, that spirit within each of us that lives and moves and has its being within the larger Spirit,[3] we can become a partner in this dying, this birthing. We can begin to trust.

SaraLeya

Under the Wings of Shekhinah

The Sabbath is identified with the Shekhinah, the Divine Feminine. It's a sense of being held and embraced ... of protection and belonging, a sense of oneness with community and other people around you.

SARALEYA SCHLEY,
RABBI OF CHOCHMAT HALEV

Rabbi SaraLeya sounds weary the evening I phone her. Her days are long, she tells me, starting with her medical practice and continuing with congregant visits and other important meetings. She is both a gynecologist and a rabbi, and although she was expecting my call, I have caught her at an in-between moment equivalent to laying aside the white lab jacket and slipping on the vestments of spiritual leadership.

She tells me that her spiritual training informs her busy practice. "I definitely think that being a rabbi has helped me to be a better doctor by enabling me to hone into the essence of what's going on with my patients. I've become a lot more centered, more balanced and quiet, more able to listen and to intuit the meta-levels of what's going on with my patients. I'm more able to say

187

to a patient, 'I'm really sorry that you're so stressed and depressed,' and to deal with things that before I might have tried to avoid."

SaraLeya studied conventional medicine, so when she became an obstetrician-gynecologist, "It was about life and death and my profession," not about the sacredness of the act of birthing. "That wasn't part of my vocabulary back then."

SaraLeya did experience the Divine in nature, however. "I used to be a mountaineer and rock climber. Whenever I was above ten thousand feet, there was a really special energy that I would feel. My parents took me to synagogue as a child, but as an adult, my spiritual life had to do with being in the mountains and climbing."

SaraLeya characterizes the activity of rock climbing as a meditative experience and one of the most intensely focused spiritual practices a person can undertake. "If you lose your focus, you fall." She is quick to add, "And there was something very deep and profound for me about being in the mountains."

I envision the beauty and challenge of the mountains she climbed: the Rockies, the Grand Tetons, the Shawangunks, the Sierra Nevada's Yosemite, and Alaska's Denali (Mount McKinley). "I never made it to Nepal before my hands got bad. I used to climb in summer and in the winter. I wasn't as hard-core as some people because I had a medical practice [and eventually a family], but mountain climbing was really important to me. It was how I spent my time."

That all changed for SaraLeya when the nerves in her arms were damaged, affecting her hands. She depicts the period when she was on disability as one of the most difficult in her life, because everything she thrived on—performing surgeries, delivering babies, mountain climbing, mothering her three small children—was now impossible or very difficult without the full use of her hands. She calls the period, "My dark night of the soul. It was a pretty significant depression because my life was pulled aside from what it had been. My climbing partner was my husband, and that wasn't working out. I was getting a divorce. I had three little kids to raise.

It was just a really challenging time. Finding a spiritual path was lifesaving for me."

SaraLeya traveled to a Jewish retreat center, and it brought her in contact with a spiritual community and practice that she embraced wholeheartedly. "I came into the spiritual practice at a time when I really needed something to help me come out of the depression. When I reexperienced Jewish community, I felt the connection to ancestors and tradition and the sense of belonging, of refinding my roots." She sighs deeply, recalling the solace that the retreats provided. "I was finding [my roots] in a way that gave me permission to experience being held, and I sensed this reality that was beyond the reality that we see with our physical eyes."

I ask SaraLeya to describe one of these moments. "The [retreat] place doesn't exist anymore, but it was called Elat Chayyim. On the eve of Shabbat, Friday night, the music was just so beautiful that people danced. There was such a communal feel of welcoming the Divine Presence and the Divine Feminine, which was so palpable I don't know how to describe it. It sort of gave me permission to connect, to be in the presence of something greater than myself. All of this was in the context of music and community, of dancing and chanting."

I ask her to say more about the Divine Feminine she experienced.

"Divine Feminine has to do with Shabbat—welcoming the Sabbath. In the Jewish mystical world, the Sabbath is identified with the Shekhinah, the Divine Feminine. It's a sense of being held and embraced. They call it 'under the wings of Shekhinah,' and that's how I sensed it when it happened that time, when she showed up. It could be an embrace of a gentle male, too. It's just a sense of protection and belonging, a sense of oneness with community and other people around you."

I admit my curiosity about Shekhinah and ask her to say more.

"Shekhinah is an old concept of an indwelling presence. It's only in the later Jewish mystical tradition, like in the last six hundred years or so, that it really became a feminine aspect of the Divine. It literally comes from the Hebrew word *shokheyn*, which means 'to dwell.' So it's that aspect of the Divine that dwells within us and around us."

I sense that Hebrew words and how they are pronounced are very important to SaraLeya. Indeed, as SaraLeya tells me more about how her life changed as a result of the retreats at Elat Chayyim, her study of Hebrew and Hebrew texts surfaces.

"[The retreats] made me want to learn how to cultivate the practice of connecting with the Divine. I relearned Hebrew in a really big way. I started studying ancient texts. It really changed my life; it gave me a focus when things were not clear. With my hands being disabled, I couldn't do all the things that I used to do that had kept me really happy and busy, which for me had been mountaineering and bike riding and needlework. I could no longer deliver babies, and I couldn't do surgery anymore, so Jewish practice gave me something else to bring meaning into my life and set me on a path of spiritual leadership."

SaraLeya studied for several years and was ordained as a rabbi in 2005. For the past few years, she has served the community of Chochmat HaLev. She describes her daily spiritual practice in the following way: "I feel that my life is infused with Spirit all the time. There's a saying in Jewish texts: 'small mind and large mind.' You can have a track in your consciousness that's always aware of the Divine, and that's what I try to cultivate. I pray every day, meditate often, and a large part of my practice is text study."

As SaraLeya speaks of the Divine, a contented serenity softens her words. "When I stop and notice, I know that I'm surrounded by love and surrounded by light and some level of reality that I can tap into by slowing down and connecting consciously and with intention. The world of Jewish Renewal offered me that gift of creating a safe space where there's music and community, where it's very easy to experience the Divine. I feel it regularly in prayer and song and holy space, when I'm able to be quiet. In that prayerful moment, I feel held with beautiful energy around me. At that moment, surrender and faith come easily. I feel very lucky to drop into it when offered the opportunity."

As for many of us, the busyness of an urban life impacts Rabbi SaraLeya's spiritual practice. "I've got about four years before I can retire from my medical practice, so my spiritual practice now is to really stay as centered and as open as possible to the small moments of the infusion of energy from higher places. It's just part of who I am at this point. It's not something that I have to constantly cultivate, which I'm really grateful for."

I want to hear more, but SaraLeya's window of availability is quickly coming to a close, so I launch into my last question. "What would your heart say to a young woman about your faith and about faith in general?"

"My words of wisdom would be to keep an open heart and mind, to love, and to try to live from a place of knowing that there's Something greater than ourselves that holds the universe together and that keeps the universe going. In my twenties, I would have just laughed at those words, but it's what I would recommend. Give faith a chance. Give love a chance. Keep the option open that there's a greater reality. And know that there are people and communities who care."

Going Deeper

1. What changes in SaraLeya's life led to her spiritual growth?

2. In what ways does she experience the Divine?

3. In what ways and areas of your life can you practice what she calls "small mind and large mind"?

Try This

Pick a routine task and do it mindfully. Keep one track of your mind open to the Divine as you undertake the components of your selected task.

Lucy
Embracing Our Imagination

Deuteronomy 32:18: "You were unmindful of the Rock that bore you, you forgot the God who gave you birth."

Poem in Honor of Destiny, Born Stillborn

O mother,
my mother,
my rock …
Tower of protection,
Cradle of the weak!
Your green-gray folds,
flint to the fire of my rage,
give way, give birth to
rivers of liquid grief,
washing across stern sheer angles,
already weathered by centuries of
mothers' tears,
metamorphosed in a second glance into
firm breasts and embraces for a child
at risk.
O mother,
my mother,
my rock …

192

who bears me through every wilderness,
the rod of my anger strikes you,
and from the cleft pour forth consoling waters.

And everywhere around you explode—
      all unexpected!—
the springtime constellations of joy,
petals of gold and mauve and white.

LUCY KOLIN, PASTOR OF RESURRECTION
LUTHERAN IN OAKLAND, CALIFORNIA

Lucy is still wearing her suit from the memorial service she has just conducted. Her hair is short and almost entirely white, contrasting with the black cloth of her clerical shirt and the silk jacket she wears over it. A pair of red koi fish swim up one sleeve; delicate green fronds wave on the other.

Lucy has been a pastor for nearly thirty years. When asked to describe an encounter with the Divine, she tells me about a deeply spiritual moment she experienced while walking a labyrinth. "The labyrinth at Mercy Center has this amazing, *amazing* rock at its center." She reaches up to outline the heft and grandeur of it. "The shape and the texture of this rock draw me, like the image of God as our mother, a rock."

The experience she recounts took place not long after her granddaughter had been born stillborn. "Obviously it was devastating for the parents, but it was also really painful for me. So I decided to take a room at Mercy Center and walk the labyrinth. I got to the center of the labyrinth where this rock was. Other times I'd looked at it or prayed beside it, but this time I was just drawn to touch it and hug it and run my hand over it. It was an experience that was so palpable to me and so intimate and very clarifying, very healing. I went afterward and wrote "Destiny" poems—that's the name of my granddaughter who was stillborn. Just being near this rock was so calming and healing that, like the writing of the poems, the moment was incredibly creative."

Gesturing outward from her center, Lucy explains, "It was like giving birth to something more. I hadn't planned on writing those poems, they just came to me, and I felt released in a way to do that. Some pain had been cleared away. And some sense of reconnection"—here, her fingers intertwine at her belly—"to God our mother, to God my rock, was made, and that gave me the ground to stand on, from which I was able to write and to create in this way."

Experiencing God as rock has been transformative for Lucy. She describes her exploration of the Divine through her preparation and elaboration of liturgies, sermons, and Bible studies. "The metaphor that finally hit me was the rock. Rocks are living for me. The rock is where water comes from, and for me, that's a breast-like image.[1] Maybe to some a rock seems more masculine, but to me I definitely felt that it was a feminine image and a maternal image. And unless it's been through a lot of water, a rock's got a lot of texture to it. God has texture like that. God is complicated. God is always more than we think."

Lucy explains that the parental images of God didn't work as well, for personal reasons. "I've always had a difficult time feeling connected to feminine or maternal images of God because, even though I know there's a difference between my own experience of growing up with a mother who didn't understand me (and who I probably couldn't understand enough to appreciate), I was still working through my own experience with a mother who found me very difficult: Who was this changeling? This person who grew up to be this woman she didn't understand? So for me, because I appreciate words and symbols and language and metaphors, I like to think about God in a number of different ways."

One of those ways is through wordless images. When Lucy was struggling with a personal conflict, she heeded her spiritual director's advice to let go of words and to rest in images and mental pictures. As background, Lucy explains, "My spiritual director said, 'What if, in your devotional time, you didn't use words? What if you just sat and looked at whatever images or pictures came to you? Could you do that for a while?' I said, 'I don't know, because I do love words a lot.' But in this instance, they were getting in the way. So there was a way in which fasting from words allowed me to be nourished by images, pictures, and faces that came to me. That eventually was the way that I found the way through the conflict."

Lucy adds, "I still care about words, how to play and create with them, but I also really care about textures and colors and different kinds of art. I like to populate the space around me with things and pictures and colors and let that stimulate whatever the Divine wants to show me."

Lucy rests her hands in her lap. The heaviness of the afternoon's service and her impending meal with the grieving family weigh on her, but she continues stoically. "I just talked about this idea in the memorial. Sometimes I think we're so heavy into Jesus that the other persons of the Trinity never get equal time or attention. Like God as creator or as artist. The memorial was for someone who was an artist. Although she was trained as a scientist, she came to painting when she turned fifty. She was very good at 'found art'—that's when you just find things or they find you, and you put them together. God also practices 'found art,' helping us see what *can* go together. I talked about that in the memorial."

The recently deceased woman was among Lucy's close grouping of friends. This comes up when I ask Lucy about her community. "The woman who just died, she was a key person, and I still feel the connection with her. There's something to be said for the community of saints and those thin places where they can be communicating to you."

Lucy's other friends are similarly interested in images as well as music. "They are women who are not afraid to use their imagination, to consider it part of their devotional practice. Imagination is one of the gifts of the Spirit." Lucy touches her forehead. "Imagine if God had no imagination. We'd be sunk a long time ago. Can we embrace our imagination and not be afraid of what can happen?"

Lucy portrays the women in her inner circle of friends, many of whom are parishioners, as collaborative and supportive. "Some of the women who I count in this circle are very connected. Some are East African. Whatever strictures they've grown up with, they themselves have a great respect for the feminine. There's a sense of how important women are. Life can't go on without women. Women bring something that is absolutely essential to the whole. These women are strong and creative because many grew up with very little, or in dangerous times when you have to use your brain and instincts and everything to make a way for your family or your community. I think about the women of Rwanda, Eritrea, Liberia, Tanzania. I feel I've gotten strength from them, especially when I look at my life through their eyes. They are elders (well, more elder than me!), so I find that I have some other mothers here. In a way, I can renew the mother-daughter relationship that didn't work too well when I was growing up. As women, they teach me and befriend me and receive me. Among them, I feel respect and love and care."

Lucy smiles wanly. The day's stress shows, but she recharges with thoughts of her friends and their support. "I feel more affirmed in being a woman and living as a woman and wanting to be fulfilled as a woman. I really embrace that and enjoy it. I feel like I have spiritual freedom, and it's related to imagination and curiosity."

When asked for her words of wisdom, Lucy folds her hands as if in prayer. She thinks for a moment. "Nurture your sense of curiosity," is her first counsel. "Pay attention to the body and the physical sense of self and learn from it. Respect it, because in those rhythms and textures and biological processes and movements, there's always something that comes to us about who the Divine is and how she's trying to be with us and play with us."

Going Deeper

1. Where do you see rebirth and growth in Lucy's experiences of loss?

2. Looking back over your own life, where do you recognize instances of "found art"? How have you grown from the experience of adapting to things you thought couldn't possibly go together or work out?

3. What do you think of Lucy's encouragement to trust your imagination? Where might your imagination lead you?

Try This

Gather images, paper in various colors and textures, and small glue-able items (like leaves or other items you enjoy but wouldn't necessarily imagine coexisting together). Before you bring these pieces together into a collage, breathe quietly for several minutes. When you open your eyes, begin to arrange the images, items, shapes, and colors in ways that are pleasing to you. Work with your materials until you feel satisfied with your arrangement. Use glue if you want a collage you can keep as a reminder of "found art" in your life.

Or, alternatively: Close your eyes in a place in which you have great familiarity (ideally your bedroom). From a seated position, reach forward and explore with just your fingertips the textures of things around you, for each item that you encounter through your sense of touch.

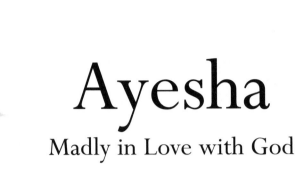

Ayesha

Madly in Love with God

Allah feels very near to me because of what
was taken away and what was given back.
AYESHA MATTU, AUTHOR AND
WOMEN'S HUMAN RIGHTS ADVOCATE

Ayesha Mattu proudly identifies herself as an
American Muslim. She is also the mother of a
two-and-a-half-year-old, who interrupts our phone call
only once, his sweet toddler voice calling out for her.
Later, she comments that she is raising him to be an
American Muslim feminist like his dad.

In a serene and steady voice, Ayesha describes a
spiritual encounter that was both inner and outer. "I
was sitting outside on a summer day in Massachusetts,
one of those beautiful New England summers that
you appreciate after a long hard winter. My eyes were
closed, and I felt the sun on me and heard the wind
moving nearby in a large old tree, and suddenly, very
strongly and viscerally all through my body, I felt that
God existed. I was curious to know the Creator of this
beauty all around me, and I wanted to connect, beyond
the dogma I'd been raised in."

As a Pakistani American, Ayesha had grown up in a Muslim tradition that she describes as judgmental and controlling, one that she chose not to practice when she went away to college in Boston. "I was brought up with a strict interpretation of Islam, both in California and back in Pakistan. [It was] a lot of rote memorization of Islamic verses and rituals. I found that my experience was actually quite shallow, because it wasn't bolstered by critical thinking; it didn't feel like something that was my own."

But the visceral experience of God in the sun's rays upon her skin caused her to reexamine her childhood faith. "I had this reawakening and connection, realizing that God was there. God was palpable." She began to read Islamic mystical literature, starting with the most famous and beloved Islamic poet of all time, Mawlana Rumi. "Rumi," she explains, "was not only an orthodox Muslim; he was also a theologian, a jurist, and a poet madly in love with God." Reading Rumi, Rabia al-Adawiyya, and Hafez, Ayesha found that Islamic mysticism resonated with her own experience. Referring to the sunny summer day, she adds, "I could feel God all through me, that he was so majestic and beautiful. His creation made me curious and made me want to commit to him and find out more about him."

She uses the English male pronoun although she says that in Arabic, Allah contains both genders, and that concept attracted her back to Islam also. "Allah is not considered male or female. Of the two parts of the word—*Al* and *lah*—one is masculine and one is feminine, so together they point to the fact that God is beyond gender."

In college she had begun working for women's human rights, motivated by the double standards and gender inequities she experienced in her own upbringing and witnessed around her in the United States and Pakistan. "The Pakistani Muslim community that my family was connected to was not very supportive of women, and that led to my wanting to work for human rights, in particular, to amplify women's voices."

Starting in the 1990s and moving into the new millennium, Ayesha began raising awareness and millions of dollars to support women and girls around the globe. In September 2001, the attack on New York City's Twin Towers that killed thousands also shattered the communities she was working with. "When 9/11 happened, I was working for a human rights and social justice organization in Boston. It was a time of great questioning for American Muslims. The question was not, 'Can I be American and Muslim?' The question was, 'How could someone do this in my name?'" The human rights organizations she was involved in stood in solidarity with her and other American Muslims during those tumultuous days in which a grief-stricken nation lashed out, looking for easy targets. She describes the post-9/11 weeks as "a very confusing time because of these external [events]. It only made me want to delve more into this very beautiful mysticism that I'd already begun to connect with and I wanted to have more of in my life. I would have meandered along this path of exploration, reading more and pondering, but 9/11 accelerated the process, quickened it."

She met her husband during that time, and although the post-9/11 context didn't encourage her to talk about her faith, her future husband was curious about it and eventually chose to convert to Islam. Five months after they married and shortly after they moved cross-country from Boston to the San Francisco Bay Area, Ayesha became very ill. "I got sick, and I was paralyzed from the waist down. The doctors didn't know if it was permanent or what was going on. And over the next couple of years, I had repeated bouts of paralysis and blindness."

She talks about the terrifying moments of turning blind, of not being able to move her legs. "It was a real crucible. We didn't have a support network, and I was so sick. Our marriage was young, and it was very challenging. It almost broke us." Her voice grows louder. "But through that time of illness, what came forward was not only the strengthening of our partnership but also this awareness of being carried by Allah. Even as my body was breaking down around me, this spiritual intensity, awareness, and growth was coming to the forefront and carrying me through this time."

Ayesha describes how she went through several episodes of paralysis and blindness before they diagnosed her with an autoimmune disease. She eventually found treatment and recovered, but her spirituality was forever altered by those moments. She says that her faith in the Divine who carried her, the Allah who is neither male nor female but beyond both, became "a really permanent and deeply rooted joy, a very beautiful and healing part of my life. When you go through something like paralysis or blindness and come out on the other side of it, there's not one day that goes by that you're not reminded of that time. You remember when you could not walk, couldn't see. Allah feels very near to me because of what was taken away and what was given back."

Ayesha continues her labors on behalf of girls' and women's human rights, working as a consultant. She is also helping to create new Muslim communities and networks, for example, her *halaqa* (Qur'an study group), which has been meeting in her home and those of other members for almost seven years now. "There's this idea that all spiritual gatherings must happen through the mosque, but I don't need to go to a gigantic mosque that everyone poured their money into. It isn't women-friendly or gay-friendly or child-friendly." She talks about the safe spaces she's helped to create and describes her study group. "My community is a very diverse group of American Muslims who are artists, filmmakers, writers, doctors, and lawyers from all different ethnicities and backgrounds. [They include] people who are converts and born Muslims, bringing an incredibly rich texture to what it means to be Muslim in America today."

She considers the *halaqa* group her closest community. "It's a gender equality environment. People are actively working to make something that is very social justice oriented, and where the

[Islamic] values of service and charity and compassion are being implemented in people's lives."

When I ask what she is doing to heal the world, Ayesha talks about the anthology she edited. "*Love, InshAllah: The Secret Love Lives of Muslim American Women*[1] is an outgrowth of both my spirituality and my work in the women's human rights field. There's a stereotype of [Muslim women], so we gathered a racially and ethnically diverse mix of women, as well as women who identify as orthodox, cultural, or secular Muslims. Gender, sexuality, love, sex, dating, relationships are [topics] not often talked about, so we're lifting them up to allow women to say what is really challenging about being a Muslim woman in America today and what's joyful and wonderful about it.

"Since 9/11, Muslim women don't have a space to critique their own community or Muslim men because we're a community under attack and therefore have to maintain a united front. When a community comes under attack, often the first thing that erodes is women's rights, their space in the mosque, their leadership in the community. This was a way to amplify our voices and to start discussions in our communities, both Muslim and with people of other faiths and backgrounds."

My final question to Ayesha, which is what her heart would say about her faith to young women, gives her pause. "Read the mystical poets of Islam," she muses. On faith in general, she adds, "It's not a straight line, and doubt is embedded in it. Loss of faith and movement away from faith are natural and not to be feared. The important part is just to keep moving toward the light."

Going Deeper

1. Describe the impact of life-threatening illness on Ayesha's spirituality. How have illness and bodily changes affected your experience of faith?

2. In what ways did 9/11 affect Ayesha's life and that of her community? How does your faith change in relation to events that unfold around you?

Try This

Ayesha talks about the ebb and flow of faith throughout one's life. She suggests that our relationship with the Divine can be experienced as a marriage, with moments of distance and reconnection. In this vein, I invite you to ponder the words of the Islamic mystical poet Mawlana Rumi:

> *Come, come, whoever you are.*
> *Wanderer, idolater, worshipper of fire,*
> *Come, even though you have broken your vows a*
> *   thousand times.*
> *Come, and come yet again. Ours is not a caravan of*
> *   despair.*[2]

Upon reading this passage, write down the first thing that comes to your mind.

Allison

Not Fearing Death

Max's passing changed everything. It was so hard for me, but once I had grieved and I realized what it brought me, it was pretty phenomenal. The change was this: I knew that there was nothing to be afraid of, to not be scared to die.

ALLISON POST, SOMATIC EDUCATOR
AND AUTHOR

Toned and sturdy, Allison sits on the waiting room couch of the office where she does cranial-sacral body work. Her blue eyes light up as she clarifies that the divine experience is not a singular isolated moment for her. "I live in that experience. Because of the work I do, it's every moment. But I will say that one of the most palpable experiences I had was when my cat, Max, was dying."

She explains that Max was only four and a half years old when he was diagnosed with type 1 diabetes. "He was very, very sick. Insulin is not manufactured for cats, because it's not economically viable. We did homeopathy. We did acupuncture. We tried pills. We tried everything."

Allison was heartbroken. "I mean literally, besides my husband Steven, who is my favorite animal, this cat was my most affectionate buddy. I mean, he used to put his paws around my neck and 'kiss' me to the point that Steven would say, 'This is getting a little too close.' And it's true, Max and I were very, very close.

"So when it was finally clear that all we were doing for Max was still not working, I went to the vet to put him to sleep. I had five people with me, including Steven. When it came time for the shot, Max literally put his paw out for it. I was holding him in my arms when the shot was given to him. He went limp. Then all of a sudden, we all looked at each other as if to say, 'What was that!' Because the whole room filled up"—Allison slowly raises her arms—"and it was an expansive energy. It was thick. You could almost see it. You could almost touch it, but not quite. It just came up, and it filled the entire room. We all felt it at the same time."

Allison smiles. "It was one of the most incredibly beautiful expansive feelings, as if we were floating, and I felt so hopeful. It also had a very particular tone, underneath what sound is, before it comes out, before the vocal cords have vibrated." She hums and lifts her hands skyward. "It was like a heaven sound. It lasted for about forty minutes. I had Max in my arms the entire time, because we were going to go bury him."

Allison recalls that even after they had buried Max, she felt that undercurrent of humming from time to time. She lit a tall candle and conversed with this new presence of Max, telling him, 'You have not only been the most unconditional love I've experienced, but I have also definitely learned that I have nothing to fear of death now. Death is welcomed, whenever its time has come, and it's a beautiful place to be. There's even singing there. So don't worry about me. I'm going to take what you taught me, and I'm going to use it in my work, and I'm going to teach it.'"

Allison feels that the experience of Max's departure is an expansion of what she feels in meditation. "He passed in 1997, and I was already meditating back then, but I hadn't really gotten that far. His passing enabled me to inquire much more deeply. I feel gifted because he told me, 'You can go much further. Don't be scared. You don't have to die to go out there; it's there, you can just touch it. And I really feel like he taught me how to touch it—to not fear death.'"

Allison says that the experience made her want to meditate every day and learn how to incorporate all that she was learning. Her daily life became her practice. "For example, when I went hiking, I could hear nature in a different way. Because I knew that's where he went. I don't think he went to an old man with a beard in the sky. I actually think he joined something that I have a sense of."

For Allison, "Max's passing changed everything. It was hard for me, but once I had grieved and I realized what it brought me, it was pretty phenomenal. The change was this: I knew that there was nothing to be afraid of, to not be scared to die."

Allison embodies this fearlessness. Her mannerisms are gentle but confident. Vibrant. When I ask her about her current experience of the Divine, she lifts her hand and places it on her chest. "I feel like my heart is the Divine. I can touch the Divine through my heart any time and through my head instead of the thoughts that kind of stop us. It's my connection to the Divine. That experience really opened my heart to a whole different dimension of understanding."

Some disagree with her. "My dad, who I love very much and who is eighty-seven, lets me know that I have very lofty ideas and that he loves me very much. He says I'm the kindest person he ever met but that my ideas will never work. He believes the world is not a nice place and that human beings—he says 'Homo sapiens'—are greedy, and they keep women down, and they create war. I think a lot of people believe that. But I just don't believe that one bit, I don't. I believe we've patterned some things, and we just need to introduce patterns that are really lofty to show our potential, and that's what we're capable of. That's what I want to do. And Max taught me all of that. Even though I think I probably had that within me like we all do, that experience was the real portal into realizing that I—that we—can do this every day."

Raised by agnostic parents, Allison says she was an agnostic until college. "College was a huge turning point for me, just realizing that I was someone religious or spiritual. I studied the Bible and decided I was Christian for about eight months. I liked the concepts of Christianity, but I didn't see why you had to be under a roof or why there had to be structure, especially when it said in the Bible, 'And the Lord said, "Be not as the hypocrites who pray in the streets but pray in thy closet [Matthew 6:5–6].'" That was my favorite line, and I thought, how come people are praying in the streets then?"

Because of those contradictions, Christianity lost its appeal for Allison, and she explored other ways of living spiritually. "I started doing yoga when I was nineteen. And then I started to hear about the Hindus' viewpoint, and I started doing meditation, and I didn't think about it as a religion either. I just thought we were breathing and feeling. After Hinduism, I went into Taoism, and I studied qigong and Chinese medicine, and again I thought the philosophy made so much more sense than *any*thing I'd studied, but it was just a collection of thoughts or philosophies."

While Allison recognizes the value that religion can offer community, she still believes that dogma and religious rules suppress what she sees as spiritual experience. "That's where we make our mistakes: making all the rules. Spirituality is not written down, it's *felt*. In order to have a true spirit of the Divine, you need to have an open mind and an open heart. You don't need any isms or structures. It's structureless and if you put a structure on it, it really doesn't exist anymore because it's structureless. It's like the Tao that can be named is not the true Tao. The minute you put a name on it, it's no longer divine."

When I ask Allison what or whom she considers her community, she answers softly, "The earth. Everything enhances my relationship to the Divine. When I hike, I see the trees swaying in the wind. When I walk in the street, I talk to every dog that passes me. Any animal connects me to that, the Divine. I talk to them, and they kind of talk back. Making love with my husband connects me to the Divine." She smiles. "He's my favorite community."

Shrugging her shoulders and opening her palms, she adds, "I think it's anywhere I *am*. I just don't have a particular community. Sometimes I choose to go into a construct, like I love midnight mass on Christmas because I love to sing, and I love to sing those songs. Talk about being connected to the Divine: Put me in a chorus with a bunch of people, and I am completely connected to that. Any community that is doing something to express themselves creatively, that's the community that I'll thrive in. The people who come to see me and visit me in my practice because they want me to hold them in the divine space, that's a community."

When I ask Allison about her efforts to heal the planet, she responds, "One of the most important ways I feel I do that is by having my mom live with me, even though I never got along with her. I mean, I really love her, but she was never really stable." For Allison, putting her parents in a nursing home unless they need constant assistance is out of the question. "I think it is so terrifying and lonely for them there." She believes that her alternative—taking care of her mother even though they never got along—is healing her mother-daughter line and helping her to become a better healer. "I feel that through it, I healed myself, which means I'm a better healer for the people who depend on me to help their pain. I also feel it has been healing for my mom and for our relationship. Understanding and compassion take time."

Allison expands this concept of spirit-centered healing to the international community. "Humans are a community. When people are dying in Afghanistan or the Sudan or any of these places where they're not being treated well, you *feel* it. Because we're in the human matrix." She feels we all have the capacity to connect and improve our human community, both in our families and globally.

"When focused, we really can make change. We can shift. And in my own life, I practice what I preach. We can all do it. When someone looks lost, I stop and help them. I will help a stranger if it's safe. When babies need help, people call me. I see them for free. I think these are things we can do within our own limitations that on a daily basis heal the planet. Taking care of children is a huge thing because they're the future of the planet. If I could sustain myself, I would work on every baby in the world for free."

Her final advice: "Feel, don't think. Just be still and know. I think that in order to experience the Divine, we really need to remove a lot of the distractions. We really need to keep stillness because it's out of stillness that we get divine."

Going Deeper

1. What losses in Allison's life enabled her to "go further" in exploration of the Divine? What is her view of death? Of change?

2. How does Allison's sense of humanity as community ("the human matrix") resonate for you personally? When do you feel connected to other humans and members of other species?

3. What do you think of Allison's opinion that spirituality is *felt* and that once it's codified, it loses its vitality?

4. What is your experience of spirituality as something that is *felt*? How has loss or other difficult experiences influenced it?

Try This

Really act on your inclination to be generous with your spirit of goodwill. Find a dog or cat to pet. Hug that beautiful tree across the way! Or simply hug your closest human, yourself included.

Viviana

All of Us Spirit

During that time [when I was in the coma], there was a moment when my mother and the doctors thought that I was going to die. That is the only time that I was fully conscious, fully aware of everything: my ability to choose, my inner power, my knowing of an existence of a different reality that is not this physical world.

VIVIANA MARTINEZ, FOUNDER OF SACRED
VALLEY RETREAT CENTER IN YUCAY, PERU

Viviana's slightly accented voice is barely discernible above the din of the kitchen clatter and conversations of nearby diners. I lean toward her to ask about her most memorable spiritual experience. Her eyes, black as a moonless night, draw me in.

"When I was nineteen years old, I was in a coma. I was at the University at Trujillo [in Northern Peru] and working for a political party. I was working in the slums, and I would eat anything, eat anywhere, and I got typhoid. I didn't know I had it. I just kept going. I felt dizzy. I felt fevers, but since I come from Cusco, from the mountains, and the university was in the hot area, I thought it was just the heat. I started to throw up, and still I didn't want to go to the doctor. I said, 'This is going to pass.' Then I went on a hunger strike with other students, professors, doctors, nurses, and that's when the typhoid got worse. But the hunger strike was very important to me. We were asking for health rights and protection for the prostitutes because in Trujillo there was a very large red-light district, and there were women coming from different parts of Peru. At the time I didn't know much about human trafficking. But we knew the levels of exploitation, and there were a lot of sexually transmitted diseases. And because of that, we wanted to organize the women and develop a union with them."

Viviana recalls that she was on the hunger strike until one day she collapsed. "When I was unconscious, they took me to the emergency room. I was in a coma for a month. During that time, there was a moment when my mother and the doctors thought that I was going to die. That is the only time that I was fully conscious, fully aware of everything: my ability to choose, my inner power, my knowing of an existence of a different reality that is not this physical world.

"The moment I remember is, suddenly I saw my mother, and the doctors and the nurse, and the boyfriend I had at the time, and a few of my other friends all gathered around me because they all thought that I was going to die. In the coma, I could see them. My mother was holding my hand, and she was pressing my hand and telling me, 'Please, feel my hand, feel my hand.' And I remember wanting to talk to her. I wanted to tell her, 'I'm not dying, I'm here,' but my body didn't respond. They were telling my mother that they couldn't keep the IV needles in me, that they couldn't find more veins. They were going to look in my feet, they said, and a nurse touched my foot. For the first time in that month, I felt my foot. I felt it in a way that I cannot describe. I cannot explain that feeling of her hand on my foot. It was like it was entering my foot. It was like it was one with my foot. After that, I had this experience of choosing, and I thought, 'What do I want? Do I want to come back?' And I came back. I chose to be alive. And after that, I changed. It changed my life completely."

I ask Viviana what she means, and she responds, "Back then I didn't believe there was Spirit, none of that. My family, we weren't practicing anything." She explains that, back at the university, she changed the direction of her anthropology major to focus on shamanic experiences, even though her parents opposed this decision. But Viviana had already developed a strong sense of self. Even before the coma taught her that she was "much bigger than this body," she knew how to fight for what she wanted.

She and her younger sister had been sent to a Catholic boarding school. "According to my parents, we grew up with more discipline there, but I was very unhappy about it. I was six years old when we were told we had to prepare for the First Communion and had to confess all the bad things we had done. I thought, 'What did I do that was bad?' And my sister said, 'Make up a story.'" Viviana laughs. "So I said it was bad that we were chewing gum in class. We were not supposed to chew gum in class. Now when I look at that, I think it's absurd how we put those concepts into children."

"Catholic school is very rigid. It made me stronger about my beliefs because I had to stand up to the nuns, to my parents. They wanted me to wear a veil in church. And I said I didn't want to wear all these other clothes, and I didn't want to go sit in church for three hours. My mom said, 'It's part of the regulation!' And I said, 'But I don't want to do that. That's not what I want for me!'"

At age twelve, Viviana refused to return to the boarding school. Her father said he was going to punish her by sending her to live in the village with the Indians he considered ignorant, and Viviana concealed her delight. She spent her twelfth year in her grandparents' home in Yucay, a village area ringed by mountains and inhabited by Quechan Indians. Viviana relished that year and the many summers she lived there. "I always loved more the Indians and their ways of relating to life and everything, to the cosmos. With the Indians, it was more beautiful. With them, the mountains, the animals, water, everything is like we are. Everything is alive."

Viviana explains that because she'd had polio as an infant, she had undergone numerous surgeries, and the woman who cared for her was Quechua. "Doña Berna was a wonderful teacher. I would be in my cast and I would see my cousins playing, and I used to get mad. She would say to me, 'You know what? The luckiest one is you.' And I would get mad at her. 'How can you say that! I can't play with them. I can't run. I can't swim. I can't even ride a bicycle!' And she would say to me, 'Why do you want to do all those things? You need to see. You are learning to see.' And I would tell her that I already see, and she would tell me to be quiet and watch. She used to tell me, 'You are going to be a *curandera* [shaman], so you need to use this experience and see. She used to say, 'Even before people tell you [their needs], you need to recognize them.' Now I know what she taught me. It's very valuable. I'm grateful.

"I was ten months old when I had polio, and I had many, many surgeries. When I was fifteen, they were going to do this surgery to stop the growth of my good leg so that both my legs would be the same size. The doctor told me about the surgery, and I said, 'I don't want that.' And he told me, 'But you will not limp if I do that. Nobody will notice that you have polio.' But I said, 'But I do. I know I have it. No matter what you do, I already have it.' Just the thought that they were going to cut again, I didn't want that. It was a big struggle, especially with my dad. It was hard for him to accept that I limp. And that I list to one side sometimes. He would come and press my shoulders and say, 'Stand up straight.' He would get mad watching me walk and say, 'You have to put your heel down first, like this.' I remember looking at him and thinking, how can I walk like that? This leg is shorter, and I cannot put down my heel first, like he says. So I would ask him, 'How can

I do that?' And he would shout, 'Just by doing it!' She laughs. "But I knew my body, what it could do."

Viviana's strong sense of self shapes her advice to young women: "Love yourself more than you love your neighbor. Be able to know *you* because that is not selfishness. It is about respecting yourself at all levels. For example, in relationships we tend to forget ourselves. We lose ourselves. It's very important to remain conscious: I am this. In order to love, I need to love me more than anything or anybody. Even more than I love my children, I need to love myself, because what can I give that is not me? The Indians used to say, '*No puedes conocer a nadie si no te conoces a ti.*' As I grew up, I understood, and I discovered that that's true. If I don't see me, I cannot see anything or anybody."

The Quechua Indians also taught Viviana how to work with the elements, "how to incorporate air, earth, fire, water, and ether in whatever I do." I ask her about ether, and she explains, "Ether is the cosmos, that Something that surrounds us and connects us and feeds us, but we think we are separate."

Viviana integrated these teachings with her university studies, and after she received her undergraduate degree in anthropology, she deepened her shamanic knowledge by working with *curanderos* in Northern Peru. "I went to the different indigenous nations and groups there. Then I went to México for seven months, and I lived with the Yaqui Indians in Sonora and learned all about how they work with plants and with animals also. I continued my connection with Spirit, deepening it in a way that it expanded beyond myself."

With her parents' encouragement, Viviana applied to and was admitted to the University of California in Berkeley. "I was supposed to do a master's degree in anthropology. I lasted six months. I went back to México because I felt the school to be very limiting and sterile. I lived in México for a few years. I worked with the Mayan *curanderos* in Michoacán, and then I traveled, working with *curanderas*, just doing what I wanted to do."

Eventually she returned to Berkeley. She completed her graduate degree in transpersonal and integrative psychology, and she decided to stay. "I had only thirty-five dollars in my pocket. Even though I had a degree, I didn't have a work permit, so I had to clean houses, take care of children. I made my way."

When I ask her about Kundalini yoga, Viviana clarifies that Kundalini is energy and that it helps connect her to her spiritual essence. "We all are spiritual, whether we have a spiritual practice or not, whether we're aware of it or not. There is a modality in Kundalini yoga when you work with the Spirit. The Quechua people call it, 'Working with your other self.' The work is about the energy that needs to be rebalanced. It's not conscious thought. It's a balancing of energy of the person. I don't call it healing, because there is nothing to heal. We are perfect beings. It's just about putting our body, mind, and spirit in harmony and balance.

"When I do my work as a *curandera*, I call on my past teachers, and they come and work with me." Viviana makes clear that she is speaking of her teachers who have died. "I feel as if they are doing the work through me. The Indians taught me that when we die, Spirit does not disappear, that we can call on [the deceased] for support and work through them, and their guidance. And I do that. Because of my own experience with death, I know that this force is there. That's how I operate. We are all spirit inside this accumulation of energy we call our bodies."

I ask how she knows they're present, and she swirls her hands by her cheeks. "It's like a very soft wind around my face, and then I feel immense calmness, and I feel my guru working through my body, through my hands." She recalls working with a man who had colon cancer, how he protested that the repression of his emotions and sexuality had nothing to do with the cancerous mass in his colon. "But," she says, "we do many things unconsciously, many things. And when we are aware of them, we can stop them, overcome them. That is my work. I have worked with people who were mentally disturbed and addicted who are now the best counselors in San Francisco. Through this work, they discovered their own spirit, their own power. And now that they know that, they don't need to rely on somebody else to be the conduit. That power is within them."

Over the past decade, Viviana has worked in several shelters for homeless women and children and for homeless single adults, in part because she has experienced (and transformed) illness, familial loss, and suffering in her own life. She depicts her work with homeless people as her practice to heal the world. "I don't call them less fortunate, because I don't believe that they are less fortunate. They are people who don't know themselves. I am a trigger for them to see who they are."

She tells stories of the many people she worked with in the shelters of San Francisco and people she recently touched on the streets of Berkeley, where she is temporarily visiting while her husband renews his visa to Peru. "I see in some of them this amazing spirit, but something's really broken in them that doesn't allow them to overcome things, and they don't have the resources. Like the young homeless man with the spikes on his jacket that everyone was afraid of. I loved that man. I knew that if he just had the proper services, he'd be such an amazing person. He would say to me, 'It's enough that you respect me. It's enough that you care.' 'But it is not enough,' I told him. 'Because if it was, you would not be here [in the shelter].' She tells of the homeless woman living on the bench outside the Rockridge BART metro station, how she noticed that she'd been on that bench every day as she passed by. "I said to her, 'I want to have lunch with you,' and the woman looked"—Viviana whirls her head around in imitation—"And she said, 'Me, you want to have lunch with me?' Viviana chuckles. "I said, 'Yes, you. I want to have lunch with you!'"

In a different way, Viviana is continuing the revolutionary vision she had as a nineteen-year-old, when she worked in the shantytowns of Trujillo. "Trotksy said that the revolution is an

ongoing process. It doesn't end when we get to power. Until everyone has power, we have not accomplished the revolution. And I
believe that. Now, I don't need to be with any party, because I
believe I do the revolution with my life."

About two years ago, Viviana felt "a knowing," a calling to
take a chance and develop a retreat center back in her homeland.
She and her husband, a rabbinic student raised in an Israeli kib-
butz, started a retreat center in the mountain-ringed village where
she spent her summers as a child. Viviana describes their organic
farm and the activities of the retreat center. "It is a place to remember your own magic, a place to educate your consciousness as you
connect with the Mother Earth and all its elements. There you
realize that the main prayer is gratitude—gratitude for everything
we are given, as well as for everything we are not given."

Viviana smiles enticingly. "In Quechua, *yucay* means
"bewitched." There you experience the oneness, the aliveness of
everything and its connection to you. It is a magical place, the
Andes. You must come experience it."

Going Deeper

1. What childhood and young adult experiences led Viviana to
   her understanding of Spirit?

2. What is her attitude toward change? Why would she say that
   "prayer is gratitude for everything we are given, as well as for
   everything we are not given"?

3. What was your gut response to Viviana's advice to love
   yourself *more* than you love your neighbor? How do you
   apply this wisdom to your own life?

Try This

Lie down and take a few minutes to breathe deeply. Sensing with
your inner faculties, locate your toes and how they feel. Without

physically touching them, feel your toes and then your heels and calves, working your way up your body. In your mind's eye, isolate each body part and feel whatever sensations it brings you, gently holding and then releasing each sensation before moving on to the next body part. From your lower legs, move up to your knees, thighs, groin, buttocks, womb/abdomen, chest, back, fingers, arms, shoulders, neck, face, and crown. When you are done, sense and hold your entire body in love.

Also, if you have a massage or other body work done, take some time to focus on the natural rhythm of your breath and then on the physical contact your body is receiving. In your mind's eye, hold those parts of your body that the body worker is touching. Think of Viviana's words: "We are all spirit inside the accumulation of energy that is our bodies." Think "energy" at each moment of touch.

Zoharah

Who Am I and Why Am I Here?

We must become the change internally that we are seeking to bring about externally.

GWENDOLYN ZOHARAH SIMMONS, PhD,
ASSISTANT PROFESSOR OF RELIGION,
UNIVERSITY OF FLORIDA[1]

D r. Gwendolyn Zoharah Simmons is a joyful and upbeat elder. When she answers my phone call, I sense a smile in her voice. She tells me that she was raised by her grandparents and describes them as "very involved black Baptists," taking her to all-day Sunday church services and midweek Bible studies and prayer meetings. But even though the black church was formational for Zoharah, she inwardly questioned the church's teachings from an early age. "It seemed very incomplete to me. I had this feeling that they weren't telling me the whole story because it didn't seem to make sense to me. I grew up poor and saw a lot of suffering, and that seemed very unfair to me. I had this feeling that there was something more to life than what I could see."

As young as nine and definitely by the time she was twelve, Zoharah would go out at night to sit under the stars. "I can remember looking up at the sky and saying, 'Who brought me here, and why am I here?' I got very interested in the UFOs craze. I would sit outside and hope that whoever brought me would come back and take me because I didn't want to be in what seemed to me to be a very difficult and unjust place. I now understand that I was propelled on a spiritual search for the answers to the questions, 'Who am I? Why am I here?' Those great questions would just fall on me"—Zoharah draws out the words—"*Who am I? What is life really about?*"

These deep questions were still troubling Zoharah when she started at Spelman College in Atlanta in 1962 and joined a Baptist church (where Dr. Martin Luther King Jr. occasionally preached) "upon orders of my grandmother." After two years, however, she dropped out of Spelman, against her family's wishes, to work full-time in the civil rights movement by joining the 1964 Mississippi Freedom Summer Project of the Student Nonviolent Coordinating Committee (SNCC) and later working with the group's Atlanta Project. Zoharah recalls, "In the Project's 'Freedom House,' we lived communally, and a lot of times we would play music and dance or play cards after our day's work, but there was this one couple who rarely joined us. They would always depart from the group and go to their room. They were also vegetarians, the first I had ever met, and I was curious about them. I started questioning them about why they never joined in with the frivolities. After quite a bit of probing, they told me that they were spiritual seekers and practiced meditation when they went to their room. I asked them about meditation, and after they explained it to me, I asked if they would teach me how to meditate."

Meditating daily in the way that they had taught her, Zoharah encountered one night a palpable, compelling Presence. "I was by now twenty and had made my first trip to Philadelphia [where she later resided], and I had been meditating in the way they had taught me. I fell asleep while meditating, and the next thing that I remembered was being outside of my body. I thought maybe I was dreaming. But then there was a Presence also without form that began to talk to me. I began to ask this Presence who it was. The Presence simply said to me that I should follow. I traveled away from the house with this Being. And then I became afraid and didn't want to go any further. I said, 'I must go back and get my body.' I started falling back, and the Presence kept going, until I no longer could feel the Presence, and in this formless state, I came back into the house. There asleep on the bed was my body. I remember lying down on the body and being submerged back into it and immediately sitting up. For the next three days, I was not able to sleep. I would sit up waiting for it to happen again. It didn't, but I knew what I had experienced, and it left a profound imprint on me. I continued with meditation, but I also got married, and I had a child, and there was much going on with the civil rights movement."

Zoharah married a fellow movement worker, Michael Simmons. Like Zoharah, he worked with SNCC and other organizations to register black voters and defend the civil rights of black Americans. Influenced by Dr. Martin Luther King and others, Zoharah and Michael began educating African Americans about the injustice of the Vietnam War and the need to resist it and the draft. "Michael, my husband at that time, refused military service. He went down to the draft board, told them that he was working for democracy in the United States and that he wasn't going to Vietnam to impose democracy there when we didn't have democracy for black people here at home. He was arrested, sentenced to three and a half years of prison, and sent to Lewisburg Federal Penitentiary [in Pennsylvania] to serve his time. We moved to Philadelphia, Michael's hometown, in preparation for his imprisonment. I was pregnant at the time, and our daughter, Aishah, was born shortly before he was imprisoned."

Zoharah describes the windy, sometimes icy roads she drove to the penitentiary and how worried she was about Michael. "In prison, Michael met this couple who were very spiritual. They were graduate students at Bucknell University, and they came to the prison to run classes for the inmates. When he found out that they were meditators, he made sure that I met them. They said that I could stay in their apartment when I came to visit with the baby." The couple encouraged Zoharah to meet their spiritual teacher, who lived in New York City. They assured Zoharah that their teacher would answer her spiritual questions and take her on as one of her pupils.

For Zoharah, deepening her spiritual life was key to enabling her to address the multiple challenges she faced: her husband's unjust imprisonment, survival in a new city with very little income, and a crippling illness her baby had developed. Zoharah drove to New York with a friend and arrived very early at the chapel of her friends' teacher, Reverend Challi. They were told to wait even though they were first in line. At first Zoharah was put off. "We were the first people to arrive, but Reverend Challi took all the other people first. I was very concerned since I think we were the only African Americans there, and given my years battling racial injustice, I could not help but wonder if that fact had anything to do with us being the last persons she addressed. But I determined to stay."

Like all the others, Zoharah was asked to write down three questions she wanted answered, but from what she could see, the questions were never handed over to Reverend Challi. "Her assistant said that writing down your questions helped you to focus your mind on why you had come and what you wanted Reverend Challi to answer. 'So she's going to read my mind? Is this a hoax?' I wondered. But I thought of my friends, who were very grounded, and I told myself, 'I'm sure they wouldn't send me here if it were.' So I wrote down my first question: 'Are you my teacher?' For my second question, I thought about my daughter, Aishah, who had a serious disease. She was only thirteen months old when she was diagnosed as having a very severe form of rickets, because when she tried to walk, she broke her leg. So I wrote, 'Can my daughter be cured?' My third question had to do with Michael. Even though I didn't write down that he was in prison, I was concerned that his activism in the prison had caused him to be put in solitary confinement, what they called 'the hole,' on several occasions. I was very afraid and worried about him and thought he could be killed in there."

Even though Zoharah suspected that she and her friend were being discriminated against, she stayed until they were the only ones remaining in the pews. Zoharah pauses, and when she speaks again, I hear her grin. "And then the teacher says, 'Now I am so pleased to have only you two here.' And she has this tremendous smile, radiating out love toward me. 'You want to know about your teacher. Your teacher is coming for you very soon. You are so blessed to have such a beautiful teacher. He will answer the question you've had since you were a little girl.'

"I'm about to fall out of my chair because I never saw that she was handed any questions, but she goes on. For my second question, she says that my daughter will definitely overcome her illnesses and that I will find the cure for her. For the third one—I'd written nothing specific about my husband's situation; only asked if he was in danger—she says, 'Your husband has no business being in prison. He is there for reasons of conscience, and it's wrong. He is in danger, and they hate him there. Please tell him that I said for him to be careful and not to enflame the guards.'"

When Zoharah next went to visit Michael, she told him about Reverend Challi's message, and she hoped he would heed her advice. She also prayed for Aishah, whose deterioration worried her sick.

When I ask if Aishah was indeed cured, Zoharah answers, "I was at a health food store, looking very, very sad. A woman I didn't know came up to me and said, 'Is there something wrong?' I told her about Aishah, and she said, 'Have you ever heard of homeopathy?' I shook my head no, but I was desperate to help my daughter. In the children's hospital they were proposing experimental drug treatments, and the doctors were nasty to me, had no respect for me as a welfare mom, a black woman, and I didn't have any confidence in them. I thought they were going to experiment on my daughter."

The woman in the store told Zoharah that homeopathic medicine was from natural substances and suggested she call the national homeopathic association to locate a homeopathic doctor. "I prayed over it and asked God to guide me to the right doctor. I picked this doctor who was way out in a part of the city I'd never been to. The seventies was a volatile time—with race riots and all sorts of things—and Philadelphia was a very racially polarized city, and his office was in a working class white area I'd never been in before. I was scared, but I knew I would do anything to get help for Aishah. I walked into the office, and the people there looked like they were shocked. I was the only black person in the waiting room, and I felt hostility toward me. The doctor was a very old man with a heavy German accent. That, too, scared me, but I was desperate. He examined Aishah and told me not to worry, that he would have her walking in less than six months." Zoharah gasps and explains that the doctors at the children's hospital had told her that Aishah would need braces and that it would take years. "And then he was literally putting these little white pills in my child's mouth, but he wouldn't tell me what he was giving her, and I thought, 'Oh mercy, what have I done?' And he said, 'Mother, don't worry, this is okay!' He told me that I should be prepared because her appetite was going to increase tremendously. He gives me these packets of these little white pills and tells me to give them to her. Well, I cried, I prayed, and I did it. Soon she was eating almost twice the amount she normally consumed. And just as he had said, her bones began to heal as shown by the X-rays taken regularly at Children's Hospital. The fracture healed, and in six months she was standing and taking steps. In less than a year she was healed."

After her daughter began to show signs of improvement, Zoharah found a yoga class to help her get back into meditating. "It was led by an African American woman, which in 1971 was very unusual. One day she says, 'I have a guest who is going to speak to the class.' The guest, a PhD student from Sri Lanka, says to the group, 'I want to bring my teacher from Sri Lanka to the United States because he will be able to help people deal with racism and the awful things that go on in this country related to race.' So the young man hands out photos of his teacher, Bawa Muhaiyaddeen,[2] and he tells us he has studied with this teacher for seven years. I was so taken with the photo of Bawa that when the young man asked for visa sponsors, I said yes without even thinking." Zoharah laughs with delight. "I was on welfare with a sick child, a husband in prison, and living on the charity of friends, and here I am signing up that I'll be responsible for somebody!"

A month later, Zoharah and the rest of the class went to the airport to welcome Bawa. She describes the small entourage that exited the plane, and the last person out was Bawa Muhaiyaddeen. "A very tiny little man, with a turban on his head, he goes right to my daughter who's in a stroller and can't walk because she has a cast on her leg, and he kisses her on both cheeks. She's looking at him in a way I've never seen her look at anybody. Her head is tipped back, her mouth is open, and it's like she's in a state of ecstasy. Seeing her face like that, I look up to see what she's looking at because Bawa was lovely but not something that was going to knock your socks off. But when I look up, I see beams of light coming from him, and I swoon—I have never swooned before or since—and I almost pass out."

Zoharah tells me that for the next seventeen years, she studied with Bawa Muhaiyaddeen. "He would come and go, and I traveled with him to many cities. But that first night, even though it was very late and he was very old and the others wanted him to rest, he gave his first discourse. I remember he said, 'If you're on the path to God, you have to ask, "Who am I, and why am I here?"' Well, that had been my question since I was twelve! 'Finally,' I thought, 'I'm going to get the answer I've had since I was twelve!' I was twenty-five then, and I've been engaged with this teaching since that time."

As is the tradition in Sufism, Bawa gave Zoharah her Sufi name: Zoharah, which means "full of light." For nearly two decades, he shared his insights and understandings with her and other students whenever he came to the United States, founding the Bawa Muhaiyaddeen Fellowship,[3] which continues to this day.

Zoharah's former husband, Michael Simmons, also studied Sufism in prison and was released after two and a half years. "He even met with Bawa in Sri Lanka, which I was not able to do!" She laughs, adding that although she and Michael eventually divorced, their lives overlapped in amazing ways.

Zoharah's travels with Bawa, as well as her ongoing human rights and antimilitarism work, took her around the world. As a leader with the American Friends Service Committee (AFSC) for twenty-three years, she headed up the AFSC delegation to Beijing for the Fourth International Conference on Women. Meeting Muslim women from many countries "set the course" for her dissertation on the impact of Islamic law on women, and she lived in Jordan for nearly two years while conducting her research. She received her PhD from Temple University in 2002.

When I ask Zoharah how her spirituality relates to social justice, she answers, "Most of my life has been engaged in social justice movements, beginning with the civil rights movement." She also emphasizes the link between one's spirituality and one's works of compassion: "We must become the change internally that we are seeking to bring about externally. I say to people, 'Explore your spirituality in any direction you are led by your heart.' I think that any religion can be a path to one's spiritual development and can lead them to the answers of the questions in their heart."

She adds that she's chosen the Islamic tradition—particularly its mystical branch, Sufism—because of her years with Bawa, but she is open to the truths found in other traditions. "This past summer I participated in a ten-day Vipassana Buddhism retreat that I found incredibly enriching. I plan on doing it every summer that I live. *InshAllah*—God-willing," she affirms, and I hear her smile again.

Going Deeper

1. How did racism and other social and economic injustices influence Zoharah's evolving spirituality? In your own spiritual development, how do social and economic circumstances play in?

2. What do you think of Zoharah's suggestion that you must become the change internally that you are seeking to affect externally?

3. Zoharah speaks about spiritual teachers. Can you think of a mentor or teacher who aided your spiritual growth? In what ways were you most impacted?

Try This

Set aside twenty minutes or more for meditation. Read "Spirit Guide Meditation" in the section "Meditations and Visualizations" (page 275). Ideally, prerecord it or have a friend read it to you as you breathe deeply and enter into the experience of encountering a spirit guide.

Kristin

Listen to Mother Earth— She Has a Lot to Tell You

I think that if you listen to Mother Earth very intently, she has a lot to tell you.

KRISTIN HANSEN, RETIRED ATTORNEY

When I ask about her spiritual experiences, Kristin Hansen looks out the window for a moment before answering. The muted sunshine lights up her weathered profile and glints on her wire-frame glasses. It sets the plaid flannel jacket she's wearing to an autumnal glow. She turns to look at me and says, "I have to say that the most powerful spiritual experience for me was when I almost died in the Amazon jungle in southern Columbia. I got an infection, but I still had to walk about fifteen miles and ford a raging river to get help. I was almost dead when we— my husband, Bear, and I—reached this little town of San Augustine, the last town with vehicular roads before one enters the jungle. Thank goddess that they had penicillin there. I was very weak, almost dead. "I remember distinctly feeling death on my left shoulder. I saw the white light that people talk about—it really

228

is like a birth canal—and I totally realized that I had the capacity to make the choice between life and death in that instant. I could relax into nothingness or I could go back to the reality. I chose to go back. Bear and I were having a hell of a fun time." She chuckles. "We were traveling all over, bumming, you know, hitchhiking everywhere. I chose life. I wanted more fun with Bear."

Yet the near-death experience changed Kristin's life and demarcated a new beginning. After she and Bear returned from South America, she went to law school, passed the California Bar, and started a practice in intellectual property rights.

But before Kristin left South America, she had several more adventures with Bear, whose given name was Donald Able Espinoza. She recounts another powerfully spiritual experience with ayahuasca, a drink that "Indians have used for teaching-learning experiences for many centuries in *Amazona*. Those present called me a *bruja* [witch] afterward, because of the way I reacted. I sort of became a mother, sensing everything. I sensed that Bear was standing by a fence and that he had to get down. I got to him just seconds before a bullet whizzed by where his head had been."

Kristin looks at me. Perhaps she senses I'm a little stunned by her tales, and she returns to the original question in a more direct way. "I consider myself an extremely spiritual person. I have altars at home. Anytime I kill anything, like plants from the garden, etcetera, I pray to it in the old Indian way. I follow the old Native ways wherever I can."

She credits her childhood—that she was an only child and that she grew up by a river—for her sensitivity to the spiritual connection of all things. "I had many spiritual experiences as a child. I had a working mother, and after school I practically lived on the banks of the Willamette, which is a very large river in Oregon. My mother used to tell a story about me running into the house shouting, 'Mommy, Mommy, the wind talked to me!'

"I've always been very connected with the animistic forms of holiness. Mother Earth has taught me so much. Just by listening, by sitting quietly for hours on the banks of the river, or in a redwood forest, or the desert, you learn. Things come to you: ideas that can be manifested and brought to life in reality. If you lay down, get comfortable, you get that warmth and you go into an alpha state. At least that happens for me. The Spirit talks to me when I get to that tranquility level. I didn't know that as a kid—that your mind goes into an alpha state. But your mind goes inward. Mine does anyway, and so it feels like a direct connection. That's the only way I know how to explain it. Rocks talk to me. Paths appear to me in the woods. I've never lost my way, have never been lost in my life. I always know where true north is." Her gaze flits to the window. "It's like I feel it from inside. I feel connected. Mother Earth tells me what way to go. If I stay calm enough and listen and look at the visions that come in, she tells me exactly what to do and where to go."

Even when she was a trial lawyer, Kristin found time for being in nature. She loved camping and hiking and climbed Mount Shasta fifteen times. Now she spends much of her time on the mountain near her home: San Bruno Mountain, also called *Ahwastes*, in the native Ohlone language.

Twice a week, Kristin tends to the native plants on Ahwastes. "I water the native plant species that help the habitat of the Pacific coast frog, callippe silverspot butterfly, and mission blue butterfly, all endangered species. Typically it's a very spiritual time for me because I'm there on the mountain around 6:30 in the morning. I have 180 gallons' worth of water in tanks rigged in the back of my truck so I can water the native species that we volunteers have planted up there from seedlings. We just water them the first couple of years till they get going and can go on their native path, this being a dry region and all. At that time in the morning, alone with the butterflies, the frogs, and the songbirds, it's always very quiet and just wonderful."

She nests one hand inside the other as she talks about the importance of growing back the native species, local food, and conservation efforts. "I love my morning shower, but I aim for the two-minute showers. This morning I thanked the universe for allowing me to have a hot shower in the morning when people are dying in Africa because they have no drinking water. It's heartbreaking, so I try to conserve as much as I can. I could do much better. We all can."

When I ask her how she contributes back to the earth, Kristin says, "I love Mother Earth and have believed in the whole Gaia thing for years. I generally try to live very simply on Mother Earth. I reuse everything. I don't want to add any more to the garbage burden that the humans are creating on this earth. I strongly believe that the magnetic center of Mother Earth is one of the principals and powers that lets us know when we're on the right and the wrong path. I think that if you listen to Mother Earth very intently, she has a lot to tell you. That's about it. I pray to Mother Earth every day with my actions."

Kristin says good morning to the sunrise every morning and good night and thank you to the sun every evening. "That started when I was a fisherman at Depoe Bay. We'd go out deep-sea fishing every day, and I was always so thankful that we got everyone back in safe and that the catch was good."

Since she's lived in so many places, I ask Kristin how she experiences community. She responds, "I have two communities. One is the Reclaiming Collective that I was a part of for years. Herchurch is obviously the other. It's much more rewarding and fulfilling to me now than anything else I'm involved in. We sing some of the same songs that I used to sing in the circles, because they come from old feminist, goddess traditions. That's what allows me to be very comfortable here in a Christian church. And it's a dynamic place to be." She chuckles and adds, "I'm happy here at herchurch. I like it here. It's the first Christian community that's ever been welcoming to me."

Kristin had only been to church once as a child, which she remembers "as a very sad experience." By the time she was a young adult, Kristin had read the holy scriptures of many traditions. But she still didn't believe in an anthropomorphic divinity. When confronted by adults in the Job's Daughters program about whether or not she believed in God, she'd countered, "I believe in a Supreme Force. I don't identify it as male or female. I identify it as a force, the wind talking, a bolt of light through the rain clouds." These days, she adds, "To me that's what all of the 'naming' words— Goddess, God—are about."

Kristin cracks a smile and waits for my next question, which is about how to pass the faith on to young women. "I feel as an elder that I do need to pass on and educate now. I've had many experiences that are different from those that most girls have. It's my dedicated goal to counter all the good hard work that mothers have put into their daughters and give them a breath of fresh air now. Their codes and mores are set by the time they're fifteen, probably by the time they're ten. When they're sixteen, eighteen, even up to twenty, it's a discovery time for them. My charge now is to teach young girls that they can take a year off from the routine and use that time for introspection and hard work. But not to spend it in pubs or something like that."

She laughs, knowing that I have a fifteen-year-old daughter and that I might find this threatening. "I firmly believe that everyone should take a year off between high school and college. Keep on learning, but take a break from formal education to discover yourself, that's what I say. It's a critical time. I want to give women the belief that they can do whatever they want to. All you have to do is just do it. It's all in the doing. Bear and I never knew where we were going to go. By the end of the day we always had a ride or an invitation to stay with somebody."

Because she'd referred so many times to Bear in the past tense, I finally ask Kristin if he is deceased. Her eyes water, and her voice becomes gravelly. "Yes. He passed on in 2004. He was killed by asbestos in the shipyards where he used to work as a kid. He got mesothelioma, from asbestos."

I feel bad for having asked the question, but Kristin rebounds and talks about the stroke she had just last year. "I've had a couple Vespa accidents, too, and then the stroke caused me to lose a lot of weight and muscle strength. I've never been this weak. I've always been very strong, Viking-strong."

When the stroke came on, Kristin says she called over Dionne, her companion and former helper for Bear's art shows. "I was talking to Dionne so she could see how I wasn't making sense. I remember lifting each leg like this"—she grabs her thigh and lifts it from the chair—"as we went down the stairs."

I ask Kristin if the stroke was like the near-death experience, and she shakes her head. "I had control of the stroke situation, and the part that I didn't have control of, I couldn't feel. But the near-death experience I didn't have control of."

Still, she sees the similarities. She claps her knee and adds, "Now that I'm retired, I've had my first warning stroke, and the rest of my life is before me once again!" Her laughter is as exuberant as that of a child playing on the banks of a free-flowing river.

Going Deeper

1. What are some of the childhood circumstances that influenced Kristin's spirituality?

2. How would you describe your feelings when you are resting or reflecting in a quiet place in nature? What do you learn in those moments?

3. How did Kristin react to the changes in her life?

4. How does Kristin distinguish between her near-death experience and her stroke? For you, what's the interplay between your ability to control and your trust in the Spirit?

Try This

On a temperate day, lay down in a quiet stretch of lawn, meadow, or beach where human sounds are limited or distant so that you can focus on your body touching the ground and the sensations of breeze, bird calls, and insect hums. Breathe deeply and focus on these sounds, letting them go as soon as your senses lay hold of them. Be open to everything but hold onto nothing. Just let the sounds enter your personal field and fall away. When you've had a chance to meditate this way for twenty minutes or longer, take a few moments to write down what you experienced.

Dionne

Drumming to Heal the Mother

My Mother Earth! I drum and pray for her. For
us healing her pain.

DIONNE KOHLER, DRUMMER PRIESTESS
AT HERCHURCH

Dionne beats out a short rhythm on her sacred
black and crimson *djembe* drum.[1] She has been
drumming since she was a child, and her biological
father before her, even though she didn't know that
until 1994. "My father is a drummer and a dancer, last
I heard, on the Hoopa Reservation by the Klamath
River. He never knew about me until I called him
one day in 1994." Dionne's wide-set black eyes grow
large as she explains that when she found her biological
mother and discovered she was part Apache, her mother
informed her that Dionne's father was Cherokee. "I
was like, 'Yay! I'm Indian! I'm Indian! I *knew* I was
Indian!'" She whoops. "I was so happy. When I called
him, I asked him, 'So am I Cherokee?' 'And he said, in
a deep voice like this, 'Cherokee? You're not Cherokee.
You're Yurok-Karuk!' And I'm like, 'What the heck is
that?' So I looked it up. The Karuk were tall … but
the beach tribes—the Yurok—were a little stockier. In

fact, I look like a Yurok." Dionne gestures to her round face and her short, sturdy build. "You can go to the museums up by Eureka and Sacramento and see my ancestors on the wall."

Dionne explains she was told that she could receive money from the government if she registered as part of the tribe, but she didn't want to. "I found this out in 1994. Now I'm fifty-one, and I figure I'm okay. Children on the reservation need those funds. Also, I wasn't raised on the reservation. I'm a half-breed. I'm a mix. I'm not an Indian. I'm not a white. I'm in the middle. I'm a mix."

I ask Dionne to describe an experience of Spirit, of the Divine, and she recalls a moment with her best friend from high school. "We had just finished singing and playing guitar at an open mike, and I was sitting next to my friend, whose sister (also a good friend of mine) had recently died. I was looking at my friend, and her face started to break up. She had glasses, and I could see these eyes looking at me through them, and it was her [deceased] sister looking at me. "Something in my face made my friend ask me what was up with me, and I said, 'She's here, your sister is here.' I was trying to describe it. There was this golden-like sunshine all around us from those eyes." Dionne cups her hands around her eyes. "These eyes looking at me through my friend were like a portal. And I heard her sister's voice saying, 'I'm right here. I'm always here.'

"At first it was just the eyes … and then it just got bigger and bigger, growing brighter and brighter … like this." Dionne draws an outline from a height of six feet down to the ground. "And I felt, 'I am in the presence of the Holy One. The Other. The Divine. The Other Side of Time.' And she said, 'I am always here. I am always with you.'"

Dionne looks at me, and for a few seconds we sit in silence. Then I ask the questions about where and how she was raised and what religion she was brought up in. "I'm a country girl!" she sings and raps out a rhythm on her drum. She tells me she was raised Roman Catholic by adopted parents, who worked on a farm in the

Central Valley. She tells me that they went to Mass occasionally and recalls her first memory of the crucifix, when she was five years old. "The first image of Jesus that I saw was bloody and hanging on a white wall. It scared me. I thought, 'That's going to happen to me.'" She extends her arms in mock crucifixion. "I thought, 'They're going to put me up there.' I was scared to death of Jesus on the cross for years."

Her words shock me into seeing the brutality embedded in the religious icon I grew up with, but I don't want to pry by asking her why she saw it that way. Dionne tells me that eventually she made her peace with the crucifix and started attending Mass regularly in her high school years. Her best friend was in a church folk group, and she loved the guitar's music. "The first time I heard my friend play the guitar, I heard angels. It was a twelve-string, and it was just different. I'd never heard anything like that before. It calmed me because I was a very angry teenager—there's stories to prove that—but the music helped." Dionne describes her feeling of being cast off as an infant, how abandonment disorder was a source of her anger and lack of trust. "They say music calms the beast. I asked my friend, 'Please teach me to play the guitar like that.' So in exchange for me teaching her to play the drums, she taught me guitar.

"It was the beginning of my spirituality because we sang folk tunes in church. We sang the Byrds." Dionne intones, "Turn, Turn, Turn," in descending notes. "And the song of Saint Francis: 'Make me an instrument of your peace," Dionne sings in a strong and resilient mezzo-soprano voice. "I never missed a single church service, because of the music. I've been to all kinds of churches. You name them, I've been to all of them! But in the other churches, I was always like, 'What about the women, hello?' There're so many powerful women, but their stories aren't being told. When I started coming to herchurch, I was like, 'Oh, this is good. I like this.' I saw the drums up there by the altar, and I asked Pastor Stacy, 'Why are the drums there?' And she said, 'Oh, someone used to play them, but she doesn't anymore.' So I asked Stacy if I could. You saw how I started with just one little drum. And now my sister drums are all here." She motions to the drum kit next to us.

"Herchurch is very important to me as a human being, spiritually and emotionally. If it was not for herchurch, I would not be going to church." I ask Dionne about this, about her ongoing relationship with the Divine. She moves the *djembe* closer to her knees and brushes her hand against it. "Every morning when I wake up and open up my eyes and see that I'm still here, I give thanks to the Divine. I know it's both male and female. In Genesis, it says that God made humanity in God's image, both male and female. But for me, the comforting voice that I hear in my head is feminine. The voice is like Julie Andrews singing. It's female. It comforts me and tells me everything is going to be okay. And because of my family issues—not having a mother— this is very important to me."

Dionne recounts a second experience, one that happened at herchurch. "When Randy [the church's elderly janitor] retired, I became the janitor, and I was here alone a lot, and I would clean the whole church. And one day I was in the sanctuary, and I had just finished sweeping and mopping the floor and putting all the chairs back. I was dripping with sweat, and I sat down in the narthex [which opens into the church's sanctuary]. As I did that, all of a sudden that golden heart of Christ-Sophia"—she refers to the over-the-altar portrait of a mestiza, called Mary by some and Wisdom or Sophia by others, whose chest bears a golden heart much like the Sacred Heart of Jesus image—"all of sudden when I sat down, the sunlight coming in just hit on that heart, and then the whole church did that big golden glow … And this whole church was just like the sun. It started with the heart, and it just got bigger and bigger, and I sat there with it.

"I am receptive to things like that. I let them happen. I say, 'Okay, don't shut your eyes. Don't run and hide. I felt I was home. I am safe, I am protected. I have this Light around me, my Creator who is looking at me and smiling, saying, 'I appreciate you and what you're doing with your creativity.'"

Dionne has done many things in her life, including serving as a medic in the navy reservists and also as a caregiver for Kristin's mom. I ask her what she considers her healing work to be now. Dionne closes her eyes and inhales a deep meditative breath. After a few seconds she speaks with an inward-looking tone of voice. "My drum. I put all of my intensity for healing into my hands and...." *Pom!* She hits her drum with a single resounding boom. "*My Mother Earth!* I drum and pray for her. For us healing her pain.

"I do everything I can to make my carbon footprint as light as possible. But the most that I can do, being the little tiny speck of human being that I am, is pray. The spiritual world has more healing power than my little human body does. So I connect through my drumming or my singing or my guitar playing or dancing. Whatever the physical expression, it's to exalt that Spirit of creation that made me, to thank it: 'Mother Earth, what can I do to heal You? What can I do?'

"I can only do what I can and then pass it on to others, saying things like, 'Don't throw your cigarette butt on the ground. Why can't you pick it up, and put it in the garbage can, because your little cigarette butt ends up in the ocean, and then the little turtle thinks it's food, and then the turtle eats it and dies.' And the person says, 'Okay, I never knew that before.' I don't want to get angry with people because it seems they don't understand the consequences of their actions unless you point it out to them in a Princess Diana-like way. I try to be more graceful so that people will respect our Mother Earth, the grounding soul beneath our feet. And to help her out a little bit. You know, She gives us so much."

I ask Dionne for her words of wisdom for young women, and she sighs like a deflating balloon. "Young women … I go back to when I was fifteen when I wanted to"—she makes a quick slice across her throat and a slitting sound—"myself. For reasons that we don't need to go into, I just felt that life was not worth living, and there's so many teenagers now killing themselves, it's sad. Because they don't see a future. They don't see anything worth living for, and that hurts me because even though it seems like this world is all messed up and crazy, there's still love.

"So children, yeah. That's tough because …" Her eyes glisten darkly. "You can't protect them. I lost my niece. First Christmas without her. She was only seventeen." She wipes her eyes with her sleeve. "You can't protect children. They think they know everything. You can't tell them anything …" She shakes her head. "So words of wisdom for children? I don't have them."

Dionne pauses before offering, "Hang in there. Live it down. Today may seem like it's the worst day of your life, but you're alive and my niece isn't. Neither is my friend's sister. And these were two beautiful girls who had a lot to give." She takes out a handkerchief to pat her face and returns it to a back pocket. "So, children? I'll just be their friend. In this youth class [at herchurch], I try to bring out their creativity, whatever it is. If they want to dance, to drum, to draw or play guitar … whatever makes them feel good."

I ask Dionne if she wants to add anything. She smiles. "Thank you for doing this." She brings her hands together and bows her head toward me. "These stories, wherever they go, however they get told, even if they just save one person, keep one person from jumping off the bridge, they're important. Thank you."

Going Deeper

1. What impact did Dionne's childhood and background have on her spirituality?
2. How do loss and other changes inform her spirituality? How do they inform yours?
3. Reflect on the ways in which your spirituality has changed due to loss(es) in your life.

Try This

Attend a drumming circle. You can search for "drumming circle" on the Internet to find one near you.

Stacy
Climbing into Her Branches

I believe that we have created what God is: metaphors that help us connect to something that's sacred within and beyond ourselves. But on the less intellectual level, I sometimes really believe that there's some kind of Being that is she.

STACY BOORN, PASTOR OF HERCHURCH

Stacy is the pastor of Ebenezer Lutheran, more commonly known as herchurch. Today, as most days, she is smiling, and her grin lights up her round, ruddy face. A front tuft of her short blonde hair is dyed purple, something that would seem incongruent with her stiff black suit and white clerical collar—until you get to know her. By then you would know that Stacy plays. A lot. Liturgy is just one of her playful arts. Photography is another.

Her photos of people, dunes, shells, flowers, and other faces of nature adorn the church narthex as well as the church's adjoining art gallery called A Woman's Eye, or AWE. Stacy leads me through the AWE gallery to a meeting room lined with framed watercolors. She says that for her, "Creativity and spirituality are two threads in the same cord. Sometimes it is music, sometimes dance, sometimes words. Mostly for me it is imagery, splashes of color and placed objects that enhance and embody the Sacred and her Presence."

As she pulls out two folding chairs for us to sit on, she relates how she is drawn by the Tree of Life. "It's a grace-filled and empowering image and metaphor for Goddess, as if we could climb into her branches and find renewal, friendship, and peace for the whole world just as the birds of the air come to the branches of their favorite trees."

Nature is a favorite subject of Stacy in her artwork. "All of nature is interdependent," she adds. "I suspect this is why I love looking through a camera lens to see more closely nature's details and mystic qualities."

I ask her to describe a time when the Divine was most palpable to her.

"My strongest connection to the Divine—that is, before I understood my connection to the Divine Feminine—was probably my actual ordination day. There was something in that day for me. Not for the first time, but more vivid than other times, it seemed that the Divine was both within and surrounding me, almost a coming-over-me experience that grounded me in a real sense of the Divine Presence."

Stacy describes standing before all the pastors and parishioners who attended her ordination ceremony. A couple of parishioners came forward with the stole, which symbolizes pastoral leadership, and in that moment, Stacy felt a Divine Presence. She describes how, as a preteen, she'd lovingly crafted "this funky red felt and burlap stole" for her hometown pastor and that he had sent it for her ordination. Stacy recalls that as the red stole was held aloft over her shoulders, she felt a strong sense of accompaniment. "It was a Divine Power—not necessarily a Being, but a Presence—that was choosing to be with me."

Stacy had wanted to be a Lutheran pastor since she was nine years old, and she'd had one or two similar experiences of this Presence. When she was ten, all the kids in her small congregation received the Lenten gift bank, a fold-it-yourself, cardboard box with a picture of Jesus and a coin slot. "I went through all my drawers at home and got all the money that my grandmothers had given me, and I just kept stuffing it in and stuffing it in. We brought the box back on Good Friday. Stacy chuckles at the memory of the tiny cardboard cube stuffed with twenty-six dollars in coinage and tightly wadded bills. She only knows how much it totaled because the pastor mentioned it in his Easter sermon. "I wasn't doing it to get recognized. I really felt it was my gift to God, and I heard very clearly on that Good Friday that God was saying, 'Thank you' to me."

Two decades later, Stacy finally fulfilled her childhood dream of becoming a pastor. While in seminary in St. Louis, she had experienced a period of depression, so she took some time off to address the issues and then transferred to a seminary in Berkeley. It'd been a long, hard journey. Stacy reflects, "So I think a part of feeling this Divine Presence at the ordination was also a sense of healing and acceptance. Approval was still a big part of my life. All of that came together at the moment of ordination.

"Another one of the major things that was an 'aha' for me— something that probably led to my interest in feminist theology— was when I had my parish in Richmond that became a predominately Laotian congregation." Stacy, who had been leaning back in her chair, suddenly rocks forward. "It was just a few years into my pastoral ministry, about 1990. A lot of the Laotian families wanted to be baptized, three or four generations at a time. After we talked about what the church was about and what Jesus was about, they began to educate me. I knew nothing about other cultures. What they told me was kind of a breakthrough. And the family baptisms were a big experience for me. Altogether I baptized around seventy-five people.

The 'wow' feeling I experienced wasn't so much from the fact that all these people became Christian. No, it was more like, 'Wow, in this ritual I'm really experiencing God, so I think the other people must be too, as they are the ones being baptized!'"

Again Stacy struggles to describe the ineffable Presence in that moment. "See, there was something not explainable about it. It was not just the ritual of baptism as I understood it, but something different. It happened in the water events somehow: the pouring, the baptizing, the splashing, the whole messy deal. There were a lot of people to baptize, a lot of water flowing onto the floor, all of that. And in this moving water somehow there was Something Beyond."

Stacy says that this breakthrough was the beginning of her understanding of the Divine Feminine, because it opened her to experience a broader dimension of God. As an explanation, she segues into another baptism story, this time just as she was beginning to make the connection of the baptismal waters with "the birthing waters."

The baptism took place right before she started using female imagery for God. "I had been here at Ebenezer Lutheran a year when there was a baptism of one of the members' grandkids. The parents were a young couple who didn't come to church at all. I met with them and said I would like to baptize the baby in the name of God as Father and Mother, in the name of Christ, and in the name of the Holy Spirit. 'Oh, that's great!' they said. And so we did that." Stacy laughs with delight recalling the baptism: the young couple's willingness, the ceremony itself, and the brouhaha that resulted. "There were two or three folks in the congregation who said that this was the work of the devil! To call God 'Mother!'"

The powerful reaction prompted Stacy to read more feminist literature and theologies. She said to herself, "'There must be something to this!' And from that time forward, I read all the things I should have read in the eighties. It was eye-opening to me, just so powerful. All the time I was in seminary, I had somehow not seen the women's movement, not heard about feminist theologies. I wondered, 'How could I have missed this and felt that I'm a proclaimer of good news?'"

She began meeting with other self-identified feminist Lutheran pastors, and this gave her a sense of community. "We'd get together for lunch and share our experiences. One month, Pamela Pond brought each of us a goddess rosary that she had made. I'd never done anything with prayer beads. It was not very Lutheran, you know. But Pamela asked each person to pick a rosary. They were Anglican style, all from gemstones. They were fascinating to me because when I was kid, I had collected rocks. I knew what every stone was. I wanted the amethyst rosary, but someone else took it, so I picked up the tigereye one. When I got home, I thought it was just a wonderful tool. Something to touch, to see the female figure on it. Wow, I thought. This is just about me as much as it is about God!"

In the meantime, Stacy continued to read, and at church, she continued to talk about what she was reading. She'd bring some of it into her homilies. "A few people at the church were interested, but it took a long time before more than a few got interested. It took a few years, when other people joined the church, and that was really fantastic."

By then those who'd so strongly opposed her use of the word "Mother" for the Divine had long since left. Stacy was employing inclusive language, terms like "the Holy Other," but hadn't yet used the G word. She doesn't remember the date of when she first used "Goddess," but she remembers the reaction of one of her longtime members. The word "Goddess" was printed right there in the bulletin. "I don't remember which Sunday it was on, but right before we were to start the service, Dorothy Hult came up to me."

Dorothy was an older member who has since passed on. Stacy, pantomiming Dorothy's in-church composure, whispers through her cupped hand, "'You know, Pastor, a long time ago my mother told me that God is *not* a man. The church wants to make God a man, she said, but remember, God is *not!* And I've been waiting for the day when the church would finally say that in some way!'" Recalling this moment, Stacy laughs. "Dorothy's day had arrived! We said Goddess for the first time that Sunday!"

Stacy admits that at first she thought it was just a language switch. "I printed God/dess—with a slash—in the bulletin. I'd gotten this form out of an academic book by Rosemary Radford Ruether.[1] It wasn't really meant to be a liturgical way of dealing with it. But I used it! Whenever I came to 'God/dess' in the text, I said, 'Goddess,' and this long front row of old Swedes[2] said, 'Goddess,' too. And I thought, 'Wow! It's happening so fast!' Afterward Dorothy told me, 'It's only because they didn't know what to do! They just followed you!' But it was a wonderful first experience for me!

"Now I think it feels completely natural for me to use the term 'Goddess' or 'Mother' or 'Midwife' or any of those terms. For example," Stacy elaborates, "with the young girls in our Saturday class, I just use the term 'Goddess.' I feel that the actual use of this word, this metaphor, is so powerful in itself that we don't need a lot of talk and explanation.

"On the other hand, there're multiple feminist theologies and multiple voices. I like to dabble in a lot of them. I think it works well in a church setting that way." Stacy points out the herchurch's use of various representations of the Divine Feminine, including Sophia,[3] Mexico's Our Lady of Guadalupe, Europe's Black Madonnas, and the venerated Mary of Magdala, the ascribed author of the second-century *Gospel of Mary*. The church is also home to numerous female icons, both modern creations and replicas of ancient figurines. "We are a bridge—from ancient to modern, Christian to not-so-Christian," Stacy asserts. "What we do here as a faith community has implications for the whole church."

But Stacy reaches farther than the church. "I also think that it's important for the whole world that the power of women—not just a few women in the United States, but women globally—be seen and that the power and the understanding of the Divine Feminine be seen. Not just feminine metaphors, but the real-life females of the world as well, women like yourself."

In a sentence, Stacy links the power of God-talk (or in this case, Goddess-talk) to real women and women's agency in the world. She expands this connection to the earth and all beings. "The world and the whole of the universe are in essence the body of the God/dess, and we jointly share the life forces."

Our conversation moves to the Divine's infinite complexity and the challenge of its articulation in the limited scope of human language. But Sunday is an exceedingly long day for pastors. Stacy smiles, just a hint of fatigue pulling at the corners of her mouth. "Actually, I go back and forth whether it is just totally metaphor or whether there *is* a Being that has just as much feminine entity and power and energy to her." Asked to clarify, Stacy says, "I believe that we have created what God is: metaphors that help us connect to something that's sacred within and beyond ourselves. But on the less intellectual level, I sometimes really believe that there's some kind of Being that is she."

Going Deeper

1. How did Stacy address challenges in her vocation and in her life?

2. Which of the images or metaphors that Stacy mentioned speak to you?

3. What does Stacy mean when she suggests that the power of women and the Divine Feminine need to be seen not just as feminine metaphors but in real-life examples, "women like yourself"?

4. How are you an example of the Divine at work and at play in the world?

Try This

Set out several hues of colored paper for collage making. Whimsically choose the colors that draw you. Let your imagination lead the way as you cut the colors into shapes. Group the shapes to your fancy. Rearrange them. Play. Take pleasure in the collage you are creating.

Or, take out your rosary. (If you don't have one, you can order a goddess rosary from www.herchurch.org. Instructions and prayers come with it.) You can pray a woman-affirming rosary by saying the "Our Mother" prayer (page 60) and the "Hail Goddess" prayer (below), alternating prayers for the small and large beads of the rosary.

> *Hail Goddess, full of grace.*
> *Blessed are you*
> *and blessed are all the fruits*
> *of your womb.*
> *For you are the mother of us all.*
> *Hear us now*
> *and in all our needs.*
> *O blessed be, O blessed be.*
> (ADAPTED FROM CAROL P. CHRIST)

Virginia

Stirring the Ashes

Faith is trust—trusting in the Universe.... If you make the best decision that you can, and then continue in that trust, having that faith that God is walking with you, you *can* go forward and God will go with you.

VIRGINIA STELLA, ARTIST

Virginia flips back her white skein of ponytailed hair and laughs. She is Sicilian, with large, deep-set eyes, and quite the storyteller. I have come to her home, a tiny abode clinging to a hill in the outskirts of San Anselmo, but I met her at herchurch's last Faith and Feminism Conference, where she displayed some of her botanical drawings.

Adorning her simple living room are a few of her drawings and watercolors. I remark on her talent, and she responds that we all are creative beings. Her own art enables her to focus on where the Spirit is calling her, she says. "It might be making a greeting card for my church members to sign for a sick person, or volunteering to coordinate an art exhibit, or attending an art association meeting, or donating my favorite oil painting to a good cause. I'm not waiting for inspiration to

250

make that $1,000 painting, but I just keeping on making art and letting the path unfold. Keep stirring the ashes, and they will burst into Spirit Fire."

Evidence of that Spirit Fire is all around us, displayed in Virginia's exquisite renderings of native flowers. But she is most proud of her picture window, which frames Mount Tamalpais. "Look, the Indian maiden, my Divine Feminine!" she exclaims, referring to the Miwok people's name for their sacred mountain.

Like her art, Virginia's spirituality has grown and changed over the last few decades. She explains that on the previous Friday, the feast day of Mary Magdalene, she'd attended a service of rituals honoring Mary Magdalene. The words and rituals had a profound impact on Virginia. "Being Catholic," she laughs, "I love ritual!"

I ask her to describe it to me, this service of Mary Magdalene.

"At the beginning of the event, I was thinking that I'd have to be here a million times before I could really believe this, and then by the end, I was just taking it in and giving it back. They were saying, 'The feminine is beautiful, and you are beautiful, and God is in you.' I had to keep telling myself, 'Just take this in. Just be open.' And then near the end of the ritual, the priestesses stood in a circle, and they said, 'If you want, you can come forward for a blessing.' I thought, sure I'll do that. I went up to a woman, and...." Virginia's dark eyes open wide. "It was a transforming experience! I *felt* to be in the presence of Jesus!"

She recounts how the woman, dressed in floor-length forest green velvet, blessed her by saying Virginia's name and encouraging her "to be filled with the Spirit but to stay grounded...." Virginia gasps. "And I was so able to take that in! Her love and her generosity and her femininity were coming to me, and I was able to take it in. See, I've always had this idea that when you hear God say your name, you will know that you are loved. That's what Mary Magdalene experienced when she went to the tomb, and Jesus came out, and he said, 'Mary,' and looked at her: she was transformed. And then he said, 'Don't cling to me; I'm going, but you have what you need within you.' And so that was Mary's transformation that he gave back to her: *herself* (John 20:11–18).

"See, Jesus blessed Mary, and that's what that woman was doing to me. She was blessing me and saying, 'You have everything you need within you.' Mary was not expecting to see Jesus, and neither was I expecting to receive this healing. And it really was healing. It was a deep healing for me."

The two previous years had been difficult ones for Virginia. Her youngest daughter had been through a lot. And Virginia herself had experienced many of the inconveniences that go with aging. She had fallen at the YMCA's pool, opening a huge gash in her leg that required stitches. She longed to get back to her swimming, but had accidentally bumped and reopened her wound three times. How long it was taking for her to heal! Other symptoms of aging aggravated her, too, especially the memory glitches that she jokingly calls "those senior moments." But altogether, these changes worked their despair on Virginia.

"There was a moment when I thought, 'Oh my God, I'm a senior!'" I ask if she recently turned sixty-five to assure myself I didn't get her age wrong. "No, I'm seventy-seven. So many people I know are going into retirement homes, and I'm like, 'Nope! I want to be in the world yet, where there are all ages of people.' So here when various things started to happen to me, both physically and with my memory—like 'Oh God, what was her name? Is that happening to *me?*'—there came a day when I said, "I'm a senior. And I acknowledged the sadness and the problems that come along with that. 'This is where I'm at,' I said. 'I really need to accept this.' So it's acceptance, letting go and trusting that this will be a good time in my life. It will be a different time, and I have to figure that out.

"And it's happening in my little church." Virginia explains that for the last thirty-plus years she's attended a small faith community called Comunitas Cristi, or Christ Community, in addition to "the big church" of St. Anselm's. In her small faith community, Virginia confides, "We are aging. People are dying—good friends—and we're grieving. People are going into retirement homes because they have to. They're moving away, moving in with their children because they have to." Virginia, who is single—her husband left her the same week their last child went off to college—takes a sharp intake of breath. "My friends can't get together because they're ill. So we're saying our little church is aging, and this is the spiritual task that we have before us. Where is God in that?" Virginia implores with uplifted hands. "Where are we being called to? As a community and as individuals?"

Virginia chronicles how their small faith community was formed in the wake of Vatican II under the Archdiocese of San Francisco. As one of many small faith communities that laypeople formed in the 1960s, it gave laypeople the permission to see, as Virginia gleefully proclaims, "that *we* are the church. Amazingly, we are over forty years old now. Our priests come mostly from the Franciscan and Jesuit seminaries in Berkeley, and they write these textbooks, and we're in all these books!" Virginia exclaims. Her laughter is mirthful, a ripple of pure joy. "They bring their students to come and see us!

"See, we do Mass, but we make our own revisions. In the Catholic Church, only the priest or deacon can give the homily, but we *all* reflect! We say that we have four or five homilies by the time we're done with Mass! Plus, we have to set up, clean up, and do everything ourselves. This is not a church you can just come and sit down. We try as much as we can for the men to work in the kitchen and the women to collect the money!"

"We're open to everyone: divorced, gays, Jewish, Indian, American Indian. Everyone is welcome if you behave with respect. Different people have different spiritualities. I've become identified as the most feminist. I always bring that information back to the community, and I feel very supported there."

"Most of the community's children are grown up and gone now. One of the children who grew up in our community was at the Magdalene service on Friday night, and she is becoming a priestess! A priestess!!! Oh, yes! I told her I was so happy to see her there. And I told people back at the community that Velda's daughter is becoming a priestess! To see one of our kids doing that is so wonderful! She's found her way just as we found our way away from the traditional church."

I ask Virginia what she would share about faith with a young woman like Velda's daughter. Virginia jumps right in. "Faith is so much a part of me, it's my lifeblood. I equate it with trust. Faith is trust—trusting in the Universe. Trusting that you can let go and be okay. Somehow I feel if you just think about what you're doing and make the best decision that you can, and then continue in that trust, having that faith that God is walking with you, you *can* go forward and God will go with you. Have that faith. Because I'm seventy-seven years old and have had all these experiences, I *know* that I can go forward into the darkness and that I will be taken care of or that I can deal with that. God will never give you more that you can deal with. I see that it my daughter's life. She's led an incredible life of challenge. She looks like one of these middle-class miracles, but no, wrong! The angels keep coming out of the woodwork to lift her up. God is taking care of her. Why is she able to do what she does? Because she has faith, and her children will learn that from her."

Going Deeper

1. Which of Virginia's experiences resonate most strongly for you?

2. Where does Virginia's inspiration for creativity come from? How does she nurture it?

3. What does Virginia say about trust and how it relates to the changes in her life? How would you characterize your own faith in terms of trust?

Try This

Find a box of finger paints and a sheet or more of paper. Close your eyes and breathe quietly for a few moments. Then let your fingers paint whatever your imagination calls forth. Have fun!

Jann

Let Justice Roll Down Like Water

Everything that I desire to see in the world—
peace, justice, freedom from oppression, equal
economic opportunities, caring for the earth,
honoring one another—we've got to have a
symbolism that will support those values. We
have denied the Divine Feminine, so the world
is all out of balance.

JANN ALDREDGE-CLANTON, PHD, MDIV,
AUTHOR, LECTURER, AND
ONCOLOGY CHAPLAIN

When Reverend Dr. Jann Aldredge-Clanton
smiles, it illumines her heart-shaped face. In
describing her spiritual experiences, she speaks with
the unhurried, lilting pulse of her native Louisiana.
"One very powerful time was right here at herchurch,
the first year I came. I felt her energy flowing in such a
powerful way through the church and in all the beautiful Divine Feminine images. Many times when I'm
[keynoting], I pray a lot ahead of time. I pray that she,
Sophia[1], is with me, helping me, but I don't always feel
her presence. But she was just so tangible that Friday
night that I told my story at herchurch."

That night, conference participants heard Jann share her struggles to become ordained when there were very few female clergy in her Baptist denomination. Jann sensed the Divine Presence in the storytelling but also in the congregation's singing of her hymns. "The way that the people sang brought tears to my eyes." Jann's voice swells. "I felt her presence. It's like the reason that I gave the hymns to you all. It's part of the reason that I created them."

I ask Jann about the inspiration for the lyrics she pens.[2]

"Writing a hymn is a kind of prayer language; that's the only way I know how to describe it. Sometimes a hymn begins with an image or a verse in scripture I want to put in. I just start it and have faith that it's going to turn into a hymn, and it almost always does. Sometimes I feel the Divine Presence much more profoundly when I am creating than when I am trying to meditate or any other ways of ritual or religious community, because I feel that it's a direct connection with the Creative Spirit."

The same Spirit that inspired Jann to write lyrics first moved her to pursue doctoral studies and then urged her into the ministry. To all of these changes, Jann opened her heart. Her vocation kept unfolding. When she was teaching English at Dallas Baptist University, she felt called to pastoral ministry. When she was in parish ministry, she wrote a book on feminist theology for the layperson and a children's book on Mother and Father God. And yet she felt called to do more. "When I realized that people's resistance many times was coming from a deep place that only ritual can reach, I felt called to write liturgy and ritual."

In all Jann's varied positions—as professor, minister, chaplain, lyricist, author—she has taken on racial and gender inequality. In preparation for her most recent book, *Changing Church: Stories of Liberating Ministers*,[3] she set out to interview twelve ministers who were each incorporating the Divine Feminine into their worship services. "My hunch was if they were doing that, they were connected to a lot of social justice issues and, oh, was that verified ten

times over. That connection was really strong. This expansive theology and an ethic of justice and equality in relationships and taking care of the earth are inextricably connected." In fact, the issues
are so intertwined that Jann states, "If I didn't think that spirituality or theology had any connection with social justice, I wouldn't
be writing or leading liturgies. I wouldn't be trying to transform
my spirituality or other people's. I think that as we transform spiritual symbols, then we, and the whole earth, *are* transformed. It's
the chicken and the egg. It all goes together."

As another example, Jann talks about her current political
work in Dallas. "Politically, I've been working on fracking. There're
some companies trying to come into the city limits of Dallas,
and we've gone to public hearings and spoken out against this.
My sister's very involved in this issue. Her grandchildren live in
Flower Mound, and their school is close to places where there is
gas drilling. She's gone out to drilling sites, and literally she's had
headaches after she's stayed out there. Drilling companies are using
fresh water that can't be used again and these chemicals that are
known carcinogens. In Flower Mound, the breast cancer rate is
higher. I got up at one of the hearings and talked about my experiences as an oncology chaplain. 'Anything that is putting carcinogens into the water or air hurts us,' I appealed to them. 'We're all
involved. One out of every two Americans has cancer sometime in
their lifetime.'

"Some of the young people at the hearing had signs with, 'We
can't drink oil' and 'People over profits,' so I quoted the biblical
passage, 'Let justice roll down like waters and righteousness like an
ever-flowing stream.'"[4] Recalling that moment, Jann grins. "Some
people say natural gas is better than coal. But [fracking] is slowing
down progress toward renewable energy. I know we need jobs. I'm
on a workers' rights board too, and gas drilling provides a lot of
jobs. It's complex, but we've got to get involved in green jobs. We
need clean energy if we're going to sustain the earth."

Asked for her parting words of wisdom, Jann says, "Find the Divine within you. I wouldn't tell you what kind of community or how to name the Divine, because I think that it's very important for that to come from within you. I would encourage women to realize the power that *we* have—the Divine within us—as we join in community, with her within and around us, the Divine Feminine, however we name her, Mary Magdalene, Sophia, Shekhinah, Ruah, El Shaddai; there're so many names for the Divine Feminine in Hebrew scripture. She's in all the traditions. I would just encourage women to find her and then feel that power to join with her in bringing all of these changes. To value what has been denigrated as feminine: the nurturing, the giving birth—whether that's physically or giving birth to creative work—beauty, caring for the earth, tenderness, all of those traits that have not been valued."

Jann lifts her hands outward from her lap. "Everything that I desire to see in the world—peace, justice, freedom from oppression, equal economic opportunities, caring for the earth, honoring one another—we've got to have a symbolism that will support those values. We have denied the Divine Feminine, so the world is all out of balance. My writing stories, lyrics, taking academic feminist theology to laypeople ... helps bring individual transformation, transformation of communities, and transformation of the world in all of these areas that we've talked about."

Jann elaborates more on the importance of working in community, and as our time together draws to a quick close, she smiles and proclaims with Southern sweetness, "And bless *you* for writing this! I think it's going to have a big part in this transformation!"

Going Deeper

1. What changes did Jann experience in her life? How did she look to the Spirit in embracing those changes? What has changed as a result for other women?

2. Where does Jann draw her inspiration for writing songs from? What moments in your life can you characterize as engagement with what she calls the Creative Spirit?

3. Jann talks about the importance of spiritual symbols. Which spiritual symbols are affirming and empowering for you?

Try This

Think of your favorite religious song or chant. Hum a few lines to yourself or play it. The next time you sing it (in community or alone), notice which words and melodies appeal most to you. How does the music deepen the experience? Are there any words or symbols that no longer resonate for you? If so, how can you change them so that they do?

Alternatively, try this: Think of a short phrase that has spiritual meaning for you and sing it, making up the tune as you go along. Repeat it several times so that you can recall it later. Sing it whenever you need to be reminded of its spiritual truth.

Katie

Would You Hug Me, Jesus?

The thing that's most important is also the most difficult: to be loving and kind to each other. I don't remember any sermons, but I do remember the kindness that people have shown me. That's what matters.

KATIE KETCHUM, AWARD-WINNING COMPOSER, ACTRESS, AND CONCERT PIANIST

Even though Katie Ketchum's hair is tinted blonde today, I think of her as the red-haired starlet in her musical *The Magdalene Stories*.[1] She has a fabulous voice and leads herchurch in everything from baroque hymns to gospel rock and earthy pagan chants. But today her energy seems more subdued. Our interview takes place directly after a croning ceremony at herchurch, and a symbol of Katie's cronedom, a purple scarf, drapes her chest. Perhaps it is the ceremony that has made Katie suddenly shy. Or perhaps it is the audio recorder, because I know her to be an incredibly talented musician. She studied as a concert pianist under Weldon Kilburn and the Royal Conservatory of Music in Toronto, and she has written scores of songs, including several musicals.

She is an outstanding example of living and creating from one's heart and soul.

But when asked to describe a time when she felt the Divine most palpably, Katie speaks softly. "The first time something like that happened, I was helping a friend by staying with her when her mother was dying. At the time, I was incredibly lonely. I had just completed a divorce. I was in a very sad place. I mentioned this to one of my students, and she said, 'You know it's lonely for me at college sometimes. But I just ask Jesus to hug me, and he does.' I was a little, you know, cynical about it, but I was sufficiently desperate that night to ask, 'Would you hug me, Jesus?' And suddenly when I closed my eyes, I saw eyes looking at me with this intense compassion, and I felt a presence over my body. It was a very visceral experience. I felt this incredible love come over me. It was really shocking. I was stunned. I wrote a song about it." She hums a line from the song.

"The next day I went to this waterfall where I hike, and I asked Jesus again. All of a sudden, I felt this incredible love and compassion. Later I asked another student of mine, someone who I knew went to church, 'Did you ever have an experience of Jesus like, hugging you or kissing you?' She said, 'Oh no! That would be the devil!'" Katie laughs. "She told me it was the devil! Anyway, it happened another time. I guess you could call it almost an altered state, a physical relaxation, a feeling of intense love. I cried because the love was so intense. I don't think I've ever felt that intensely loved or accepted or forgiven."

I asked about Katie's religious upbringing, and she epitomizes it as "confusing." Her mother, a second-generation Englishwoman, was a strict, somewhat fundamentalist Presbyterian, and her father, who was part Native American but in denial of his roots, referred to himself as an "existentialist." A Seventh-Day Adventist woman babysat her most days, including Saturdays, when Katie went to the Seventh-Day Adventist church with her. So Katie didn't know what to think or believe. When she became a professional musician, she played in hundreds of churches but didn't really connect spiritually with any of them. Until Mary Magdalene.

"About five years ago I was at a dead end artistically. I wasn't getting bookings. I didn't know what I was going to do next. I realized that the last time I did something really big, that even won the National Endowment for the Arts Award, was when I wrote about a woman's life.[2] So I started going through lists of women, and when I looked at the name of Mary Magdalene, I felt chills throughout my body."

The Magdalene Stories was a hit. Katie believes it was Mary's guidance. She describes a number of instances when Mary spoke to her. "Mary was my muse. I heard her voice in my head. For example, at one point, I perceived that she said, 'I want you to put a rap song in your musical,' and I said, 'No way. This is ridiculous. I'm not a rap singer.' So I didn't put a rap song in, and then after I'd performed the musical quite a few times, one night I got up and went to the computer, and this entire rap song came out. It was almost as if it were dictated. After I performed it, I thought about taking it out because I was still not sold on this idea of including a rap song. I'm mean, I'm from a different generation. I'm not a rapper. I mentioned this to a friend, and she said the rap song had brought her to tears. 'Don't take it out,' she told me.

"But do you see what I mean about Mary's guidance? A rap song was the last thing that would occur to me. It was Mary's work. Mary was really there guiding this project. Another time I remember that I was asking her, 'What do I do next?' And the answer I received was, 'I don't want you doing anything unless you're rested. Take care of yourself.'" Katie claps with delight in retelling Mary's insistence. "This is not something I would typically tell myself, but Mary says it: 'Don't keep pushing yourself, Katie. Go take a nap. I don't want you working when you're exhausted.'"

For the first time, Katie smiles broadly. She leans forward to confide, "I always had issues about being successful and yet remaining true to my own spirit. The Mary Magdalene project, of all my projects, was the most successful financially. It ended up in the Sacramento Theater Company twenty-eight times. I made the most I'd ever made in a month and a half. I kind of think that was Mary too. She wanted the project to be out there, to get attention.

"And it's not just that it was successful financially. I'm not talking about—what do they call it?—'abundance spirituality.' What I mean is that it made me *feel* successful. Whatever it was that I felt I needed to be 'successful,' that project did it. *She* did it. She anointed me: 'Here you are.' She was telling me, 'You're worthy to be successful, Katie. You can lay that worry to rest.' I had always worried about success, and now I didn't have to anymore."

Katie beams. I am amazed that a woman who is such a vibrant performer and worship leader could have appeared almost timid at the start of the interview. But when she is in her element, she has flair, like when she is singing Mary Magdalene's story, her red curls cascading over her piano.

Herchurch has also opened spiritual moments of connection for Katie. "I've played professionally in churches all my life, and yet I do not connect to the Divine when I'm in church. There's so much involved in delivering the music. Even if you're not cuing others, there's still a lot involved. It's very left brain. It's hard to relax enough so that you're feeling the spiritual connection. But then something happened while I was playing at herchurch. I connected. Somehow I was able to do both. Suddenly I wasn't just singing, wasn't just leading. I felt a Presence...." At a loss for words, Katie uses her hand to gesture from her heart outward. "An analogy would be that I felt my heart pulled."

I ask Katie for other moments when she connects spiritually, and she responds, "I connect when I'm writing a song, when suddenly that spark of creativity comes. And then of course, in nature.

And the community of priestesses, that's enriched my life, too. I think it's important to have a balance of male and female in spirituality."

In light of the recent croning ceremony, I ask Katie for her wisdom. What would she share with young women? What has her spirituality taught her?

Katie is moved by the thoughts this question inspires. Her eyes moisten. "The thing that's most important is also the most difficult: to be loving and kind to each other. I don't remember any sermons, but I do remember the kindness that people have shown me. That's what matters."

Going Deeper

1. What changes was Katie going through during the time of her mystical experiences?
2. Katie is now painting in addition to composing. What strikes you about the changes in her life and the way she has grown with them?
3. How can you adapt so that opportunities and challenges that come into your life can facilitate growth?
4. What are your stories of the Spirit at work in your life?

Try This

Not everyone has the type of spiritual experience that Katie encountered, but anyone can take a few minutes to connect with a deeper sense of Spirit. Do that now in meditation. After breathing deeply for several minutes, call upon your spirit guide, and observe what happens. Or notice what's happening for you physically and emotionally. What do you sense in your body, and what does it tell you? What do you sense emotionally or intuitively? After a time that feels right to you, write down your observations.

EPILOGUE

A few days after finishing the interviews for this book, I went out to San Francisco's Ocean Beach and planted in the sand a symbol of each woman in this book. With a stick of *palo santo* wood from the Peruvian Amazon, I pressed our names into the damp, sandy firmness. There by the waters that gave birth to life millennia ago, I spiraled our names like an inverted wreath, indenting the sand with letters and bits of shell and sea-polished glass. As I stood back to dedicate this powerful weave—this symbol of rebirthing ourselves and our ways of understanding the Divine—the ocean rippled out a slow-spreading wave that took hold of our names and sucked them back into her substance, our original birthing waters.

Most of us have been taught that God creates life, breathing our days into existence, our nights into being. We have been taught that Spirit, however we name it, births all that exists. And this is true. Yet we also birth the Divine, as the women in these pages have shown.

All encounters and understandings of the Divine are essential to the whole. In bringing to light women's spiritual experiences, we increase our day-to-day awareness of the Divine and enhance our global consciousness of God. And when we see in ourselves and others the divine connection between us all, we increase the level of goodwill and equanimity in the world. As Viviana says, "All of us are spirit in this accumulation of energy we call our bodies." All of us are spirit, nestled within the larger Spirit: the ether, the cosmos, the blue planet we call home.

Not too long after the ocean took back our names, I found myself completing the last few pages of this book and dedicating them to the Spirit who gave us birth and receives us back again. In great appreciation, I offer our narratives to the Spirit that infuses all of humanity, so that each of us, far and wide, may be renewed, en-spirited, and blessed.

ACKNOWLEDGMENTS

I thank Divine Mother Wisdom for the truth that she has inspired within me. *Mil gracis*—a thousand thanks and more—to all the women who shared their stories and spiritual truths with me. Deepest gratitude to Jan, who encouraged me to write even when I felt without hope: you showed me my wings and nudged me to use them.

Kudos to my editors, Emily Wichland, vice president of Editorial and Production, and Justine Earnest, assistant editor, as well as the entire SkyLight Paths' team, who worked diligently to enliven and beautify the text. To Kathleen, Kay, Kathe, and Women of Spirit and Faith—thanks for your support and collaboration!

To family … how can I adequately thank you for putting up with my choices to hole up in my room and not use vacation time for real vacations? And my sisters—both biological and spiritual, especially Denise, Nelly, and Jann—who read my first chapters and listened to my aggravations? Again, mil gracias!

Lastly, to you, magnificent readers: may you see the truth of your stories and the beauty of your spirit-inspired life.

Meditations and Visualizations

For all of the following visualizations, it is best if you pre-record or have a friend read them out loud to you. Plan on at least fifteen minutes for each guided visualization. Sit or lie comfortably, and allow yourself the time you need to enter and return from the experience.

For the guided visualizations to be effective and allow the listener to relax deeply and enter her imagination, the reader (whether that is you or a friend) needs to proceed much slower than normal and allow plenty of silence in between the meditations' phrases. A good rule of thumb is to pause two to three seconds after every period, five or more seconds after every ellipses (...), and up to seven or eight seconds between paragraphs. Even if it feels like too much intervening silence, the listener is using that silence to enter very deeply into a meditative experience.

Greeting Silence Meditation

Close your eyes and relax your body. Take all the time you need. Get comfortable. Shift your muscles, stretch, and relax. Wiggle out the tensions. Raise your shoulders and drop them back again. Make sure your spine is straight but soft, comfortably aligned.... Feel the calm. Feel your muscles relaxing.

In this relaxed state, breathe deeply. In and out. In ... and out. Slowly begin to notice your breath. Hear it entering your body ... and leaving your body. In ... and out.

Inhale and exhale thoroughly, like ocean waves, waves that surround you. Or, like soft heavy clouds, clouds that fill you with silence....

Inhale slowly and deeply. Exhale slowly and thoroughly. Let your breath sink in ... and out. In ... and out. Your breath is a rhythm of calm, exhaling in ... and out. In ... and out, in and out.

Feel your breath, moving in ... and out. In ... and out.

Now feel your heart, rhythmic like your breath. Listen ... to your breath. Listen to your heart. Relax into your body's rhythms.... Bask in silence....

Trust. Listen. Breathe. If words come, receive them.... If images come, receive them.... Receive what comes.

Feel yourself imbued with the presence of the Divine. Ask the Divine to speak to you. Listen....

When you are ready, open your eyes. If you are prepared to write, do so now.

Meditation on Divine Love

Breathe in and out, in and out.

Hear in your breath a prayer. Hear in your breathing in and breathing out an acknowledgment of the Divine.

Breathe your prayer in ... and out. In ... and out....

🌿 Feel within yourself the touch of the Creator, the wisdom of the Divine.... You are divinely inspired. You are loved into being. You are a gift.

🌿 Feel your giftedness.... This breathing, living, loving being: a gift to be alive; a gift to others.

🌿 Feel the touch of divine love in the expansion and contraction of your lungs, the pulse of the universe.

🌿 Feel the love-inspired heft of your being, your weight upon the chair or floor, your grace.... Feel the love that brought you here into being with this spinning planet, this web of life....

🌿 Give thanks. Express your gratitude from the tips of your toes all the way up to the crown of your head.

🌿 You are a gift.... You are loved ... cherished... caressed into being.... You are a gift to yourself ... to others ... to this world, and to God.

🌿 To the Divine, you are a gift ... a gift giving back.

Gratitude Meditation

🌿 Close your eyes and relax your body. Breathe deeply, in and out. Let your breath enter your body slowly and calmly, filling up your lungs ... bringing vitality, oxygen, life. Then exhale, emptying your lungs, releasing toxins and waste.

🌿 Inhale slowly and deeply, filling all the way up, and exhale slowly and thoroughly, emptying back out into the air around you.

🌿 Inhale and give thanks for this breath, this breath that nourishes you. As you exhale, give thanks again for life, for your life, for the lives of your loved ones....

As you take air into your lungs, give thanks for your body.... As you exhale, place your attention on the crown of your head. Caress it in your mind's eye, expressing gratitude for your intelligence, your creativity.

Now place your attention upon your spine, giving thanks for it, the way it supports you and allows you to move.... See your ribcage, your heart, and your lungs. Thank the Divine for all of your organs, for your life.

Move to your hips and thighs, calves and toes, all tingly with vitality. Caress those toes with overwhelming gratitude to your Maker.

Bask in gratitude, giving thanks for your body.... Giving thanks for your spirit, your connection to the Divine and all beings around you.

When you are ready, take up your pen. Let your appreciation pour from your heart through the pen and onto the paper.

Visualization for Creating

Get comfortable. Breathe in deeply, counting to five if you wish. Relax your neck, your shoulders, your back.

Feel yourself sinking into the chair. Inhale slowly. Feel your stomach round out.... Exhale. Feel your diaphragm pushing the air out. In ... and out.

Inhale. Feel your lungs expand slowly. Exhale. Feel them release.

With each breath, sink deeper, deeper with each release. In ... and out. In ... and out.

- Now think of something you have brought into being. Something you have lovingly and painstakingly created.

- Conjure this creation, and give it voice.... Let it speak its name and anything it wishes to tell you. Listen....

- Express everything in your heart for this your creation. Hold it close.... Then, when you are ready, let it go.

- Return to your breath, moving quietly, calmly, peacefully within you.

- When you are ready, pick up your pen and write.

Wisdom of the Body Meditation

- Close your eyes and relax your body. Shake out a few muscles. Loosen up your tense shoulders. Envision your torso in a relaxed straight posture, your feet touching the ground, the chair firmly supporting your bottom.

- Breathe deeply, counting to five if you wish: five counts on the way in, five on the way out. Take in the air, slowly and calmly. Allow it to fill your lungs, bringing vitality, oxygen, life.... Exhale the air, slowly and calmly, allowing it to carry out those elements you no longer need.

- Inhale slowly and deeply, filling all the way up.... Exhale slowly and thoroughly, emptying your breath back into the air around you. As you inhale and exhale, acknowledge this breath, this bodily wisdom that nourishes you without your even having to think about it....

- As you exhale, place your attention on the crown of your head. Caress it in your mind's eye, acknowledging its beauty, its wisdom....

🌿 Behold, in your mind's eye, your face, your neck and
shoulders, your lungs, and your heart. Acknowledge
their beauty, their wisdom, the way that they sustain
your life....

🌿 Allow your mind's eye to travel down your arms and
torso, your hips and thighs, calves and toes, all tingly
with vitality, overflowing with wisdom.

🌿 Acknowledge this wisdom, your body's wisdom. Stop
and listen to this magnificent body of yours ... this gift
of the Divine. Hear what it has to say to you now....

🌿 When you are ready, take up your pen and begin to
write.

Meditation on Being a Vessel

🌿 Breathe deeply, in and out ... in and out. Let your
breath resound within you, as you breathe in deeply,
expanding your belly and then your chest.... Exhale
and feel your chest empty out, and then your belly....
This is your breath, your sustenance, the rhythm of
your life, the pulse of your existence.... In ... and out.
In ... and out.

🌿 Breathe in fully and deeply. Breathe out calmly and
completely. Like the whispering of wind in the pines,
the splashing of ocean waves....

🌿 Listen to your breath, the sound it makes entering and
exiting your body, renewing and replenishing your
cells.... Your breath takes in nutrients and expels waste.
Your body cycles, in time with the earth. Cycling in ...
and out. In ... and out.

🌿 Now imagine you are on a boat, drifting with the
waves—restful, peaceful waves.... Now you are the

vessel, this sense of wholeness and peace voyaging on the waters....

Fill yourself up with this calm: the calming rock of the waves; the placidness of the lake or ocean; the expanse of it all; its beauty....

Sense yourself as a vessel, a container, filling up with each breath, relaxing with each exhalation. A vessel filled with goodness, filling up with divine love, expelling all toxicity.... Stay here as long as you like....

Then slowly, gently, let the rhythm of your breath bring you back to awareness. Breathe softly as you awaken.

When you are ready, pick up your pen to capture your emotions, the insights just as they are, before they slip away.

Spirit Guide Meditation

Breathe in slowly, with ease and comfort. Breathe out calmly, releasing whatever needs to be released.... Breathe in, taking in love. Breathe out, releasing negativity. Breathe in kindness, magnanimity. Breathe out fear and distrust. In ... you are held tenderly. Out ... you are calmly releasing. In ... and out. In ... and out.

A path arises before you. Take a step. And another, until you are walking along this path, moving peacefully, with purpose, walking, taking in the sights and sounds around you. Smiling or singing, enjoying what is....

After a while, you pause. Way off in the distance, you see someone approaching.... As the person or being nears you, you make out the features ... contours ... a sense of their being....

When he or she is near, you reach out, a gesture of peace. You listen. You share. You converse.... You take in the words, the gestures.... You feel the truth in your heart.

Stay a while, listening.... Experience a gift, whatever he or she brings you ... Be with the person yet a little while longer....

When you are ready to leave, say thank you.... Say goodbye to this place, acknowledging that you may return at a time of your choosing. Savor your last moments....

When you feel like you have gathered all that you experienced to bring back with you, say thank you to your guide.

Let the pulsing of your body, the sounds of this room bring you back slowly ... to this place where your pen and pencil await to capture the essence of your guide's message. Express the images, words, or emotions that are present. Put them to paper now. They are a gift.

Guided Visualization of the Open Door

Close your eyes and relax your body. Breathe deeply, in and out. In ... and out. Let your breath enter your body slowly and calmly, filling up your lungs and slowly draining away. Inhale slowly, filling all the way up. Exhale slowly, emptying back out.

As you inhale, count to five, and as you exhale, count to five again. Let the counting guide your breath in ... and out. In ... and out.

Now imagine you are counting your steps down a staircase or a walkway or a path. You are stepping and counting as you inhale and exhale.... In ... and out. In ... and out.

Now imagine a door or a passageway. As you come closer, examine it. What does it look like? Is it light or dark? Open or closed?

Step closer so that you are in or by it. What can you see? Can you see the other side? What do you hear? Smell? Sense?

What does this place mean for you? What significance does it hold? Ponder this place.... Ask yourself or the Divine, "What is the purpose of this threshold? What am I to do?"

Linger here ... thinking, questioning, asking, examining....

When you are ready, pick up your pen and write.

THE INTERVIEW QUESTIONS

Eliciting Spiritual Stories

Questions often prompt stories, and I found that the following questions and a listening attitude encouraged participants to share from their hearts about their spirituality. The questions were simply jumping-off points, giving them the chance to reveal their experiential understandings of the Divine in relation to their lives as women, their communities, and the larger community of planet earth. The questions also guided me in exploring my own spirituality. Try using the questions as prompts for your own writing and see what comes up for you!

1. Think of one instance when you felt in a very palpable or otherwise powerful way the presence of the Divine. Describe it to me.

2. Tell me how you felt to receive this experience. Did this experience change you? Did it change your activities and your aspirations?

3. What was happening in your life at the time of this experience?

4. What had been your religious experience up to that point?

5. Tell me about your ongoing relationship with the Divine and what it means to you today.

6. Do you have a community that enhances your relationship with the Divine?

7. For you, what's the relationship between spirituality and social justice?

8. What are you doing to heal the world? If you could contribute a single thing to this world, what would it be?

9. What are you doing to safeguard the health of the earth?

10. What would your heart say to a young woman about your faith and about faith in general?

NOTES

PART I: DIVINE LOVE AND LOVE OF SELF

1. Henry Liddell and Robert Scott, *Liddell & Scott's Greek-English Lexicon* (Oxford: Clarendon Press, 1996). In Philippians 2:7, "kenosis" is used to describe Jesus's self-emptying.

2. Masao Abe, Patrick Henry, and Wayne Teasdale, "Sunyata and Kenosis: The Rise of Universal Compassion in the Spiritual Journey," *Monastic Interreligious Dialogue*, bulletin 48, October 1993, http://monasticdialog.com/a.php?id=704. See also Bernadette Roberts, *The Path to No-Self: Life at the Center* (Albany, NY: State University of New York Press, 1991).

3. Luke 1:38, New Revised Standard Version.

4. Ebenezer Lutheran Church in San Francisco, or "herchurch." For more information, see www.herchurch.org.

Esperanza: Great Courage within Me

1. In a *guinda*, people are fleeing from military assault, running and hiding in unpopulated areas to save their lives.

Lindsey: Where We Find God

1. Bishop's Ranch is an Episcopal retreat center in Healdsburg, California.

2. Lindsey Crittenden, *The Water Will Hold You: A Skeptic Learns to Pray* (New York: Harmony Books, 2007).

3. Gospel of Thomas is one of the "sayings" Gospels, along with the Gospel of Magdalene and the Gospel of Phillip, discovered near Nag Hammadi, Egypt, in 1945. They are dated to be writings from the second and third centuries.

4. Crittenden, *Water Will Hold You*. pp. 46, 48.

Lori: Rocking in Mother's Arms

1. Lori Eickmann, "In Search of God: One Woman's Quest Leads Her to Change Her Life and Answer the Call to Become a Minister," *San Jose Mercury News*, May 2, 1998.

2. Virginia Ramey Mollenkott, *The Divine Feminine: The Biblical Imagery of God as Female* (New York: Crossroad Publishing, 1994).

3. Leonard Swidler, *Biblical Affirmations of Women* (Philadelphia: Westminister Press, 1979).

4. Isaiah 42:14; Hosea 13:8; Isaiah 49:15; Proverbs 1:20–33; Matthew 11:19.

5. Eickmann, "In Search of God."

6. Ibid.

7. Lori Eickmann has a PowerPoint presentation available on these and other scriptures where God is referenced with female metaphors, pronouns, and images.

8. Eickmann, "In Search of God."

Hyun Kyung: From the Palms of God into the Vortex of Becoming

1. In Korean names, the last name is spoken first, Chung is Hyun Kyung's last name.

2. Chung Hyun Kyung is the author of *Struggle to Be the Sun Again: Introducing Asian Women's Theology* (Maryknoll, NY: Orbis Books, 1990). Her other writings include *In the End, Beauty Will Save Us All: A Feminist Spiritual Pilgrimage*, vols. 1–2, published in Korean; *Letter from the Future: The Goddess-Spell according to Hyun Kyung*, also published in Korean; and *Hyun Kyung and Alice's Fabulous Love Affair with God*, written in conjunction with Alice Walker.

3. Quan Yin is the bodhisattva of compassion. Sculptures and other artwork depicting Quan Yin have been found in many parts of China as well as other Asian countries.

Susan: Worthy to Stand Here with God

1. Women of Spirit and Faith includes local WSF circles, the Young Leaders Council, and the Mentoring Project. They can be reached at www.womenofspiritandfaith.org.

Sridevi: Rooted in the Divine Feminine

1. Ebenezer Lutheran Church in San Francisco is also known as herchurch.

2. Sridevi Ramanathan, "What the Goddesses Did for Me," *Vision Magazine*, Living Arts, May 2010, www.visionmagazine.com.

3. Ibid.

4. Sridevi teaches Zumba dancing, which draws from collective dance forms in Latin American and African cultures.

Arisika: The Body as Gateway to the Divine

1. 1 Corinthians 13:12, King James Version.
2. Alice Walker, *In Search of Our Mothers' Gardens* (San Diego: Harcourt Brace Jovanovich, 1983).
3. Alice Walker, *Her Blue Body Everything We Know: Earthling Poems, 1965–1990 Complete* (San Diego: Harcourt Brace Jovanovich, 1991).
4. Oshun is an orisha in the Yoruba tradition of Africa. Aphrodite is an ancient Greek goddess. Both are goddesses of love.
5. Marge Piercy, *Woman on the Edge of Time* (New York: Alfred A. Knopf, 1976).

Rachel: The Sacred within Me

1. *Pachamama* in Quechua and Aymara means "Earth Mother." She is the ancient mother goddess of the Inca and today's indigenous people of the Andes.

Anna: Circling into the Womb of the Mother

1. Miriam Therese Winter, adapted.
2. Prayer attributed to Joan Borysenko.
3. The labyrinth pattern named for the Chartres Cathedral in France dates to the thirteenth century. Many churches in Europe have ancient labyrinths in their naves.
4. A croning ceremony honors women past menopause by bestowing on them gifts symbolic of their wisdom and magnanimity, by asking them to speak their wisdom to those assembled, and by allowing them to publically proclaim the next steps they would like to take in their lives.

Alice: Resonating like Home

1. See note 4 from previous chapter.

Sarah: Hanging Out the Wash like Prayer Flags

1. Celebrate Living: Enhancing Christian Communities can be found on the web at www.celebrateliving.org.

Ann: Seeing Ourselves with Love

1. Zen Monastery Peace Center, www.livingcompassion.org/zen-monastery-peace-center.
2. Houn Jiyu-Kennett (1924–1996) was a highly venerated Buddhist teacher and the first female to be sanctioned by the Soto School of Japan to teach Zen Buddhism in the West. Quote originally attributed to

Meister Eckhart, a thirteenth-century German theologian, philosopher, and mystic.

3. Stillheart Institute, just off the coastline in Woodside, California.

4. Buddhist reading practice.

PART II. DIVINE CONNECTION

1. Carter Heyward, *Our Passion for Justice: Images of Power, Sexuality, and Liberation* (Ohio: Pilgrim Press, 1984), p. 49.

2. In his book *Quantum Theology: Spiritual Implications of the New Physics* (New York: Crossroad Publishing, 2004), Diarmuid O'Murchu posits that our essential human nature (indeed one universal to life) is that of attraction and repulsion of subatomic particles, a longing or yearning for union. Many discoveries in the field of quantum physics point to unity and interconnectedness at the level of the atoms that compose our bodies and all visible matter. See also Amit Goswami, *God Is Not Dead: What Quantum Physics Tells Us about Our Origins and How We Should Live* (Charlottesville, Va.: Hampton Roads Publishing, 2008).

Irma: A Mother's Embrace

1. Luke 8:42–48.

Elena: Celebrating the Mother's Diversity

1. Isis is an important Egyptian goddess; Kali and Durga are Hindu goddesses.

Belvie: Who Can We Become Together?

1. Seeing these connections between the earth's degradation and children in urban environments, Belvie Rooks produced *Hey Listen Up: A Sense of Self, A Sense of Place*, a multimedia-based curriculum that encourages youth, particularly from marginalized urban communities, to explore an expanded sense of who they are within the unfolding evolutionary context of family, community, bioregion, and the larger universe. For more information, see www.journeyoftheuniverse.org/ ed-series-2/2010/8/26/belvie-rooks.html.

2. Alice Walker, *Her Blue Body Everything We Know: Earthling Poems, 1965–1990 Complete* (San Diego: Harcourt Brace Jovanovich, 1991).

3. Rooks, Growing a Global Heart website, http://growingaglobalheart. weebly.com/index.html.

Malisa: Seeing the Divine in Each Other (*Namaste*)

1. *Namaste* in Hindi means "I acknowledge the Divine in you." It is often used as a greeting, with a slight bow and hands held together over the heart.

2. Seuss, *Oh, The Places You'll Go* (New York: Random House Children's Publishing, 1960).

3. Ganga is a great mother goddess of the Hindu religion associated with the Ganges River. Millions participate in pilgrimages to the Ganges headwaters in celebration of the Goddess Ganga.

Sadaya: The Womb of God through Which We All Come

1. The Dances of Universal Peace combine chants of sacred phases from various traditions. The movement was founded in 1967 by Samuel Lewis, an American mystic also known by his Sufi name, Sufi Ahmed Murad Chisti.

Debbie: Experiencing the Divine in the Multitude

1. Proposition 8 on the California ballot, which banned same-sex marriage in California, has been overturned in federal court and may be appealed to the Supreme Court.

2. The Dream Act is pending legislation granting legal status to students and members of the U.S. military who entered the United States as undocumented children. It has not yet been approved by both houses of Congress.

Susan: Appreciating the Sacredness of Life

1. *Sophia* is ancient Greek for Wisdom, mentioned several times in the book of Proverbs and other canonical books, as well as the name of a book in the Apocrypha.

PART III. DIVINE CHANGE

1. Diarmuid O'Murchu, *Quantum Theology: Spiritual Implications of the New Physics* (New York: Crossroad Publishing, 2004), p. 63.

2. Carol P. Christ, *She Who Changes: Re-imagining the Divine in the World* (New York: Palgrave Macmillan, 2003).

3. Acts 17:28, attributed to Saint Paul, likens our relationship with God as a child in the womb of the mother.

Lucy: Embracing Our Imagination

1. See Exodus 17:6.

Ayesha: Madly in Love with God

1. Ayesha Mattu and Nura Maznavi, eds., *Love, InshAllah: The Secret Love Lives of Muslim American Women* (Berkeley: Soft Skull Press, 2012).

2. Amin Malak, *Muslim Narratives and the Discourse of English* (Albany: State University of New York Press, 2004), p. 151. M. Fatih Citlak and Huseyin Bingul, eds., *Rumi and His Sufi Path of Love* (Clifton, NJ: Tughra Books, 2007).

Zoharah: Who Am I and Why Am I Here?

1. Gwendolyn Zoharah Simmons has authored several publications and has been featured in a PBS series, *This Far by Faith*, which examines the African American religious experience of the last three centuries. Her soon to be published works are *Muslim Feminism: A Call for Reform*, being reviewed by NYU Press, and *Islam Does Not Equal Fundamentalism*, also forthcoming.

2. Shaikh Muhammad Raheem Bawa Muhaiyaddeen, a Sufi mystic and philosopher, first traveled to the United States from Sri Lanka in 1971. Bawa, as he is known by his followers, authored over two dozen books, created numerous works of art, and recorded a meditation album.

3. Bawa Muhaiyaddeen Fellowship, founded in 1971 in Philadelphia, is located at 5820 Overbrook Avenue, Philadelphia.

Dionne: Drumming to Heal the Mother

1. A *djembe* drum is a rope-tuned, goatskin-covered drum. In the African Bambara language, *djé* is the verb for "gather," and *bé* translates as "peace."

Stacy: Climbing into Her Branches

1. Rosemary Radford Ruether has written scores of books, including *Sexism and God-Talk: Toward a Feminist Theology* (Boston: Beacon Press, 1993); *Gaia and God: An Ecofeminist Theology of Earth Healing* (New York: HarperCollins, 1994); and *Goddesses and the Divine Feminine: A Western Religious History* (Berkeley: University of California Press, 2005).

2. Ebenezer Lutheran (herchurch) is originally of the Augustana Lutheran Synod, founded by Swedish immigrants to the United States in 1860 and merged with other Scandinavian Lutheran synods to form the Lutheran Church in America in 1962, which is now part of the Evangelical Lutheran Church in America.

3. *Sophia* is ancient Greek for "Wisdom," mentioned several times in the book of Proverbs and other canonical books as well as the name of a book in the Apocrypha.

Jann: Let Justice Roll Down Like Water

1. See note 3 from previous chapter.

2. Jann Aldredge-Clanton is the author of several hymnodies and books. *Inclusive Hymns for Liberating Christians* (Austin: Eakin Press, 2006) and *Inclusive Hymns for Liberation, Peace, and Justice* (Waco: Eakin Press, 2011) are her two hymnals.

3. Jann Aldredge-Clanton, *Changing Church: Stories of Liberating Ministers* (Eugene, OR: Cascade Books, 2011).

4. Amos 5:24.

Katie: Would You Hug Me, Jesus?

1. Katie Ketchum, *The Magdalene Stories, A Musical*, www.katieketchum.com/press.html.

2. Katie Ketchum, *Mary Cassatt Musical*, www.katieketchum.com/bio.html.

SUGGESTED RESOURCES

SUGGESTIONS FOR FURTHER READING

Aldredge-Clanton, Jann. *Changing Church: Stories of Liberating Ministers.* Eugene, OR: Cascade Books, 2011.

Bolen, Jean Sinoda. *Urgent Message from Mother: Gather the Women, Save the World.* Boston, MA: Conari Press, 2005.

Bourgeault, Cynthia. *The Wisdom Jesus: Transforming Heart and Mind—A New Perspective on Christ and His Message.* Boston, MA: Shambhala, 2008.

Christ, Carol P. *She Who Changes: Re-Imagining the Divine in the World.* New York: Palgrave Macmillan, 2003.

Faulkner, Mary. *Women's Spirituality: Power and Grace.* Charlottesville, VA: Hampton Roads, 2011.

Hunt, Mary E. and Diane Neu, eds. *New Feminist Christianity: Many Voices, Many Views.* Woodstock, VT: SkyLight Paths Publishing, 2010.

Johnson, Elizabeth A. *She Who Is: The Mystery of God in Feminist Theological Discourse.* New York: Crossroads, 1997.

Mollenkott, Virginia Ramsey. *The Divine Feminine: The Biblical Imagery of God as Female.* New York: Crossroads, 1994.

Novick, Leah. *On the Wings of Shekhinah: Rediscovering Judaism's Divine Feminine.* Wheaton, IL: Quest Books, 2008.

Ruether, Rosemary Radford. *Goddesses and the Divine Feminine: A Western Religious History.* Berkeley, CA: University of California Press, 2005.

Schaaf, Kathe, et al, eds. *Women, Spirituality and Transformative Leadership: Where Grace Meets Power.* Woodstock, VT: SkyLight Paths Publishing, 2012.

Shapiro, Rami. *The Divine Feminine in Biblical Wisdom Literature: Selections Annotated and Explained.* Woodstock, VT: SkyLight Paths Publishing, 2005.

Winter, Miriam Therese. *Paradoxology: Spirituality in a Quantum Universe.* Maryknoll, NY: Orbis, 2009.

PARTICIPANTS' RETREAT AND HEALING CENTERS, CONGREGATIONS, AND OTHER MINISTRIES

Chacra Emek Sacred Valley Retreat Center

www.sacredvalleyretreatbb.com

Founded by Viviana Martinez and her husband, this bed-and-breakfast retreat center is located halfway between Machu Picchu and Cusco, Peru. You can take in the magic of the Andes, enjoy organic food grown on site, and opt for meditation or touring activities.

Chochmat HaLev

www.chochmat.org

An independent Jewish Renewal center for Jewish learning and meditation, Chochmat HaLev is known for its high-energy services that integrate music, prayer, and silence. Rabbi SaraLeya Schnel is one of the rabbis.

Ebenezer Lutheran ("herchurch")

www.herchurch.org

Herchurch introduces inclusive language and imagery for the Divine in liturgies, programs, and celebrations. Reverend Stacy Boorn is pastor.

First United Lutheran Church

www.fulc.com

Previously expelled from the Evangelical Lutheran Church of America (ELCA) for ordaining an openly gay pastor, First United is now a full participant in the ELCA and is active in interfaith circles. The Reverend Doctor Susan Strouse is pastor.

Growing a Global Heart

www.growingaglobalheart.weebly.com

Founded by activists Belvie Rooks and Dedan Gills, Growing a Global Heart is an organization committed to social justice, ecological restoration, and the greening of the inner and outer spirit.

herHealing

www.herHealing.net

Reverend Alice Martin facilitates healing and personal growth by enabling the recipient to clear obstacles from his or her energy system.

Interfaith Coalition for Immigrant Rights (ICIR)

www.icir-clue.blogspot.com

Led by Reverend Debbie Lee, ICIR champions the civil and human rights of immigrants living in the U.S.

The Reverend Doctor Jann Aldredge-Clanton

www.jannaldredgeclanton.com

Reverend Doctor Jann Aldredge-Clanton's ministry includes preaching, teaching, hymn-writing, and chaplaincy work. She encourages use of inclusive language and images in all forums.

Katie Ketchum

www.katieketchum.com

Katie's hilarious, award-winning solo performances lift up heroines like Mary Magdalene and American painter Mary Cassatt. Katie directs music and leads chanting in many settings, including herchurch.

Stillheart Institute

www.stillheart.org

Located in a coastal redwood forest not far from Silicon Valley, Stillheart offers retreatants a harmonious space where they can expand their self-awareness of body, mind, and spirit.

Unwinding the Belly

www.allisonpost.com

Allison Post's healing arts include her Unwinding the Belly techniques, along with qi, massage, and cranial-sacral body work.

Yoga in the Belly of the Goddess

www.yogainthebellyofthegoddess.org

Kundalini yoga utilizes intense movement, powerful breath-work, and the chanting of primal sounds to tone the body, strengthen the nervous system, and calm the mind. Alison Newvine is instructor.

Women's Spirituality Program

www.ciis.edu/Academics/Graduate_Programs/Womens_Spirituality_.html

Arisika Razak is program chair and a member of the core faculty of the Women's Spirituality Program at the California Institute of Integral Studies.

Women of Spirit and Faith

www.womenofspiritandfaith.org

WSF is a national collaboration of women committed to strengthening women's organizations and leadership capacities utilizing circle processes, deep listening, mindfulness, and compassionate action.

BLOGS

The Divine Feminine

www.patheos.com/blogs/thedivinefeminine

A sacred space for the voices of women from all faith traditions and spiritual perspectives to explore and express the many dimensions of the Divine Feminine. Coordinated by Women of Spirit and Faith.

Ella's Voice

www.ellabakercenter.org/blog

UCC minister and immigrant activist Rhina Ramos blogs on Ella's Voice for the Ella Baker Center for Human Rights, a community and social justice organization in Oakland, California.

Lindsey Crittenen

www.lindseycrittenden.wordpress.com

Writing instructor and author Lindsey Crittenen posts writing tips, inspiration, and other writing aides.

Love, InshAllah

www.loveinshallah.com

American Muslim feminist author and leader Ayesha Mattu blogs in this community of American Muslim writers sharing their perspectives on life, relationships, and the search for love.

Proud Member of the Religious Left

www.progressivechurch.wordpress.com

Reverend Doctor Susan Strouse, pastor of First United Lutheran Church in San Francisco, blogs about inclusive church, current events, and life.

A Woman's Eye Gallery

www.stacy.awegallery.com

Pastor Stacy Boorn's photography blog. Visuals to feast on!

Women, Spirit, and Faith

www.womenspiritandfaith.com

Author Lana Dalberg provides ongoing stories of women's spiritual experiences and other inspirational pieces.

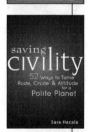

Spiritual Practice

Fly-Fishing—The Sacred Art: Casting a Fly as a Spiritual Practice
by Rabbi Eric Eisenkramer and Rev. Michael Attas, MD; Foreword by Chris Wood, CEO, Trout Unlimited; Preface by Lori Simon, executive director, Casting for Recovery
Shares what fly-fishing can teach you about reflection, awe and wonder; the benefits of solitude; the blessing of community and the search for the Divine.
5½ x 8½, 160 pp, Quality PB, 978-1-59473-299-7 **$16.99**

Lectio Divina—**The Sacred Art:** Transforming Words & Images into Heart-Centered Prayer *by Christine Valters Paintner, PhD*
Expands the practice of sacred reading beyond scriptural texts and makes it accessible in contemporary life. 5½ x 8½, 240 pp, Quality PB, 978-1-59473-300-0 **$16.99**

Writing—The Sacred Art: Beyond the Page to Spiritual Practice
By Rami Shapiro and Aaron Shapiro
Push your writing through the trite and the boring to something fresh, something transformative. Includes over fifty unique, practical exercises.
5½ x 8½, 192 pp, Quality PB, 978-1-59473-372-7 **$16.99**

Dance—The Sacred Art: The Joy of Movement as a Spiritual Practice
by Cynthia Winton-Henry 5½ x 8½, 224 pp, Quality PB, 978-1-59473-268-3 **$16.99**

Everyday Herbs in Spiritual Life: A Guide to Many Practices
by Michael J. Caduto; Foreword by Rosemary Gladstar
7 x 9, 208 pp, 20+ b/w illus., Quality PB, 978-1-59473-174-7 **$16.99**

Giving—The Sacred Art: Creating a Lifestyle of Generosity
by Lauren Tyler Wright 5½ x 8½, 208 pp, Quality PB, 978-1-59473-224-9 **$16.99**

Haiku—The Sacred Art: A Spiritual Practice in Three Lines
by Margaret D. McGee 5½ x 8½, 192 pp, Quality PB, 978-1-59473-269-0 **$16.99**

Hospitality—The Sacred Art: Discovering the Hidden Spiritual Power of Invitation and Welcome *by Rev. Nanette Sawyer; Foreword by Rev. Dirk Ficca*
5½ x 8½, 208 pp, Quality PB, 978-1-59473-228-7 **$16.99**

Labyrinths from the Outside In: Walking to Spiritual Insight—A Beginner's Guide
by Donna Schaper and Carole Ann Camp
6 x 9, 208 pp, b/w illus. and photos, Quality PB, 978-1-893361-18-8 **$16.95**

Practicing the Sacred Art of Listening: A Guide to Enrich Your Relationships and Kindle Your Spiritual Life *by Kay Lindahl* 8 x 8, 176 pp, Quality PB, 978-1-893361-85-0 **$16.95**

Recovery—The Sacred Art: The Twelve Steps as Spiritual Practice *by Rami Shapiro; Foreword by Joan Borysenko, PhD* 5½ x 8½, 240 pp, Quality PB, 978-1-59473-259-1 **$16.99**

Running—The Sacred Art: Preparing to Practice *by Dr. Warren A. Kay; Foreword by Kristin Armstrong* 5½ x 8½, 160 pp, Quality PB, 978-1-59473-227-0 **$16.99**

The Sacred Art of Chant: Preparing to Practice
by Ana Hernández 5½ x 8½, 192 pp, Quality PB, 978-1-59473-036-8 **$16.99**

The Sacred Art of Fasting: Preparing to Practice
by Thomas Ryan, CSP 5½ x 8½, 192 pp, Quality PB, 978-1-59473-078-8 **$15.99**

The Sacred Art of Forgiveness: Forgiving Ourselves and Others through God's Grace
by Marcia Ford 8 x 8, 176 pp, Quality PB, 978-1-59473-175-4 **$18.99**

The Sacred Art of Listening: Forty Reflections for Cultivating a Spiritual Practice
by Kay Lindahl; Illus. by Amy Schnapper 8 x 8, 160 pp, b/w illus., Quality PB, 978-1-893361-44-7 **$16.99**

The Sacred Art of Lovingkindness: Preparing to Practice
by Rabbi Rami Shapiro; Foreword by Marcia Ford 5½ x 8½, 176 pp, Quality PB, 978-1-59473-151-8 **$16.99**

Sacred Attention: A Spiritual Practice for Finding God in the Moment
by Margaret D. McGee 6 x 9, 144 pp, Quality PB, 978-1-59473-291-1 **$16.99**

Soul Fire: Accessing Your Creativity
by Thomas Ryan, CSP 6 x 9, 160 pp, Quality PB, 978-1-59473-243-0 **$16.99**

Spiritual Adventures in the Snow: Skiing & Snowboarding as Renewal for Your Soul
by Dr. Marcia McFee and Rev. Karen Foster; Foreword by Paul Arthur
5½ x 8½, 208 pp, Quality PB, 978-1-59473-270-6 **$16.99**

Thanking & Blessing—The Sacred Art: Spiritual Vitality through Gratefulness
by Jay Marshall, PhD; Foreword by Philip Gulley 5½ x 8½, 176 pp, Quality PB, 978-1-59473-231-7 **$16.99**

Women's Interest

Women, Spirituality and Transformative Leadership
Where Grace Meets Power
Edited by Kathe Schaaf, Kay Lindahl, Kathleen S. Hurty, PhD, and Reverend Guo Cheen
A dynamic conversation on the power of women's spiritual leadership and its emerging patterns of transformation. 6 x 9, 288 pp, Hardcover, 978-1-59473-313-0 **$24.99**

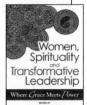

Spiritually Healthy Divorce: Navigating Disruption with Insight & Hope
by Carolyne Call A spiritual map to help you move through the twists and turns of divorce. 6 x 9, 224 pp, Quality PB, 978-1-59473-288-1 **$16.99**

New Feminist Christianity: Many Voices, Many Views
Edited by Mary E. Hunt and Diann L. Neu
Insights from ministers and theologians, activists and leaders, artists and liturgists who are shaping the future. Taken together, their voices offer a starting point for building new models of religious life and worship.
6 x 9, 384 pp, HC, 978-1-59473-285-0 **$24.99**

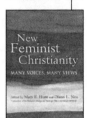

New Jewish Feminism: Probing the Past, Forging the Future
Edited by Rabbi Elyse Goldstein; Foreword by Anita Diamant
Looks at the growth and accomplishments of Jewish feminism and what they mean for Jewish women today and tomorrow. Features the voices of women from every area of Jewish life, addressing the important issues that concern Jewish women.
6 x 9, 480 pp, Quality PB, 978-1-58023-448-1 **$19.99**; HC, 978-1-58023-359-0 **$24.99***

Bread, Body, Spirit: Finding the Sacred in Food
Edited and with Introductions by Alice Peck 6 x 9, 224 pp, Quality PB, 978-1-59473-242-3 **$19.99**

Dance—The Sacred Art: The Joy of Movement as a Spiritual Practice
by Cynthia Winton-Henry 5½ x 8½, 224 pp, Quality PB, 978-1-59473-268-3 **$16.99**

Daughters of the Desert: Stories of Remarkable Women from Christian, Jewish and Muslim Traditions
by Claire Rudolf Murphy, Meghan Nuttall Sayres, Mary Cronk Farrell, Sarah Conover and Betsy Wharton
5½ x 8½, 192 pp, Illus., Quality PB, 978-1-59473-106-8 **$14.99** Inc. reader's discussion guide

The Divine Feminine in Biblical Wisdom Literature
Selections Annotated & Explained
Translation & Annotation by Rabbi Rami Shapiro; Foreword by Rev. Cynthia Bourgeault, PhD
5½ x 8½, 240 pp, Quality PB, 978-1-59473-109-9 **$16.99**

Divining the Body: Reclaim the Holiness of Your Physical Self
by Jan Phillips 8 x 8, 256 pp, Quality PB, 978-1-59473-080-1 **$18.99**

Honoring Motherhood: Prayers, Ceremonies & Blessings
Edited and with Introductions by Lynn L. Caruso
5 x 7¼, 272 pp, Quality PB, 978-1-58473-384-0 **$9.99**; HC, 978-1-59473-239-3 **$19.99**

Next to Godliness: Finding the Sacred in Housekeeping
Edited by Alice Peck 6 x 9, 224 pp, Quality PB, 978-1-59473-214-0 **$19.99**

ReVisions: Seeing Torah through a Feminist Lens
by Rabbi Elyse Goldstein 5½ x 8½, 224 pp, Quality PB, 978-1-58023-117-6 **$16.95***

The Triumph of Eve & Other Subversive Bible Tales
by Matt Biers-Ariel 5½ x 8½, 192 pp, Quality PB, 978-1-59473-176-1 **$14.99**

White Fire: A Portrait of Women Spiritual Leaders in America
by Malka Drucker; Photos by Gay Block 7 x 10, 320 pp, b/w photos, HC, 978-1-893361-64-5 **$24.95**

Woman Spirit Awakening in Nature: Growing Into the Fullness of Who You Are
by Nancy Barrett Chickerneo, PhD; Foreword by Eileen Fisher
8 x 8, 224 pp, b/w illus., Quality PB, 978-1-59473-250-8 **$16.99**

Women of Color Pray: Voices of Strength, Faith, Healing, Hope and Courage
Edited and with Introductions by Christal M. Jackson
5 x 7¼, 208 pp, Quality PB, 978-1-59473-077-1 **$15.99**

The Women's Torah Commentary: New Insights from Women Rabbis on the 54 Weekly Torah Portions *Edited by Rabbi Elyse Goldstein*
6 x 9, 496 pp, Quality PB, 978-1-58023-370-5 **$19.99**; HC, 978-1-58023-076-6 **$34.95***

* A book from Jewish Lights, SkyLight Paths' sister imprint

About SKYLIGHT PATHS Publishing

SkyLight Paths Publishing is creating a place where people of different spiritual traditions come together for challenge and inspiration, a place where we can help each other understand the mystery that lies at the heart of our existence.

Through spirituality, our religious beliefs are increasingly becoming a part of our lives—rather than *apart* from our lives. While many of us may be more interested than ever in spiritual growth, we may be less firmly planted in traditional religion. Yet, we do want to deepen our relationship to the sacred, to learn from our own as well as from other faith traditions, and to practice in new ways.

SkyLight Paths sees both believers and seekers as a community that increasingly transcends traditional boundaries of religion and denomination—people wanting to learn from each other, *walking together, finding the way.*

For your information and convenience, at the back of this book we have provided a list of other SkyLight Paths books you might find interesting and useful. They cover the following subjects:

Buddhism / Zen	Global Spiritual	Monasticism
Catholicism	Perspectives	Mysticism
Children's Books	Gnosticism	Poetry
Christianity	Hinduism /	Prayer
Comparative	Vedanta	Religious Etiquette
Religion	Inspiration	Retirement
Current Events	Islam / Sufism	Spiritual Biography
Earth-Based	Judaism	Spiritual Direction
Spirituality	Kabbalah	Spirituality
Enneagram	Meditation	Women's Interest
	Midrash Fiction	Worship

Or phone, fax, mail or e-mail to: SKYLIGHT PATHS Publishing
Sunset Farm Offices, Route 4 • P.O. Box 237 • Woodstock, Vermont 05091
Tel: (802) 457-4000 • Fax: (802) 457-4004 • www.skylightpaths.com
Credit card orders: (800) 962-4544 (8:30AM–5:30PM EST Monday–Friday)
Generous discounts on quantity orders. SATISFACTION GUARANTEED. Prices subject to change.